Models and Metaphors in Language Teacher Training

Loop input and other strategies

Tessa Woodward

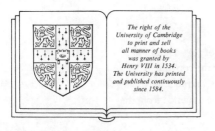

The right of the
University of Cambridge
to print and sell
all manner of books
was granted by
Henry VIII in 1534.
The University has printed
and published continuously
since 1584.

Cambridge University Press
Cambridge
New York   Port Chester
Melbourne   Sydney

To Mum and Pete

An earlier version of Part One of this book, entitled *Loop Input*, was
originally published by Pilgrims Publications, Canterbury, England.
In this Cambridge University Press volume, Part One has been
considerably reorganised and revised; Part Two is completely new.

Published by the Press Syndicate of the University of Cambridge
The Pitt Building, Trumpington Street, Cambridge CB2 1RP
40 West 20th Street, New York, NY 10011, USA
10 Stamford Road, Oakleigh, Melbourne 3166, Australia

© Cambridge University Press 1991

First published 1991

Printed in Great Britain by Bell and Bain

Library of Congress catalogue card number

British Library cataloguing in publication data
Woodward, Tessa
Models and metaphors in language teacher training: loop
input and other strategies. – (Cambridge teacher training
and development).
1. Language teachers. Professional education
I. Title
407

ISBN 0 521 37418 9 hard covers
ISBN 0 521 37773 0 paperback

WD

Contents

Thanks

I would like to thank the following groups and individuals very much indeed, in chronological order:

- The teachers on the Royal Society of Arts Diploma for Overseas Teachers' Course – for understanding and enjoying so many experiments from 1983 to 1985.
- Mario Rinvolucri – for asking me to write a book and then making me 'go and talk to the man from CUP!'
- Seth Lindstromberg – for his patience and faith and typing.
- The Arrow 'family' – for such generous cooperation especially in the matters of the Blue Book and the disks.
- Roger Bowers – for making me write more and more, and for learning to like my diagrams.
- Annemarie Young – for putting up with being badgered over the telephone.
- Alison Silver – for her sensitivity and diplomacy.
- Colleagues and friends who have sustained me in important ways through the years before this book finally came out.

Acknowledgements

The author and publishers are grateful to the authors, publishers and others who have given permission for the use of copyright material identified in the text. It has not been possible to identify the sources of all the material used and in such cases the publishers would welcome information from copyright owners.

Heinemann Publishers (Oxford) Ltd for the extract from *Discover English* by R. Bolitho and B. Tomlinson on p. 10; Cordon Art for the Möbius Strip by Escher on p. 14 © 1990 M. C. Escher Heirs / Cordon Art, Baarn, Holland; Basic Books Inc. and Scott Kim for 'Figure-figure' on p. 15 from *Gödel, Escher, Bach: An Eternal Golden Braid* by Douglas Hofstadter, copyright © 1979 by Basic Books Inc.; Oxford University Press for the extract from *A Training Course for the Teaching of English as a Foreign Language* by P. Hubbard et al. (1983) on pp. 85–6; Longman Group UK Ltd for the adapted illustration and exercises on p. 120 from *Guided Composition Exercises* by D. H. Spencer.

Introduction

Who is this book for?

- For any modern language teacher trainer, whether you have the title 'teacher trainer', have your own office, have special training and extra pay, whether you are called something else such as 'inspector', 'director of studies' or 'principal' or whether you are the sort of teacher that people turn to in the staffroom in moments of pre- and post-lesson panic.
- For anyone planning or running a pre- or in-service workshop or course.
- For groups of teachers wanting to share ideas in informal and less institutional settings.
- For teachers and teacher trainees who have been through or are undergoing the process of training and who are interested in how it can be done.
- For lecturers interested in getting away from a lecture-based approach to training.
- For trainers in any field who are interested in the *how* of training as well as the *what*.

What is the book about?

The book is about the process of training language teachers. One particular process option is described in close practical detail in Part One, and in Part Two there is broader discussion of how we classify and define teacher training events, the parameters surrounding them, the matching of process options to parameters, and, finally, how we can evaluate any process experiments we might make. In simpler language, Part One is about loop input, and Part Two is about what's inside the trainer's head (mental schemata), what's outside the trainer's head (parameters), juggling the inside with the outside (making process choices), and what the experiments are worth (evaluation).

How is the book organised?

The book is divided into two parts. The first part introduces the idea of loop input gradually, so that by the end of Part One the reader will be able to plan, run, assess and adapt training sessions in this new way. This first

1

part is practical and informal, and gives many ideas in sufficient detail for you to use them in the training room immediately if you want to. The reader stops reading, takes an idea from the book, tries it out in the training room, and eventually comes home to do some more reading. Part One is also interactive in a more conventional manner, with plenty of opportunities for readers to stop and think or join in with the process of the book. Part Two takes a broader perspective and a wider view of process and training generally.

Why is the book organised in this way?

In some training sessions, the steps of the session are carefully explained first so that nothing happens that participants have not been warned about or told the rationale for. So, there is introduction, and talk, and explanation first. The doing comes second. At the beginning of a course run like this, there will be 'welcomes' and 'introductions of personnel', timetables will be handed out, and the structure of the course outlined. There will then, perhaps, be an explanation of how important it is for people in the group to get to know each other, and an underlining of the importance of experiencing things first hand. After this careful, step-by-step introduction, after an hour or so of talking through, the group may be invited to do a warm-up. They may stand or sit and start to talk. The room will start to buzz with voices.

In other training sessions, the activity will be experienced first. There might be a brief word from the trainer as an introduction, but within minutes of the session opening people will be moving about and talking. They will do the activity first and talk about it later. This basic choice of 'explain first' or 'do first' can be made by the trainer or, once the trainees have tried both ways, put to the trainees so that they can express their preferences.

In this book I had a similar choice to make. There are two parts to the book, and one is highly practical and interactive. I had to decide which part to put first. I have decided to invite you to plunge straight in. I want to share with you a particular vision of training, first of all. I know that you will have your own ways of training. So, just as we might all come together in a room at a conference or on a trainers' course, we are, in fact, all meeting via this book. This book will be our shared experience. I'd like to invite you to join me in Part One, so that I can share with you some things that I have found useful. Then, in Part Two, we can slow down a bit and discuss things more widely.

The wonderful thing about meeting via a book, rather than meeting at a conference or on a course, is that you can, if you wish, choose to read Part Two first. If you are the sort of person who likes broad background, time to think, and explanation before demonstration, then you might well want to read Part Two first. It's up to you. But I'll take the 'experience first' people straight on to Chapter 1.

Within Part One I have taken a course of action mid-way between the choices outlined above by setting out some information in the first chapter. If you are a 100% 'experience first' person, then dive straight in at Chapter 2.

Finer details

a) *References*

As you read through the book you will meet small figures, for example [1]. At the end of the chapter you will meet the number again and you will sometimes find a single reference to an individual, an article or a book, and you will sometimes find a group of books all on a related topic, in case you want to do further background reading.

b) *Style*

In Part One you will find many contracted forms such as *don't*, *I've*, and *they'll*. I have used them because they are natural and because they allow me to express emphasis in a natural way, by simply decontracting as in *I do not mean*.

Throughout the book, I usually refer to the teacher and the trainer as 'she'. There are two reasons for this. Firstly, the majority of teachers, and many trainers, are women. Secondly, very few books use the pronoun *she* to denote women at all or women in mixed groups (that is, *he*, etc. is used in these cases). The usage in this book is thus designed to be a refreshing change.

PART ONE

1 Essentials

A FEW TERMS

Content and process

Regardless of which particular combination of course type, trainee type and trainer you are involved with, two things will be especially important to you if you are going to train teachers of English as a foreign language (EFL) or people thinking about entering the field. One is *content*, that is, what information, skills or knowledge are to be taught or learnt. The other is *process*, that is, how this information or knowledge is going to be taught or learnt, or, in other words, what 'vehicle' will be used to 'convey' the content.

I will be saying very little about *content* in this book. It will only be discussed in Part One when different ways of training are being exemplified or explained. I am interested here primarily in the different ways of eliciting, sharing, conveying and working with information, skills and knowledge in a language teacher training context. These different ways I call *process options*.

Process options

There are many different process options available, but very few teachers, trainers or lecturers have themselves been trained in using a variety of options or, in fact, in using even one to its fullest potential. There are very few courses or books available to help a trainer who decides that, for example, simply lecturing is not enough. It is often the case then that trainers work from a store of old process models gained from their own experience as students, plus a few ideas gleaned from colleagues, conferences and their own creativity. This may lead to the trainer overusing a rather thin repertoire of techniques. There will be nothing wrong in the techniques themselves but there may be ways of varying them and more appropriate techniques to choose from to accomplish the aims of a particular training session.

If this is the case, then two types of work are necessary. One is a compilation and discussion of already existing techniques and the other is the development of new techniques.

I would like to tell you about a new set of training strategies called *loop input*. It's not right for all people in all situations, but it represents a fresh option for those interested in widening their range of training choices. Trainers reading this book will already have repertoires of their own and I wouldn't want them to lay these repertoires aside just because they meet a new idea. If experimenting with process is new to you then trying loop input may feel strange or exciting at first, but after a while it may find a place in your repertoire. Trying out an unfamiliar process and taking it on board may lead you to look for other processes and to your developing your own. Our professional pool will then be richer.

Before I start explaining what loop input is, and how it works, I'll cover some background.

The EFL teacher training group: different roles and levels

Because there are so many groups involved in EFL teacher training, and in order to avoid confusion when writing about the various roles and classrooms, I will use the terms in Figure 1 *The stack* throughout this book. The terms are explained below.

1. **Students** of EFL
2. **Teachers** of EFL
> **The language classroom**

3. Teacher **Trainees**
4. Teacher **Trainers**
> **The training classroom**

5. Trainers' **Trainers** or **Tutors**

Figure 1   The stack

Much training work is done with experienced in-service groups of teachers. One would not normally refer to these teachers as *trainees*, but for ease of reference in this book and to distinguish between times when the experienced teacher is actually teaching a language class and other times when she is attending a training seminar, the term *trainee* will be used to cover any person at a seminar or on a course whether they be experienced or inexperienced, employed as a teacher or not. Thus we have a chain with five links, or a stack with five levels.

The first point I'd like to make is that any individual can belong to different levels of the stack at the same time, e.g. a trainee could be a non-native speaker of English and thus a student of EFL at the 'same' time as training. A trainer can be an EFL teacher and a tutor and a student of, say, Japanese at the 'same' time. In other words, a person in the EFL teacher training stack can have, in fact usually does have, more than one role or one face at a time. Alexia, shall we say, is a part-time EFL teacher. Her classes are on Wednesday and Friday morning. She also attends a teacher training course on Thursday evenings. Thus, she has two different roles a week in her EFL world.

The second important point is that any one person in the stack can learn from any other person in the stack. The stack is an expression of roles and organisational complexity. It is not meant to imply status differences. As lines in stacks are often interpreted hierarchically, however, I have attempted to disturb this image by putting the student at the top (the one who pays the most?) and the tutor at the bottom (the one who earns the most?). The point of the diagram is simply to remind us of who is involved, to give each role a simple name so that terms are clear throughout the book, and to show that we all have multiple roles and so can learn from each other.

Trainees and students

TRAINEES

There are important differences in confidence, status and language awareness between native and non-native trainees. Non-native trainees may be wary of expressing themselves in the target language in the training classroom or may consciously use the training sessions as language improvement sessions too. Thus they may be working on their teaching techniques and language ability at the same time.

It's easy to forget, however, how ill at ease some native speakers are when writing out their thoughts. This lack of ease may show up, for example, in the number of times you redraft an important letter, or in an inability to start writing on a blank sheet paper. A particularly bad example comes from this piece of homework, unsolicited, handed in by a young man on a pre-service teacher training course held at a British adult education college. The trainee took great care to correct the mistakes and handed it in a second time with most of the original mistakes changed but not necessarily rectified. Thus 'on there own' became 'on thier own' and finally 'on three own'. Here is an excerpt from his work:

```
Ice-breakers

This i feel was very important, as we were all strangers,
i feel the combination of the two games was just enough,
three i think would of been too many, the breaking of the
ice was skillfully done, you got to know a little about a
lot of people, but most importantly there names, and of
course putting faces to the names.
        This would be a good idea for foreign language
students if it was written down in thire language with
maybe the English version next to it, and being left on
three own to go around and ask questions.
```

STUDENTS

Despite individual and group differences in language awareness and interests, there are some parallels between students and trainees.

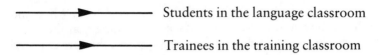

Both groups are studying something and thus are in a room with other people who they may or may not like. They have to do homework and suffer having it corrected. Members of either group may be motivated or uninterested. Being at different levels in the stack at any one moment, however, they may have a different viewpoint of the proceedings. The more students are helped with study skills to get the most out of input methods, and the more trainees are helped to improve their input methods, the more the two parallel lines will represent mirrors reflecting each other's interests, as mirror images of each other's concerns.

Using the parallels

Trainers often capitalise on the parallels between trainees and students. They do this in five main ways:

a) Trainers might ask trainees to take part in the 'ball game for names' (Frank and Rinvolucri, 1983), for example, as a warm-up at the start of their course. After the game has been played, some names learnt, and the ice broken a little, trainees will often be encouraged to discuss the game, its advantages and disadvantages, the language that's needed by students in order to play it in the target language, the equipment needed and so on. They might be asked to remember their feelings (of newness, or forgetting, of fun) and to try to recall them later in their own classes so that they can empathise better with their students. In this way, trainees remain trainees, with their own needs (e.g. to get to know each other's names) and statuses, but a game is borrowed from the students' line in the stack simply because it fits the situation.

b) Trainees might be asked to play a game taken from EFL teaching, and be required to play the game in a language foreign to them all. Thus the 'Find someone who . . . ' game might be played in French, if you happen to have native English-speaking trainees who know a little French. For example:

≫→

Cherchez quelqu'un(e) qui a | une bicyclette
un chat
une maison à la campagne
une amie japonnaise, etc.

Here, the trainees are required to suspend disbelief for a while and change from the trainee level in the stack, pretending that they now belong to the students' level. In computer language, they are required to *push*, i.e. to suspend operations on the task they are currently engaging in, which is learning to be EFL teachers, without forgetting where they are, and to take up a new task, which is practising French. The new task is usually said to be on a lower level than the first task. Once this second lower level task is completed they *pop* back up to the first level again, i.e. they resume their previous roles as trainees and go on as before, discussing the relative merits and demerits of the exercise. This is a simple kind of recursion.

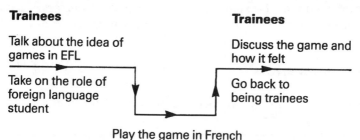

Trainees

Talk about the idea of games in EFL

Take on the role of foreign language student

Trainees

Discuss the game and how it felt

Go back to being trainees

Play the game in French

Figure 2 Push and pop

A little time is necessary to allow trainees to understand that they are *popping* or leaving one role and taking on another. Time is necessary, too, on their return to their own role after the exercise. Unless the time is taken and the process made overt, trainees are liable to suffer confusion over who they are supposed to be at any one time. To take the metaphor of deep sea diving, going down or coming up too fast can give you 'the bends'.

Pushing and *popping* are terms I gained from Douglas Hofstadter (1979)[1]. Leaving one role, and entering another for a time, represents a valid way of capitalising on the parallels in the situation between student and trainee. The example of the 'find someone who' game, however, is rather artificial since the trainees probably don't really want to learn French, at least at that time, nor are they likely to learn much from a quick, sample exposure. Aleksandra Golębiowska (1985) has argued that the experience provided by this foreign language (FL) learning 'simulation' is less than valid since: (a) the motivation experienced by the trainee is different from that of the real FL learner, (b) the frustration caused by this change of roles so early in a course can be counter-productive, (c) the novelty of FL lessons soon wears off, (d) the time could be better spent discussing the difficulties of learning English rather than learning another language, and (e) one lesson can never characterise a whole teaching/learning process. (Her article does contain some interesting suggestions, however, for helping trainees to experience what it's like to be learning English, rather than any other language.)

c) A less artificial extension of the above point comes from Argondizzo et al. (1986/7). They suggest taking games and activities often used in the foreign language classroom, but instead of changing the language they change the content. Thus, the game above now looks like this:

Find someone who | can name the phases of the lesson
                   | can define *mentalism*
                   | can explain *pre-lexis*
                   | etc.

Here, the trainees can see how the game operates and feel some of the advantages and disadvantages by actually experiencing it, but they also get time to review some of the content of their own training syllabus. They stay on the trainee line of the stack and do not take on the phoney role of language student, but simply borrow the frame of a game used at the student level.

d) Another idea that uses the similarities between the roles of individuals at different levels of the stack is what could be called *open process*. Here, the trainers open up their course to the extent that they make visible to the trainees all the constraints and decision-making procedures that they engage in. They take the wraps off their own level of the stack and make public their own concerns. Thus, a trainer might say, 'at this point in the course we have a choice. We could either hammer away at "concept check questions" for another week, until we feel you've got it, or we could leave it and come back to it in the hope that the dust will have settled in your minds and that there will be less confusion. All the trainers met yesterday and we decided to come back to "concept check questions" later because . . . '

Trainers can also take the wraps off their ongoing decision-making processes. For example, a colleague told me of a time when he was asked, 'Why did you sit on the floor to tell the story?' and found himself answering, 'Because I had to bring you closer to me (it was a very large room, with the chairs all round the walls) and I wanted you to do it quickly, which meant coming without the chairs and sitting on the floor with me.'

Trainees are not invited to join in the decision making but are 'viewing' it and can ask questions about it. They can relate this to decisions they have to make as teachers. No change in level is required. One level simply takes its clothes off and has an X-ray, so that another level can see its internal workings better. Trainees attempt to store the

X-ray image in their heads so that when they are in the body of 'The Teacher' they will have helpful information about their own working processes.

This way of working amounts to a demystification of the training and teaching process. It involves the trainer in removing some protective clothing and it also means that the trainer has to know why she does things, to be able to express this, and explain it clearly and concisely to others. This is a skill in itself.

e) Many people in language teacher training have come to feel that lecturing is somehow wrong. I don't believe this. There are many different types of lecture and they are all appropriate for different things. Trainers nowadays seem to favour discovery group work and are often slightly embarrassed when caught lecturing. I feel that discovery group work is simply another tool, equally varied in type, under-utilised in practice and just as inappropriate in some contexts as the lecture is in others.

But thanks to the recent attitude to the lecture, and in an attempt to prepare trainees for different roles in the language classroom, trainers have been experimenting with more experiential workshops and sessions. This has led to a utilisation of the parallels between students and trainees either by asking trainees to experience activities borrowed from another level, or by asking trainees to *push* down to another level for a time before *popping* back up again or by asking them to look carefully at another level with its clothes off.

Another development to arise out of lecture-shyness could be called 'X-raying yourself'. Here the eye is turned, not outwards towards other levels, but inwards to find out what is inside you as a person (at any level of the stack). These types of exercise are often termed *awareness activities*[2]. These can be directed to allow the trainees to discover more about themselves at the level of language ability, memory store, teaching beliefs, individual character or other issues. Here are some examples:

i) To help trainees find out what their hidden beliefs about 'good' English are:

In the following exercise (Bolitho and Tomlinson, 1980), compare the statement in A with the evidence in B and then comment critically on the statement.

A 'I want my students to speak only the best English so I encourage them to read only the classics of English literature.'

B I've tried a long time, and 't'nt got better. But thou'st right; 't might mak fok talk even of thee.

Hard Times, Charles Dickens

The robbery at the bank had not languished before, and did not cease to occupy a front place in the attention of the Principal of that establishment now.

Hard Times, Charles Dickens

ii) To help trainees find out what their sub-conscious images of teachers are:

'Think back to your most hated or most loved teacher at school. Try to remember what they wore, how they stood, what their gestures were. How did they enter a room? What did they carry? What did they say? Once you've remembered, tell your neighbour and tell them too how you feel you are similar or dissimilar to this remembered teacher.'

iii) To help teachers to understand the atmosphere they (want to) create in a classroom:

'Cover a page with adjectives that could be used to describe an atmosphere, e.g. *cosy*, *challenging*, *frightening*. When you've done that, circle the ones that represent the atmosphere you would like to have in your classroom. Then note down two things you do that help to promote one of the adjectives and two things you do that you think hinder the promotion of the same atmosphere.'

This interest in awareness raising has arisen, I believe, out of a rejection of the idea of the trainee as a *tabula rasa* (i.e. a human mind with no innate ideas) or 'empty pot to be filled'. If trainees are not just to sit still in lectures and passively absorb information, but are to participate in workshops and make discoveries, then there must be something inside them already. Let the trainees themselves find out what that something is.

Guiding awareness activities confronts a trainer with some difficult choices. Each trainee needs to find out different things and thus the activities have to be open-ended. There is no one right answer. The trainer has to have a light touch in order not to close down options. Too light a touch, however, can frustrate trainees who might feel that the trainer is being too non-committal, always saying that everything is all right, never putting herself on the line. A trainer has therefore to strike a balance between joining in on activities wholeheartedly (so that she does not ask trainees to do things she is not prepared to do herself) and being prepared to state what she feels or believes is right in a particular situation, but not doing that so strongly that trainees feel they necessarily have to imitate or model their answers or behaviour on the trainer's. It is, then, like the teaching of any subject, a question of balance.

All the process types mentioned above can be initiated by the trainer, but once trainees have become familiar with the different options, they can state their preferences for doing things one way rather than another. Just as we can ask trainees what content they would prefer, we can also offer a menu of process choices so that they can decide how they would like to work.

LOOP INPUT

What is it?

I want to explain what loop input is by giving some short examples (immediately), and some fully-fledged examples (later).

A brief example

Imagine that as a trainer you wish to get across to your trainees the importance of different spatial arrangements in the classroom. Before the session starts you could go into the training room and stack it so full of tables and chairs that no one could move in there. When the trainees arrive, before they even know what the aim of the session is, they will be confronted by furniture. They'll ask you how you want it arranged. In return, you ask them how they want it arranged, and discussion and furniture moving will follow.

A second example

In another session, let's say of 45 minutes, where you want to get across the idea of student concentration spans and the importance of warm-ups and breaks, give trainees a graph such as this one at the start of the session:

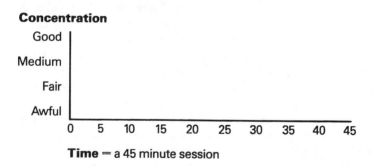

Ask trainees how they feel before you do anything else, and again without telling them 'the point'. If the majority mark concentration as only 'fair' or state that they are hungry or tired, etc. do a warm-up with them. Then teach them something completely different, asking them to note their concentration levels every five or ten minutes. When most people are experiencing a drop in concentration, perhaps after fifteen or 25 minutes, do a lively one-minute break exercise and then get them to note if they feel better afterwards (Woodward, 1988*a*).

A fuller example

Let's imagine you'd like to do a session on jigsaw listening. You make three lists headed: 'The principles behind jigsaw listening', 'How to set up and run a jigsaw listening session' and 'Materials available for jigsaw listening'. You then make three separate tapes. On one you give a lecturette containing the points on list one. On another you get two colleagues to have a conversation about the points on list two and on the third you record a telephone conversation where a publisher explains why they want to visit a school to do a session on listening materials. You run the session as a jigsaw listening session complete with these three tapes, and with listening task sheets, comprehension checks, initial grouping, cross-grouping and plenary.

The trainees have remained trainees. They have not changed levels in the stack. An EFL activity frame has been borrowed so that to some extent the trainees can feel what it would be like to experience a jigsaw listening exercise as a student. The exercise is not done in a foreign language nor is the content irrelevant. It is content suitable for a teacher training course. The content is carried by the process, but the process is also part of the content. That is the loop.

Explanation of the name *loop input*

In loop input, an activity frame is borrowed from another level. It is brought back up and used by trainees for the purpose of their own syllabus. This could be diagrammatically represented thus:

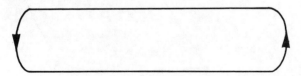

The content is aligned with the process so that the whole acts like a Möbius strip.

Figure 3   Möbius Strip
© 1990 M. C. Escher Heirs / Cordon Art, Baarn, Holland

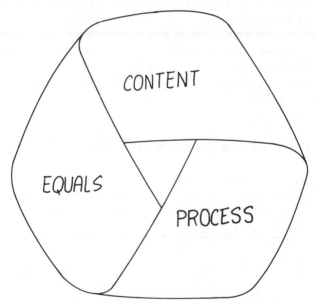

Figure 4   Möbius strip – content = process = content

The technique was named *loop input* because the Möbius strip looks like a strip of paper that has been looped.

Background and foreground

There are two threads to Part One of this book: *content* and *process*. The content is there to highlight the process, just as black silhouettes show up white spaces or white shapes show up black surroundings. If the black shapes and white shapes are fairly similar, as they are in Scott Kim's illustration below, the eye will dance between the two colours, sometimes seeing one as predominant and sometimes seeing the other.

Figure 5   Figure-figure by Scott Kim

It is possible to look at Scott Kim's pictures and only be aware of seeing the black shapes. If we equate black with content, just for now, this would be like the trainer who only thinks about content. ('I'm going to do some work with them tomorrow on coursebook evaluation.') It is also possible to look at the picture and only be able to see the white shapes. If we equate white with process, just for now, then this would be like the trainer who only thinks about process. ('I'm going to have them in groups working on tasks tomorrow.') There is another awareness possible with the picture. It is possible to switch visions, from seeing only the black to seeing only the white, at will. With this kind of awareness, the picture becomes much more interesting. This gives us, by analogy, the trainer who is capable of thinking about content and process at will.

The black shapes and white shapes in the illustration are fairly similar. In loop input, content and process are similar. For example, the content might be jigsaw listening and the process might be jigsaw listening too. There are times when one will seem to be in the foreground and other times when it seems to be in the background depending on which you happen to be concentrating on at the time.

In the picture, if you 'go into' the white and lose yourself in the white shapes, you tend to become preoccupied with them, incapable in fact of seeing the black as shapes at this time. If you concentrate on the black, on the other hand, it becomes very difficult to remain aware of the white shapes at the same time. Similarly, if you stay on your own level of the stack (see Figure 1) it is easy to become preoccupied with your own experience. If you change position in the stack, you can experience things from someone else's point of view. Switching from one line of the stack to another will make you more flexible and give you new experience although, just as in the picture, it is very difficult, if not impossible to be aware of both experiences at precisely the same moment. This is another good reason for making changes of level overt to trainees.

Some people looking at the picture may have a tendency to decide what the picture is about. They may decide that it is 'a sort of picture of reindeer'. They may project a judgement onto the picture and this projection may become fixed so that they miss the painter's point of the picture entirely.

I hope that readers of this book will not be prevented by strong feelings about what content should or should not have been included from understanding the main point of this book. For example, the chapter on dictations does not include dictations used for examination purposes. You might think this should be included because it is in your own training course. I hope this will not preoccupy you to the extent that you miss the point of the chapter. The point is not dictation but one way of telling trainees about dictation. You could use the process I describe to teach the very content you think is missing or to teach adapted content. Part One of this book is about painting two colours so that they interact to enhance each other.

EXPLANATION OF THE CHAPTERS IN PART ONE

Most chapters in Part One deal with subjects that you might want to or have to include in your teacher training course syllabus, so that content has, broadly, been chosen. I have solved the question of which vehicle to use to convey the content by choosing *loop input*. Thus, the subjects of the chapters are used to exemplify this process of input. Other styles of input could of course have been used to express the content.

Chapters might include the following:
- Some sort of diagram giving an overview of the field in which the subject of the chapter is located.
- Information, either separate or integrated, on what you might want to include in a session or sessions on the subject.
- A practical skills checklist that outlines some of the skills a trainee will need to be competent in to give language classes involving the topic of the chapter. It's a reminder that simply having input or experiencing techniques does not mean trainees will be able to handle the technique relevantly or competently in a classroom themselves.
- An overall lesson plan or path for you, the trainer.
- Material ready for use in a training classroom if it fits your situation and purposes.

The chapters are not necessarily in the order in which the subjects might come up on your training course. I have chosen to structure Part One of this book in such a way that it follows the 'Presentation – Practice – Production' or 'three Ps' model[3] of language learning and teaching, which is often used on training courses. I have chosen this model because it is so familiar to many trainers, and also because I feel we need to think about whether it is effective. The 'three Ps' model rests on the belief that language can be chopped up into little pieces and the pieces can be isolated, fed into students, practised and digested and that this will lead to their becoming part of the students' repertoire. (See also Chapters 15 and 17.)

I have organised the chapters of Part One, to some extent, according to the 'three Ps' model. Thus, using the terminology of a standard EFL presentation – practice – production lesson, I'll explain on the next two pages the way I have structured the book.

Chapter 1 At the beginning of a language presentation lesson some time is often devoted to scene-setting and an explanation is given of the situation in which the target language is going to occur. So in this present chapter I have endeavoured to give some context to the idea of loop input.

Chapter 2 This chapter contains a swift explanation of what mind maps are. This is the equivalent of pre-vocabulary work where words that are used in later work are clarified first before the target language items. The main subject of the chapter is the use of loop input in a session on using texts.

Chapter 3 Loop input is tried out on a new content area in this chapter, namely dictation. This is similar to moving, in a language presentation lesson, to a fresh picture on the board or a fresh mini-conversation where the same target form is used in a fresh situation.

Chapter 4 This chapter sets out, step by step, the way to prepare and run a loop-input session. Thus, in the terminology of language presentation, the form is 'highlighted' or broken down into little pieces for analysis and clarification.

Chapter 5 The use of loop input in the content area of classroom management is the subject of this chapter. The reader can add her own ideas to slot into the framework. It is equivalent to some 'controlled practice'.

Chapter 6 In this chapter I work backwards from session notes to session aims in order to get to some important thoughts on observing other people teach. The equivalent to working backwards, in terms of controlled practice in a language lesson is 'back chaining' where the form is practised in words and phrases from the back of the sentence in an oral drill.

Chapter 7 The idea of the 'foreign language lesson', often used at the start of teacher training courses, is discussed. The equivalent to this chapter, in a 'three Ps' language lesson, would be 'concept checking', since my aim here is to get to the heart of why we use these foreign language lessons and what we really mean by them.

Chapter 8 It is not necessary or advisable to use loop input all the time, any more than it is necessary or advisable to use, say, the present perfect tense all the time just because you've had a few lessons on it recently. Thus, this chapter, which shows how loop input can be abbreviated or contracted for faster use in everyday situations, attempts to stop me from over-teaching and you from over-generalising or using loop input too much or too often.

Chapter 9 In the first part of this chapter there is a general discussion of the advantages and disadvantages of using models. This represents a short break or change before the reading and writing stages.

Chapter 10   This chapter is about the use of loop input in sessions on role play. Usually when students get to a role play phase within the guided practice stage of a 'three Ps' lesson, more creativity and spontaneity is encouraged from the participants. Similarly, in this chapter, there is more work for you to do if you wish.

Chapter 11   This appropriately brief chapter is about the use of loop input in a session on student talking time.

Chapter 12   This chapter deals with the use of loop input in sessions on vocabulary teaching. Vocabulary teaching thus comes quite late in Part One of the book. In language teaching, too, people say that vocabulary has been rather neglected until recently.

Chapter 13   Reading mazes are useful in 'integrated skills' or 'skills-chain' lessons. Within the 'three Ps' model, their use would thus come quite far down the pyramid. This chapter, quite late in Part One, shows how they can be used and discussed via loop.

Chapter 14   By this late stage of Part One the inessentials have been shed. The mind maps and practical skills checklists are still mentioned but they are touched on and assumed rather than dealt with in detail. Thus, this chapter on listening sessions and loop input is a 'free-stage' chapter.

Chapter 15   This chapter is about the 'transfer' of learning. According to the 'three Ps' language learning model, provided the teacher sets out the target language clearly and the students work hard through all the stages, then by the end of the model, or by the bottom of the pyramid, the learners should be able to use the target item in any situation they wish to transfer it to. To parallel that idea in this book, by the time I have laid out the loop input idea and by the time you have worked your way through the first fourteen chapters, you should be able, if you wish, to set up your own loop-input sessions whenever you feel it is appropriate. The question is whether the model does accurately reflect what really happens in teaching and learning.

Chapter 16   This chapter is about evaluation. I find that I have the tendency to leave evaluation to the end of courses, though I am trying to break this habit and do more evaluation, usefully, in the middle of courses. Thus, although Chapter 16 is at the end of Part One, it is also, in fact, in the middle of the whole book.

Chapter 17   In this chapter I consider the ideas of learning and changing and how they might come about. There is discussion of mental models, metaphors and the 'chunking' of experience and how all these relate to training in general and to loop input in particular.

1. Although those very familiar with computers will be able to spot some differences here between the *stack*, *pushing* and *popping* and temporal stacks in computer programming, the borrowed language remains a very useful tool for discussing recursions in training sessions.

2. Further reading on **awareness activities**:

   Kenny, G. & Tsai, B. (forthcoming). *Resource Book for Teacher Training*. Cambridge University Press.

   Melville, M. (1981). English Through Drama. In L. Spaventa (ed.), *Towards the Creative Teaching of English*. Heinemann Educational.

   Moskowitz, G. (1978). *Caring and Sharing in the Foreign Language Class*. Newbury House.

   Wingate, J. (1984). *Open Up a Teacher*. Pilgrims Publications.

3. Further reading on the **'three Ps' model**:

   Grundy, P. (1989). A critique of pre-service training courses: Parts 1 and 2. *The Teacher Trainer*, 3, 2 & 3.

   Hill, L. A. & Dobbyn, M. (1979). *A Teacher Training Course*. Cassell.

   Hubbard, P., Jones, H., Thornton, B. & Wheeler, R. (1983). *A Training Course for the Teaching of English as a Foreign Language*. Oxford University Press.

2 Mind maps and using texts

Mind maps

As there will be quite a few mind maps in Part One, I'll spend a short while explaining what they are, in case you haven't met them before.

Most people tend to take notes in linear fashion, for example:

1. ....
   a) ....
   b) ....
   c) ....
2. ....
   ....
   ....
   a) ....
   b) ....
3. ....

There's nothing wrong with linear notes, but some people feel that they impose too much of a specific order on your thoughts. If you happen to think of 2 (b) first when you're brainstorming or reviewing a topic, you have to store it in your memory until you've thought through 1 (a), (b), (c) and 2 (a). The chances are that by that time you'll have forgotten it, or that fear of forgetting it will stop you from concentrating fully on the previous points. Mind maps or branching diagrams are a way round this. You start with a central concept in the middle of the page. You don't need to box it in, though I find I often do. The major ideas relating to the central title are written in capital letters on branches radiating from the centre. Smaller ideas relating to these main branches go on sub-branches or twigs. When you've made a mind map, you'll start to see connections between branches that perhaps you hadn't thought of before. Then you can either reorganise, draw arrows or use colour to highlight the links (Buzan, 1974).

On the next page there is a mind map about mind maps.

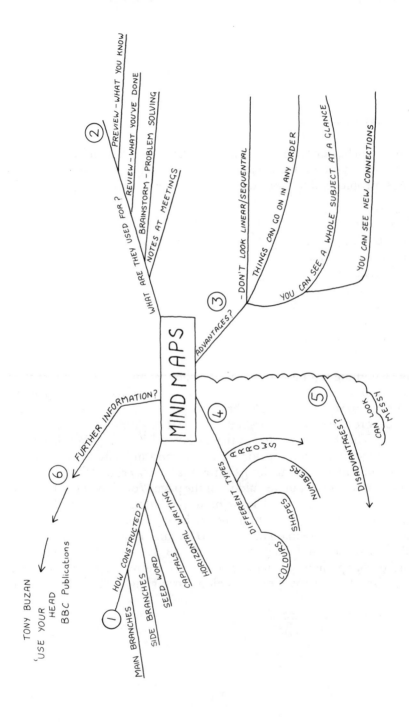

Figure 6   A mind map about mind maps

Using texts

As you can see from the following mind maps, there are plenty of things you could teach your trainees about reading. I haven't put this chapter on using texts first because I feel it's the most important or first thing that trainees need to know; I've chosen it because it's a complete loop and thus will give you a good idea about what loop input is.

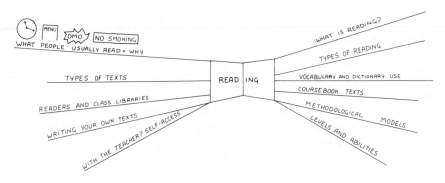

Figure 7   A reading mind map

As you see, this mind map is still pretty linear and only contains main branches. We could take one branch, e.g. 'What people usually read + why' and use that seed idea for a new mind map.

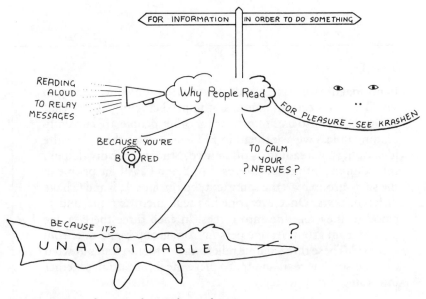

Figure 8   A why-people-read mind map

Mind maps and using texts

Let's say that as a trainer you've decided that you'd like your trainees to know what jigsaw reading exercises are and what it feels like to do them from the student's point of view. You'd also like to give them a basic methodological model for a reading lesson based on the idea of pre-, in- and post-reading tasks. Later on, of course, you'll want to check that they can actually handle the techniques with a real class, but first you want to feed the ideas in. (You might like to try out anything between * * * and * * * in a teacher training session.)

Reader activity

WHAT YOU DO   *   *   *

Step 1
Bring in some pieces of a jigsaw puzzle. Ask trainees to discuss what similarities there could be between jigsaw puzzles and a reading activity in a language classroom.

Step 2
Divide trainees into three groups using some imaginative system, e.g. smokers, non-smokers and those who are trying to give up, or brown, black, and white shoe wearers, or January to April, May to August and September to December birthdays, etc. Give Text 1 to group A, Text 2 to group B and Text 3 to group C. Ask them to read their text and check their understanding of it by using the questions on their sheets. Here are the texts:

Text 1

In normal life we don't usually know what someone is going to say. There's a certain amount of unpredictability in any chat we have. We also can't know what other people are currently reading unless we ask them. In EFL classrooms these days the idea of 'jigsaw reading' is often used. Students are divided up, for example, into three groups – A, B and C. All the people in the same group read the same text, but groups A, B and C have different texts. Once everyone has read their text and understood it, they regroup into threes. In each three there is one person from group A, one person from group B and one from group C. These three people talk to each other to find out what each person has read and try to piece the information together into some sort of whole.

Questions

1. To check that you have understood the two different kinds of grouping, could you now draw two diagrams to indicate them?
2. Everyone in the class has the same text.   T/F
   Everyone in the class has a different text.   T/F
   Some people have the same text as each other.   T/F
3. After people have read their text they
   a) stay in the same group
   b) move into a different group
   c) go home.
4. When the students are in threes they know what each person is going to say.   T/F   Why (not)?
   When the students are in threes they don't know what each person is going to say.   T/F   Why (not)?
5. What do they do in groups of three?
6. What are the disadvantages of 'jigsaw reading'?

Text 2

The following quote was overheard in a staffroom one coffee break: 'I really hate doing jigsaw readings with my class. Finding good texts takes a while and the photocopy machine is always on the blink and then I never have a pair of scissors or any white-out. Then I always get the texts muddled up so that I give people the wrong ones. The grouping for the first reading is OK, but then there's chaos when I try and get them into the second sort of grouping. It takes ages. Just when you think you've got them sorted out it turns out that one person hasn't understood what they read anyway! Hopeless!'

Questions

1. What's jigsaw reading?
2. Why do you need a photocopier, a pair of scissors or white-out to do a jigsaw reading?
3. How could people get the 'wrong' texts?
4. Why is arranging the second grouping a problem?
5. Can you think of a way round it?
6. How could you solve the last problem?

Text 3

In the old days teachers used to just whack out reading texts like hot dinners. No instruction. No arousing interest. Just eyes down. Nice and quiet for the teacher, of course.
(*Q: What's the writer's attitude to the old approach to reading skills lessons?*)

Then there were millions of comprehension questions for students to answer. Open, closed, true/false, multiple choice. Most of them fatuous and either answered mentally long before the students got to them or else needed long before students got to them. No such thing as an 'in-question', of course.
(*Q: What are open, closed, true/false, multiple choice and in-questions? Could you give an example of each type? If 'in-question' is a new term for you, you'll find two of them in this text.*)

And then when the text was over, questions answered and checked, and a few people scolded for getting them wrong, it was bang on with the next thing. Some processing of language perhaps, but no content processing at all.

Questions

1. Have you ever had a reading lesson like this in a foreign language?
2. What did you think of it?
3. Can you think of a different way of doing one?

Step 3
While the trainees are reading, go round and give everyone in group A a counter with a △ on it, everyone in group B a counter with a □ on it and everyone in group C a counter with a ○ on it (or some other marker, e.g. a coloured rod or a card of a particular suit).

Step 4
Once reading has finished, encourage the trainees to check within their groups that they understood their text, and tell them that whilst they can answer some of the questions on their sheet there will be others that they can't answer.

Step 5
Hold up a △, □ and ○ and ask the trainees to form groups of three with one each of the different counters. Once they have regrouped, hold up some pieces of jigsaw and fit them together. Explain that they have read different things and can now pool information.

Step 6
Once the swapping of information in small groups has finished, ask the whole class these questions:

1. What is jigsaw reading?
2. What are the advantages?
3. What are the disadvantages?

Trainees can be given a few minutes' reflection time before coming up with streamlined definitions or points which 'scribes' can write up. Answers to the three questions can be written on three different surfaces, e.g. blackboard, a combination of OHP and a blackboard or, if equipment is short, on posters made by cutting rolls of wallpaper into lengths and writing on the blank side of the wallpaper.

* * *

Step 7
After these questions have been dealt with, and this may take some time, ask the trainees to write down, step by step, all the activities they have done so far, starting from the point at which you held up the jigsaw puzzle pieces. Then invite them to divide all the various steps into three groups or sequences. The sequences can be represented in different ways, perhaps like this:

1. ....
2. ....
3. ....

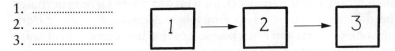

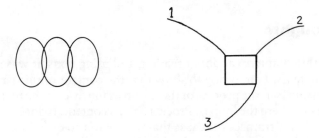

Everyone visualises things in different ways. The important thing is not which layout people use, but arriving at three phases. Once groups have discussed this and come up with something, write or draw the different suggestions on the board.

An example of a diagram some trainees might come up with is:

Anything can be accepted. They are all possible methodological models. You might like to tell them what *you* had in mind. My own phases looked like this (Woodward, 1988*a*):

The use of the three-phase methodological model is, of course, optional but I find it makes a neat framework for a lot of activities whose purposes could be difficult for trainees to remember. Models save tricks from remaining one-off ideas and bring people closer to being able to generalise and then create new ideas of their own.

*   *   *

Last thoughts

Although this chapter was about reading and using texts, it was not *just* about using texts. I am trying to show that the content of this particular training session is in the process of the lesson as much as in the texts themselves. This is where the loop is. Process equals content. It does take some time and help for trainees to realise that the answer to question 5 of Text 2 is in what has just happened and not in the text or in words coming from the trainer's mouth. Once the trainees have become sensitive to the idea of loop input, however, they have always (in my experience) found it deeply satisfying and intellectually tickling. The next chapter will give you another example of a total loop, applied to a new subject. But just as a reminder, here are a list of skills trainees will need before they can manage a jigsaw reading exercise in their own classrooms.

Practical skills checklist

Trainees will need to be able to:

- Spot, make or adapt texts useful for exploitation in this way.
- Divide texts so that the contents and the pair or group work make sense.
- Be organised in demarcation of first and second groupings.
- Check that people in the initial groups understand their text.
- Monitor group work appropriately.
- Know what they want to happen in second groupings and in the plenary if there is one.
- Respond to questions of different sorts on the organisation of the task and content of texts from individuals and groups at different times.
- Decide what information needs to be planted during group work and what should wait until the plenary.
- Give clear instructions by voice or other means.

3 Dictations

In Chapter 2, the idea was to teach trainees about jigsaw reading and a (pre-, in- and post-) reading model whilst the trainees were exposed to both of these. The content of the texts was on the same subject: jigsaw by jigsaw. And the session was run according to a pre-, in- and post- model. So you can guess that a loop session on dictation would be done by dictation.

Depending on how much time you have to spend on the subject, or how experienced the trainees are, you can use different ideas from the selection within the *Reader activity*. Sections which stand on their own are divided up by the symbol * * *.

The first section gives help with these aspects:
choice of text
breaking up a text
the speed of giving dictations
the standard way of giving dictations
reading aloud clearly and naturally
watching when people are ready to go on
cutting texts
the concept of student-to-student dictation
dealing with punctuation
experiencing what it's like to take dictation
checking by swapping papers

All the other sections introduce rather less conservative dictations, plus different ways of checking, for example, one person writing on the OHP or blackboard or reading aloud in pairs. They also mention student choice in level of dictation and how dictated texts can be used after a session. First, here's an overview of some thoughts about dictation:

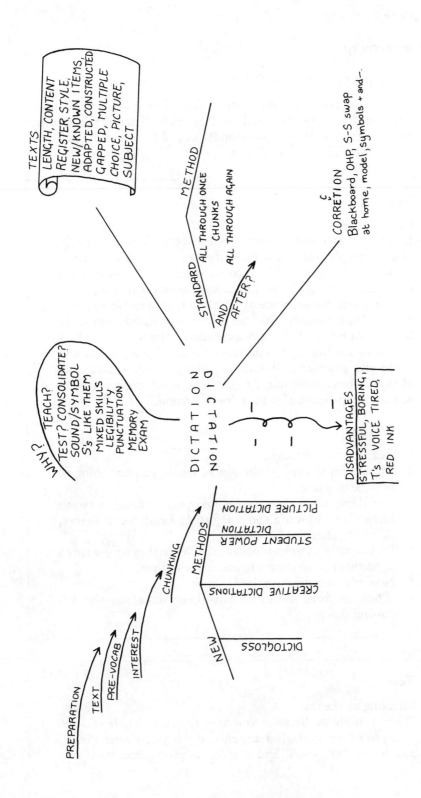

Figure 9 A dictation mind map

Dictations

Reader activity

First divide trainees into groups of three. They all need some blank paper and something to write with. Tell them they will be dictating to each other in a minute. Give out Text 1 to person A, Text 2 to person B and Text 3 to person C. The texts are as follows:

Text 1

Choice of text

It's important to select a text which is not too long or difficult, and preferably one that is interesting or useful to students. It could be one that is likely to be dictated in real life, for example, a business letter, phone message or instructions.

You could choose, write or rewrite a text to reinforce structures or lexis students have met before in different contexts or through different skills such as reading. The text could be a lead-in or a follow-up to a discussion topic. Equally well, a text could give practice in different spellings of one sound or in phonemic discrimination. At more advanced levels, texts can present samples of different styles of writing.

To the trainee:

1. Read the text through.
2. Mark with slashes (/) the places where you are going to breathe or pause.
3. Are there any words you think your colleagues won't know? If so, how are you going to deal with them? Before, during or after the dictation?
4. Dictate the text to your colleagues. When they have written it, let them swap papers to check each other.
5. Now it's your turn to take dictation.
6. When all three dictations have been done, see the discussion sheet.

Text 2

Breaking up the text

When you give a dictation you have to decide where you are going to pause. In the last sentence, if you pause after 'going' and before 'to', you'll find that 'to' is pronounced as if you

---

were reading it from a dictionary and not naturally as spoken at speed before a consonant as in /tə/. It's important therefore to divide texts up into meaningful groups of words or into sense groups as well as to read normally.

Another thing you have to decide is whether to give punctuation as you go along. Maybe if you say, 'full stop', the students will write out 'full stop'.

To the trainee:

1. Read the text through and decide where you are going to put your pauses, but don't read it aloud yet.
2. Take dictation from person A in your group.
3. Swap papers with colleague C to check.
4. Now dictate the text above to your colleagues.
5. Take dictation again.
6. When all three dictations have been done, see the discussion sheet.

Text 3

Reading dictations
Try reading this sentence very slowly, word by word, enunciating unnaturally clearly. Everybody understands, but you sound like a robot and the stress, rhythm and intonation are completely altered. It's not really English. When dictating, speak at normal speed, allowing pauses between sense groups. Keep your eye on how the writing is going. Make sure everyone's ready before you go on reading.

To the trainee:

1. Read through your text twice, deciding where you're going to pause and whether you want to read the first sentence differently from the rest.
2. Are there any words that might be new to your colleagues? If so, are you going to deal with them before, during or after your dictation?
3. Now take dictation from your two colleagues. Swap papers after each to check your work.
4. Next, dictate the text above to your colleagues.
5. When all three dictations have been done, see the discussion sheet.

All three trainees get the following sheet to discuss after completing their dictations.

Discussion sheet

1. What are your dictated texts useful for?
2. Are they the sort of texts you'd expect to have dictated in 'real' life?
3. How did you deal with unknown items in the text? What other ways can you think of?
4. How many different procedures did you use to dictate the texts?
5. How was the speed?
6. Why did the texts have titles?
7. What did you feel about taking/giving dictation?
8. What are the advantages and disadvantages of giving each other dictation?

---

* * *

STUDENT POWER DICTATION[1]

As a trainer, you might like to introduce to trainees some of the many interesting new dictation techniques now in use. The one in this section is good fun, quite noisy, and when used with language students gets them into the habit of interrupting native speakers when they need to. Here are some possible steps:

1. Explain that there are less traditional ways of using dictation.
2. Explain how the student power dictation works (see the explanation in the text).
3. Ask one trainee to take dictation like the others but to write it on the blackboard (masked from the rest of the class) or OHP (switched off). This is the 'OHP or B/B person'.
4. Dictate the text FAST!!
5. Check the work of the class against the work of the OHP or B/B person by switching on the OHP or unmasking the blackboard.
6. Discuss the advantages and disadvantages of this type of dictation and checking process.

Text

First, check your students know how to ask questions such as: 'Could you stop, please?', 'Can you say that again?', 'What does that mean?', 'How do you spell it?', etc. Next, explain that you're going to read a text at full speed. Students must stop you often and repetitively in order to get the text written down. You'll do anything they like, for example, spell words, give punctuation or read words singly, but they must ask you to do this.

This type of dictation gives students practice in getting the information they need from the teacher as well as changing attitudes about what teachers are for and how students should behave.

---

* * *

PICTURE DICTATION[2]

1. Explain that trainees have to listen and draw what they hear.
2. Start dictating Text 1.
3. After a few words go round to check that everyone is drawing and not writing.
4. Finish dictating.
5. To check if dictees have understood the text, you can take in the drawings, flash up your drawing on an OHP, have trainees compare pictures or, if you want to show a correction technique that uses oral skills, ask trainees to describe their own picture and to pick out any differences between each other's pictures.
6. Discuss.

Text 1

I once lived in a little two-storey wooden house in a large garden. The windows were very large and there was a balcony on the top floor.

An alternative way to do picture discussion is to give people a drawing and then dictate a text that describes the picture in some ways but is different in other ways. The picture has to be altered, and the feedback gives useful practice of negative forms. See Text 2.

Text 2

The picture given to trainees:

The text read out:

Jane's very short. She's got black hair and large eyes. Today she's wearing a long-sleeved jacket with three large buttons down the front.

Examples of feedback: 'She hasn't got black hair in the picture' or 'She hasn't got blonde hair now. I made it black.'

* * *

GAP DICTATION

Give out the following text to all trainees.

A text .... handed out ....students. They .... given .... little time to guess .... in the gaps. Then the .... reads aloud and the students .... in the gaps. Dictations .... checkled against a full, completed .... flashed .... on .... OHP or uncovered .... blackboard or handed .... on photocopied .... method of checking .... be .... template over the printed .... , or for the teacher .... write the missing words, jumbled .... , on a companion sheet. What do .... think of these gaps, ... the way?

Once they have had time to guess what's in the gaps, dictate the text. In case you're in a hurry, here it is. (Other plausible answers should be accepted.)

Complete text

A text **is** handed out **to** students. They **are** given **a** little time to guess **what's** in the gaps. Then the **teacher** reads aloud and the students **fill** in the gaps. Dictations **can be** checked against a full, completed **text** flashed **up** on **an** OHP or uncovered **on a** blackboard or handed **out** on photocopied **sheets. Another** method of checking **would** be **a** template over the printed **sheet,** or for the teacher **to** write the missing words, jumbled **up,** on a companion sheet. What do **you** think of these gaps, **by** the way?

For ease of reference the words missing from the trainees' sheets are in dark type in the complete text above.

To check this dictation you could do any of the things mentioned in the text. For example, you could give out the following list of jumbled words and then discuss.

Missing words – jumbled

to	teacher	what's	up	you	is	a
text	another	out	to	are	fill	by
sheet	can	a	be	an	a	up	on
sheets	would					

---

*   *   *

MIXED ABILITY DICTATION

1. Divide the class into three groups, each representing a different level of language ability.
2. Give out Text 1 to the trainees who are representing the lower level language students, and allow them a little time to look at it.
3. While they are looking at it, give out Text 2 to the trainees representing medium level students.
4. Check that the final group of trainees, representing the highest level of language students have a piece of blank paper and something to write with.

5. Read out Text 3.
6. Before checking the dictations, allow time for trainees to find out what the other groups have been doing, and be prepared to explain why you gave some trainees the 'highest' version and others the 'lowest' version!
7. Discuss the distractors and gaps to see if they are good ones (Hubbard et al., 1983).

Text 1

In mixed ability | groups, classes, schools, | you can | use employ give out

different texts to different | groups. individuals. students. | The

highest level lowest level medium level | group can be given | a whole a normal their own

dictation and thus all they need is a(n) | blank empty white | sheet.

The middle level group can get a | full gapped | text and

the lowest level can be given a text | with by in | multiple

choice frames. The same dictation is read out

by the teacher to | all. everyone. someone. | The highest write

down everything. The middle ones fill in | gaps. spaces. holes.

The lowest | mark tick circle | which of the choices they hear.

Text 2

In .... ability .... , you can .... different
.... to different .... The .... group ....
be given .... normal dictation and .... all they
need is a .... sheet. The .... level group can get a
.... text and the lowest level can .... given a text ....
.... frames. The .... dictation is read .... by
the teacher to .... The .... write down .... The
middle .... fill in .... The .... which of the
.... they hear.

Text 3

In mixed ability classes, you can give out different texts to different students. The highest level group can be given a whole normal dictation and thus all they need is a blank sheet. The middle level group can get a gapped text and the lower level can be given a text with multiple choice frames. The same dictation is read out by the teacher to everyone. The highest write down everything. The middle ones fill in gaps. The lowest circle which of the choices they hear.

A possible way of checking all the previous dictations except *Picture dictation* is to give dictees access to a large text in which the dictated text is embedded either whole or in pieces, that is, a few words here and there. An example of an embedded dictated text, in pieces, at the start of *Mixed ability dictation* Text 3 might be: 'In mixed ability classes, where you have some students adept at taking down dictations and others hardly able to write down a word, you can, given enough preparation time, give out different sorts of texts to different ability students or student groups.'

* * *

MUTUAL DICTATION

1. Put trainees in pairs facing each other, each with a pen and something to rest on. Tell them that the only rule is that they must not peep at each other's texts. Advise them to spend a few minutes guessing what might fill the gaps in their own texts before they start dictating back and forth with their neighbour.
2. Give out Text 1 to person A and Text 2 to person B.

Text 1

Mutual ....
Since students .... and B have the .... text, differently
.... , they'll need language such as '..?'
or 'I've got a gap next' before they can do a .... dictation.
The teacher can make .... or interesting
.... The texts can also be gapped .... by
.... , at phrase level, ... for specific items like
.... prepositions. .... have to be given
.... A '.........................' can be a language item
.... physical space on a page ....
or an unanswered question.

What do you think are the advantages and disadvantages of
doing a mutual dictation?

Why might you do one with your class?

Have you stopped the dictation or are you still taking notes?

Text 2

.... dictations
Since students A and .... have the same .... , ...
gapped, they'll need language such as, 'What have you got
next?' or '...' before they can do a mutual
.... the text itself useful
.... to the dictees. The texts can also be gapped
word .... word, ... , or .... specific
items like conjunctions or .... Certain instructions
.... carefully beforehand. A 'gap'
.... fitted into a .... on a page or
can be an unfinished point ....

What do you think are the advantages and disadvantages of
doing a mutual dictation?

Why might you do one with your class?

Have you stopped the dictation or are you still taking notes?

After they've finished a mutual dictation, trainees will, if you've allowed
enough time, already have started to chat about the content of the text or
to check it against their neighbour's. They may also suggest other
activities such as checking the dictation against a whole text or model to
be handed out by the teacher.

On the issue of the model handed out by the teacher, you might hand out a list of advantages and disadvantages of using mutual dictations or of reasons for doing mutual dictations with a class. Here is a possible list:

Reasons for doing a mutual dictation in a language classroom

1. It gives everyone a chance to read aloud in a moderately realistic sort of setting, to ask questions about spelling, meaning and punctuation and to pin things exactly to paper.
2. It raises the proportion of student talking time and promotes student-to-student interdependence. It also increases the noise level.
3. It can prove to people that they are comprehensible or incomprehensible to others.
4. Different pairs or people can have different texts or gaps according to their needs.
5. It weans people away from standard dictations.
6. It can review vocabulary, structures, syntactic issues or functions that have been met before.
7. It can be a sneak preview of items to be met later.
8. It can allow people to hide their ignorance or forgetfulness before a whole-class review.
9. 'Creative' or open-ended gaps can provide a balance to closed, 100% accuracy-based gaps.

Discuss whether it would be assumed by most that Point 1 was the most important, whether the teacher's use of a fully filled-in version or model makes people compare their own performance unfavourably with this model, and whether anything can be done to allow space for student contributions on the model.

*   *   *

OTHER DICTATION IDEAS

After any of the above dictation types have been done, you could add other dictation ideas, similarly looped, or alternatively un-looped, for five or ten minutes in other sessions. For a wealth of good ideas on new types of dictation, see Davis and Rinvolucri (1988).

After the sessions you could ask trainees to fill out a mind map similar to the skeletal one at the start of this chapter in order to record their discoveries so far. They could also cut out and paste their various dictated texts into a handout for themselves entitled 'Dictation'.

* * *

Practical skills checklist

Before doing dictations in their own classrooms, trainees will need to be able to:
- Find and adapt suitable texts.
- Decide what to do with new lexical items (I have not touched on this).
- Pause and read naturally and audibly.
- Choose a method of dictation and checking appropriate to needs.
- Decide on what to do as a follow-up to dictation.
- Note dictees' writing-down-speed.
- Make gapped texts for specific purposes, e.g. for prepositions or for verb form practice.
- Gap texts for mutual dictation.

1. This is adapted from an idea by Larry Cole.
2. This idea is from James Duke.

4 How to prepare and run a loop-input session

Now that you've read through and perhaps tried out the material in the previous chapters, you'll see that I am concerned to achieve a congruence, a consistency between what we say as trainers and what we do. By aligning process and content in the way explained, trainees can experience techniques for themselves without moving to the work site (that is, to a language classroom), without entering into a lengthy apprenticeship with an experienced teacher (this may be desirable but is often impossible), and without taking on the artificial role of the student who is studying content unrelated to the trainee role.

In loop input, the content is as much in the process of the session as in the handouts, texts or trainer's talk. As mentioned earlier, it does take time and help for trainees to realise that answers to questions can be in what has just happened and not in the texts or in words coming from the trainer's mouth. Once trainees have become sensitive to the idea behind loop input, however, they begin to look for information everywhere within the session. Very little is lost and there is less boredom since the trainees search for signs of practice during the preaching and see tips and points in everything. If they also see it when it isn't there or isn't meant to be there then this keeps the trainer on her toes! Inconsistencies are soon spotted and the trainer is often asked to explain the significance of things that she had thought insignificant. Honest discussion at this stage means that both parties learn and the trainer is discovered to be a normal teacher, that is, a person making decisions fast in the face of evolving practice. This breeds honesty and takes commitment.

Planning to work with information using the loop technique means that you have to think carefully about the process of sessions. This may take longer than planning a session where content is 'transmitted' by lecture. Lectures are thought, somehow, to take care of themselves. Deliberately thinking over both content and process to gain consistency between the medium and the message in loop sessions leads, however, to tremendous course credibility. After all, how credible is a trainer who lectures for long periods on student centredness or short attention spans?

Steps in producing a loop-input session

(Not necessarily in chronological order)
1. Arrive at a topic for a session (something you've noticed trainees need, or that they have requested, or something from the syllabus).
2. Brainstorm what you know about the subject. You could use a mind map (see Chapter 2).
3. To fill in the gaps, or to remember things you've forgotten, go through a related experience (e.g. become a dictee!) or do some reading or talking to people.
4. Simmer. Decide what to put in and what to leave out depending on how much experience your trainees have, how long the session will be, what trainees need most, etc.
5. Draw up a 'laundry list' of all the things the trainees need to be able to do as teachers in the area of your topic and to what level of competence. See the *Practical skills checklists* throughout this book for one way of doing this.
6. Think over the ideas for your input until you see where there is a chance for a loop.
7. Put together the materials you need.
8. Do the session.
9. Think about it, add trainee feedback and refine it.
10. Try it out, adapted, on another group.

Let's take these steps and apply them to a problem. Imagine, for example, that you'd like your trainees to get a taste of Counselling Learning[1], sometimes called Community Language Learning or CLL. Most trainers have not been thoroughly trained in the methodology of CLL, but there are many staffrooms where one or more teachers or trainers have heard of CLL, read some articles, tried the method out and adapted parts for their own classes. This, in fact, is my own position, although I've also been lucky enough to experience some language classes in CLL as well. The method has some very interesting underlying tenets and is useful on training courses too, not least because its differences point up very clearly the assumptions behind more mainstream methods.

Let's imagine that, drawing from your own experience and/or the knowledge and experience of your colleagues, you come up with an initial brainstorm on CLL. I've done one which you can see in Figure 10. You can also see that my own knowledge of the subject isn't spectacular! So, it's obviously time for Step 3 of the above. After Step 3, I would probably both add to the mind map and take linear notes. Let's imagine that my trainees will be working with students who, even after years of school lessons in the target language still feel insecure about actually speaking it. I'm thinking here, for example, of adults who have been through the Japanese school system or English office workers needing French. Or,

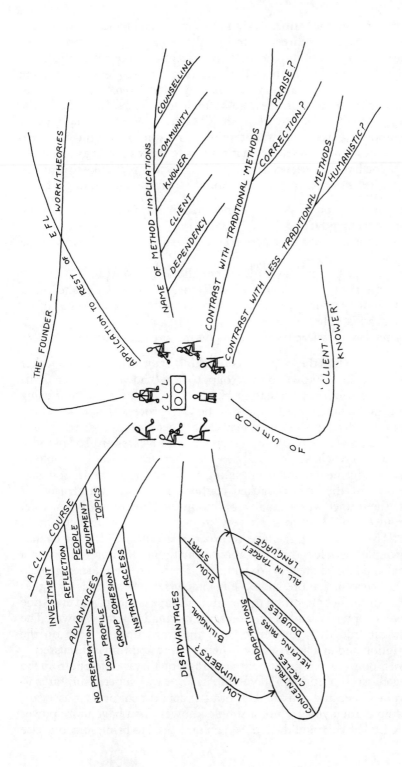

Figure 10 A CLL mind map

looking at it from the trainees' point of view, let's imagine that they have been fed a standard 'three Ps' model (Presentation – Practice – Production)[2] but are beginning to be a little sceptical about the efficacy of language learning by the teacher's selection and sequencing of small pieces of the grammatical system. You may, alternatively, have trainees wrestling with the tension they feel in their jobs from always being the initiator, the centre of attention, the 'Teacher'. Whatever the type of trainee and language student, and thus the reason for wanting to introduce CLL onto the course, the next stage is to draw up lists as in Steps 4 and 5. If you have experienced some CLL, then you might like to draw up your own lists now before you read on. My own content list might be:

- Brief introduction to names of method, founder's rationale and the influences behind CLL.
- Information on a session where everyone is round in a circle with a tape recorder.
- Make it clear that the circle idea is not all there is to CLL.
- Information on main points of difference between CLL and other methods, for example, group dynamics, attitude to silence, translation, the 'teacher's' role and so on.
- Information on where trainees can go for more information.

Now we need to find the loop. We could think of priming a native speaker (of a language little known to the group) to be a 'knower' and then inviting the trainees to learn Russian or Hebrew or Czech for one hour using the 'all round a tape recorder' part of the CLL process. There is nothing wrong in this although, as mentioned earlier, people have started to have doubts about this type of one-off language learning session. The pseudo-knower has to be chosen carefully so that they are someone capable of being non-judgemental and maintaining a low profile. If the session goes wrong because the knower lacked confidence or was overintrusive or because the trainer was incapable of letting the knower fulfil their role, then trainees are likely to get a very strange view of CLL. Let's think further. The 'circle with the tape recorder' sessions in CLL are a chance for a group of people to find out about something they don't know, in a practical and immediate way – by doing it. There is someone there to help them, an expert in that one subject but someone whose status is no higher than that of the people sitting in the circle. A tape is made, and everyone can have a copy of it and of the transcription made by the knower. The knower can add extra information to the transcription, both on the transcription and in a later session when the transcription is discussed.

There is only one thing in the above paragraph that is different from the training classroom situation. If you are in some way superior in status to your trainees because you are their head of department or their assessor, for example, then you are not a simple knower. You have more power than a CLL knower would have. So you may need to bring someone else in. As for the rest of the paragraph, it stands as well for your training classroom as for a language classroom run in CLL style. This is where your loop can be.

Let's say you've decided to get a Czech speaker in to help with a CLL session. After the session you can again have trainees in a circle with a tape recorder in the middle. They can discuss their feelings, express what they've found out, their doubts, questions, etc. They can record any part of the discussion they wish and can refer to the trainer/knower if they wish. The trainer/knower can be outside the circle, and must be unobtrusive and undominating in mood, expression and stance. You could make a decision on whether the trainer/knower should whisper the answer to a trainee's question in her ear so that the trainee then has to restate it for the rest of the group, or whether the trainer/knower says the answer loudly enough for the whole group to hear. The group can then decide how much or how little of the discussion to restate and record. The transcription would be longer, probably, than in CLL, but if trainees had their own copies of the tape produced, the transcription could be partial or condensed. The transcription/handout could look like this:

Transcription of trainees' tape

A: I like this, being able to discuss and ask anything we like without a set programme.[1]

B: I don't! It feels artificial to me. Why don't we just get a lecture or a handout? I mean, where do we start?[2]

C: Well, one thing I'd like to ask people or our knower is what the whispering was for in the Czech lesson.[3]

Trainer/knower's comments (added later)

[1] 'Deep-end' approach; nothing kept from learners; access to what they want, when they want it.

[2] Groups take time to settle. Some groups or individuals never do; some insist on teacher responsibility.

[3] Information given from inside your 'personal space' goes deeper, comes almost from you. Also you really have to listen!

A transcription plus comments such as the one above can be given out, studied and then discussed. The knower could also add references to books and articles.

My experience of running groups in the above way is that some groups will take to the hour of Czech happily, knowing that they are experiencing something for later methodological discussion, but others become frustrated not only for all the reasons mentioned earlier but also because they are reacting emotionally to the fact that the learning, especially in the first hour, is structureless ('How does my classmate's knowing how to say "Two strawberry ice creams, please" in Czech help me?'), or because they receive no overt praise, or for other reasons. Similarly, a lecturette on CLL will not have prepared them for the emotional reality of the circle work. Because of this, I have recently kept the foreign language work till later and started with some information about CLL but done in the circle method. Thus, trainees are told that I know a little about CLL and that they can ask me anything they like. The whole session is taped. I stay sitting in my chair but assume a lower profile, venturing and initiating nothing on my own but only answering questions. Here's an excerpt from a tape of one such session, about seven minutes into the session. (T = trainer, A, B, C, etc. are trainees, in this case all teachers of very varying types and lengths of experience.)

T: . . . and then comes . . . then the learner gets to the so-called adult stage. That's when the learner knows what she or he knows and, but, also knows what she doesn't know and feels that she can ask the knower, er . . . for help . . . you know really feels that she can go and ask and doesn't lose any face by doing that.
    (*pause*)

A: This is assuming that second language acquisition is the same, or similar, in the way it happens, er . . . to mother language acquisition. Do we know this?

T: Um . . . I don't think . . . er, I think it's used as a possible parallel or a . . . er, possible metaphor to explain some of the emotional feelings that hap . . . that you go through when you're learning a new language . . . rather than as scientific exactitude in terms of exactly what happens in second language acquisition, you know, the exact process.

B: Yes, well, I felt like that often. I mean, I think it's very well . . . this feeling . . . they say you know you get irritated when somebody corrects you and so I believe, I . . .

C: But what do they do with the tape?

D: She told already . . . before. They trans . . . she tr . . . The knower makes a transcription from the tape.

E: And then they can all study it.

F: Same day? I mean same time? Do they . . . ?

E: Oh! It doesn't matter, I think. Heh?

T: Well . . . probably in the next session. But, yes, they make it, that's input, and use it later.

D: But I don't understand. Why are we talking about it now? Why don't we just do it?
    (*pause*)

G: Well . . . we are doing it actually!

D: What? What did you say, G?

G: I said we are doing it!

A last word

In this chapter, I've laid out the steps involved in doing a loop-input session. The next few chapters will give you practice in going through the process. Later on we'll need to discuss the times when you might choose loop input and the times when you might decide that it isn't appropriate.

1. Further reading on **Counselling Learning**:
   Curran, C. (1972). *Counseling Learning: A Whole Person Model for Education*. Grune & Stratton.
   Curran, C. (1983). Counseling Learning. In J. Oller and P. Richard-Amato (eds.), *Methods that Work*. Newbury House.
   Krashen, S. (1981). *Second Language Acquisition and Second Language Learning*. Pergamon Press.
   Stevick, E. (1980). *Teaching Languages: A Way and Ways*. Newbury House.
2. For further reading on the **'three Ps' model** see pages 117–18.

5 Classroom management

You may, at this point, like to join in with some of the passages in this book. For example, we could do this unit together. I've chosen the topic and I've written a list of things I think trainees should be able to do as competent teachers moving around their own classrooms. Before reading my list, you may like to compile your own.

In my list below, the points aren't in any special order. I've probably missed out some points that you have down. It's good to compile these lists with other people when possible. Unfortunately, if you're working alone, that may be a real luxury.

Practical skills checklist

To be successful at classroom management, trainees need to be able to:

- Attract attention.
- Start – warm students up, greet, socialise.
- Deal with different space and furniture arrangements.
- Deal with early arrivals and latecomers.
- Mark changes of phase in a lesson.
- Ask people to do things.
- Thank people.
- Elicit information.
- Praise.
- Indicate error.
- Explain things.
- Check understanding.
- Move on.
- Describe, narrate.
- Interpret, accept interpretation, outline.
- Query meaning.
- Handle discipline problems.
- Offer and accept help and apologies.
- Move to closure.
- Close.
- Predict what's coming next time.
- Set homework.
- Vary style of voice, movement and manner.
- Be normal and human.[1]

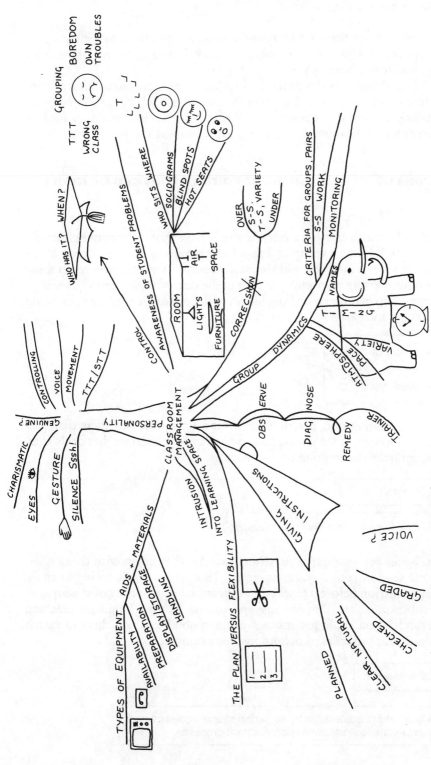

Figure 11 A classroom management mind map

51

All these points take certain types of language to effect, as well as social and physical skills. The language skills constitute a large area of work for non-native teacher trainees.

I'll go straight to the process of trying to find the chance for a loop. Before reading on, you might like to think about where the loop is. I see the loop as this: everything you tell trainees that they could try in their classroom, you can be trying in your own training classroom with them.

Areas of classroom management that can be looped

WARM-UPS

Let's take warm-ups for a start. If you believe that it takes time for individuals to become a group and to achieve maximum concentration at the start of a class, then you will want to encourage your trainees to do some short, interesting warm-up exercises at the start of their classes[2]. One type of warm-up involves matching halves of dialogues. For this one you write out cards such as:

Give the halves out. People mill around trying to find their dialogue partner. Another idea would be to do a matching exercise that deals with content from the training course, such as:

> A: What's a drill?

> B: It's a form of controlled oral practice.

But better yet would be a matching exercise that fits in with the content of the session you're warming-up to. Thus, if you were trying to run a review session before a teacher qualification exam and wanted people to be able to name the various approaches behind language teaching methods[3], you could get trainees in the mood by asking them to match names of approaches to definitions, for example:

> Behaviourism

> A belief that people learn by acquiring sets of habits gained from a stimulus-response-reinforcement process.

Suppose you wanted to do a session on reading games, what activity could you use for a few minutes at the start to get people into a group and into the content of a session?

One possible idea here would be to write out a sentence with as many words in it as there are trainees, for example, 'This is a little reading game called jumbled words that you can use in class to practise coherence and cohesion.' Put each word on a separate card. Give one card to each trainee. Trainees stand up and have to get themselves in a line, in the correct order, to make the sentence.

ATTRACTING ATTENTION

If we take this item from the *Practical skills checklist*, we can make sure that we attract attention in a different way at different times in one session or from session to session. We can do this by voice, sometimes with a musical instrument, switching the lights on and off quickly and so on.

DEALING WITH LATECOMERS

This is an easy one to loop. Let's imagine you have a session on vocabulary teaching. You can make a latecomers' hat containing cards. As people come in late they pick up a card from the hat and think about it while they settle down and wait for others to finish their group work.

On the cards, since it's a vocabulary teaching session, you can have short tasks such as:

How many words can you make from 'head'?
e.g. <u>headache</u>

Finish the series.

First I sorted the wash, then I opened the machine door.
Next I . . .
After that I . . .
Then I . . .

Think of all the words you can that start with:

inter-

para-

pre-

Which of these words are said in the same way?

rough, cough, bough, through, tough, dough, enough

For other sessions you could prepare different cards to fit the content of those sessions or use different latecomer ideas. Could you write latecomers' cards for people arriving late at a training session on correcting written work?

Repertoire lists

In the little kit I carry about with me are some lists of warm-ups, one-minute breaks, different ways of checking meaning, etc. so that I force myself to use a variety and to choose appropriate ones for each session instead of relying on my selective and shrinking memory. Here's an extract from my list on different ways of splitting classes into pairs or groups:

smokers / non-smokers   glasses / no glasses   January–June birthdays / July–December birthdays   toothpaste tube rollers / tube stabbers   tension stomachaches / tension headaches

Ways of splitting that are more appropriate for training classrooms might be:

regular homework doers / sporadic homework doers   trainees concerned with accuracy / concerned with fluency   drill-haters / closet drillers   trainees learning a language / not learning a language lesson planners / non-planners

Here's an extract from my list of one-minute break ideas:

1. *For sessions on vocabulary*
   - Make new short words using letters from one long word, e.g.
     VOCABULARY   CAB   BAR   BOY
     Other good long words are 'collocation' and 'semantic'. Can you think of some more?
   - Last letter / next word association game, e.g. *words, semantic, collocation, noun, n . . .*
2. *For sessions on phonology*
   - Go round the circle finding all the words that rhyme with 'ash' (in sound), e.g. *crash, bash, splash, rash*, etc. Are there any similarities in meaning between them?

With these lists by me, I can check when I'm planning a session that the type and content of my classroom management fit the basic message of the session. You might like to add ideas to these lists or start new lists of your own.

Making classroom management conscious

I'm trying to show that a lot of techniques in the area of classroom management can be worked quite naturally into the fabric of training session management by simply using them consciously as a trainer yourself. You will know that you are doing this. Trainees, however, will not necessarily notice that this is happening except by way of a vague feeling that classes are well-organised and lively in their arrangements. You will have to make the sorts of decisions you are taking conscious, visible, and overt in some way.

Pat Mugglestone's article 'Mirroring classroom procedures' (1979) shows how, by using a form, trainees can record the less concrete aspects of a training session. I have adapted the form and find that it can be used for review purposes later, for reminding trainees of administrative details, or simply as a way of making overt and conscious the processes of the session. The basic format of my 'record and review' sheet follows. You can, of course, adapt it to suit your purposes.

RECORD AND REVIEW SHEET

Session name   Date   Term   Session no.

1. **Warm-up idea**

2. **One-minute break idea**

3. **New vocabulary**

Word in original context	Meaning in EFL	Own sentence

New meetings of the words in fresh context (from reading, etc.)
Usual collocation

4. **Pair work organisation**
   How split up
   How started
   How finished
   Point of pair work

5. **Group work organisation**

Activity	Criteria for grouping	Size	Role of group members	Tutor's role

   Reason for splitting into groups

Integration of group work and individual work	Evaluation of work done in groups	Own comments / reactions

6. **Reading associated with session**
7. **Homework**
8. **Quotes of the week**
9. **Other things**

Are there other things you'd like to include on the form?

The form can be introduced in different ways. You could reveal it point by point each time, that is, the first week, at the end of the session, invite the trainees to recall the warm-up and to discuss how it was set up, what it felt like, how it could be adapted, and its advantages and disadvantages. Jointly or separately you or the trainees could write some notes by the first heading. After the second session, you could briefly recap and discuss the warm-up for that week and make some notes. Then the one-minute break idea could be discussed. Were any used during the session? Did they work? The trainees make notes. Using the form this way, it would become longer and longer each time until after nine weeks the whole form would have been explained. An alternative way of using the form is for the trainer to fill out a form for each of the first few weeks and then, after some discussion, to hand over the use of the forms to trainees so that in groups or individually, they can fill in one after each session. In this way, they gain a good, reviewable record of the classroom management techniques they have experienced each time as well as a record of homework and any other administrative points necessary. Some groups prefer the system where a different trainee has responsibility for filling in the review/ record form each time.

The form is useful for a number of reasons. First, it encourages trainees to look back and recall what happened in a session. As teachers, they will need this skill of recall as much as the skill of forward planning and preparation. Secondly, it encourages trainees to keep notes and ideas from the course in an organised, tangible way. Some people are comforted by this, especially come exam time. Thirdly, it underlines on paper the fact that you can learn about teaching while you're being taught. Once trainees are sensitised to this by using the form, they will begin to see much more in sessions than previously. Their minds will be working on several levels at once. They will be thinking not only about what they have to do for homework but about how the homework was given out, marked, handed back, consolidated and so on. They will tend to reflect on the various techniques used and start thinking about effecting a transfer (or not) of these techniques to their own classrooms. If you have a chance to include some microteaching on the course or if you observe their normal classroom teaching, then of course the transfer of these techniques can be planned, monitored, encouraged or noted as desired. The appropriacy of the transfer can be worked on too, in practice.

Trainees can, of course, change the design of the form. It may change three or four times during a course as they decide to concentrate on different things.

It is not only the idea of, say, including a warm-up at all, that can be underlined by using the 'record and review' form. One can encourage warm-ups that are in line with the content of a language lesson, for example, students who are about to read a text on famous cities can be warmed-up by playing the 'last letter / next word' game, like this:

'Chicago – O – Ottawa – A – Atlantic City – Y – York – K – Kyoto – O . . . Oh, help! Out!'

One can also discuss how a loop can be introduced into a warm-up, as when a group of students, all given one word each on a card, are given no help at all in putting themselves into a line to form the sentence: 'If we find *that we can put ourselves into the correct order and also make *lots *of other sentences like this one, *with *if *and *will *or *won't, we won't need to spend *much time on *that *particular *piece *of grammer *in this lesson!' (This sentence is for 44 students if all the words are used. If all the words with an asterisk before them are removed, it's for 29 students.) The loop here can be discussed with trainees. Thus, if the students perform well but the teacher keeps to the lesson plan and does a lot of work on the second conditional, is that a loop? Why isn't it? At which point isn't it?

By making your own classroom management style accessible, by working on it, recording it, discussing it and encouraging trainees to use it in their own lessons you start to acquire and pass on, not only techniques of classroom management, but also the skill of being consistent and the technique of looping. After all, why should the power of the loop stay in the trainer's hands?

Classroom language

For many non-native-speaker trainees, the language involved in accomplishing all the manoeuvres mentioned in the *Practical skills checklist* at the start of this chapter will prove quite a problem. By hearing you, the trainer, handling these manoeuvres, they will have the chance to listen to a trainer's repertoire of classroom management language. This chance should not be lost but it must also be made conscious.

For native-speaker trainees, too, there is the question of how they can modify their language to a level that is comprehensible to their students, without sounding totally unnatural, or how they can, almost at the flick of a switch, stretch their students by increasing, be it ever so slightly, the speed or sophistication of what they say. This ability to fine-tune your metalanguage (see Gower and Walters, 1983) requires practice. Native speakers often find that, for example, giving clear instructions is difficult. Listening to an experienced trainer can give pointers on how, or how not, to go about it. Once again, this noticing has to be made conscious.

c

Making it conscious

If you are working on the area of giving instructions, you can include in your sessions some times when you give instructions to trainees. You can video or sound tape these instances. You can then, either in class or as homework, ask trainees to:

- Analyse the tape and see and/or hear what gestures, phrases, facial expressions and aids were used to give instructions.
- Judge whether these worked and how they could be improved.
- Compare the language used with the language in the 'giving instructions' chapters of books like *Teaching English Through English* by Jane Willis (1981).
- Gather predictions of the language to be used by brainstorming before the session. Compare these with the language actually used.
- Compare the language actually used with a typed sheet of possible exponents for a particular function as given by a communicative grammar book.
- Note any language or gestures used so often as to be irritating.
- Note any phrases particularly liked, for incorporation into the trainees' own repertoire.

You may like to think of other tasks that would sensitise trainees to classroom instruction language and their own personal repertoires.

Remedial work

If particular trainees have specific problems with some aspect of classroom management, they can be set a project that involves investigating the trainer's (and other trainers' and trainees') methods of dealing with the problem in their own work. For example, a trainee who has problems timing phases of the lesson can be given an investigation project during a session. You, the trainer, take care to do one or more of the following: write a session plan with predicted and actual time columns marked on it, bring in a clock face with coloured zones on it, mark parts of your session material 'deletable' or 'expandable', keep a list of fillers on your desk, or use other devices that you find useful for timing or deliberate non-timing. The raw material, the data for the trainee's project is the trainer and the session itself. This has the marvellously salutary effect of preventing trainers from making glib suggestions that they've never tried out themselves, and of preventing trainees from being able to say that something would or would not work without reference to reality.

Let's imagine you have a trainee who talks so much in class that students hardly get any time to talk themselves or listen to each other. What could you do in your own training session to demonstrate ways of handling the problem? What tasks could you give the trainee to complete before, during and after your session? A useful reference here is the RSA manual (Davis, 1979, pp. 13, 14 and 22).

The wise trainer will choose a problem which she also has difficulty with, since this will give her the chance to improve and to realise that change in teaching behaviour is often slow and that areas of weakness need to be thought about and worked on without impatience or tension.

What problems do you feel you have as a teacher? Is your eye contact bad or your voice inaudible? Are your mannerisms annoying? Are you too intrusive into group work? Do you correct too little? Do you set up group work sloppily and then get bored? Do you overuse pair work? Working on your own problems in an attempt to give ideas to a trainee with a similar problem can be a great way to empathy, honesty and better teaching.

We often think of peer teaching, microteaching and full lesson observation as being the only way we can really check whether input and sensitisation have filtered through into classroom practice and behaviour. Another way is to invite trainees to help out in training sessions. Trainees can listen to each other's errors of omission in language used in group work and then slip each other cards with suggestions for new phrases on them, work out the best spatial arrangements for plenaries, organise the furniture, practise interrupting people to clarify instructions the trainer has not made explicit enough, and so on. It's quite possible for fifteen or more trainees in a group of eighteen to be working on individual projects of a classroom management kind without necessarily knowing what their colleagues are up to.

Here's an example of a task card that could be given to a trainee who has problems keeping eye contact with people:

> In the session there will be two occasions when you're asked to do pair work. Do it with the same partner each time. Don't tell them why. On the first occasion do not look into your partner's eyes much. On the second occasion force yourself to do so at least sometimes. Feel the difference emotionally in yourself and in the amount that your partner talks to you. Ask your partner later if they noticed anything.

Can you think of a trainee in a group of yours who has a specific problem? You might like to write out a task card for the trainee and think what type of session and what time in a session would suit the task best. Another idea is to produce a task card jointly with the trainee.

Another way of looping peer teaching or peer help into a session is by feeding some ideas into a few trainees before a session starts. These small groups of two to four people then communicate these ideas to the rest of the trainees in any way they like. This frees the trainer to act as an observer while losing no time within the session itself. It gives the trainer feedback on the effectiveness of her own transmission of ideas (before the session) and equalises the criticism of how teaching is done[4].

This chapter has attempted to show how you can weave the whole subject of classroom management into your sessions in the training classroom. It takes forethought, organisation and honesty, but those are surely some of the things that education is about.

1. Further reading on **classroom management**:
   Davis, R. L. (ed.) (1979). *RSA Cert. TEFL Courses: Teacher Training Techniques and Problem Areas.* Hilderstone English Language Centre.
   Dawson, C. (1984). *Teaching English as a Foreign Language: A Practical Guide.* Nelson.
   Gower, P. & Walters, S. (1983). *Teaching Practice Handbook.* Heinemann Educational.
   Harmer, J. (1983). *The Practice of English Language Teaching.* Longman.
   Haycraft, J. (1978). *An Introduction to English Language Teaching.* Longman.
   Hill, L. A. & Dobbyn, M. (1979). *A Teacher Training Course.* Cassell.
   Hill, J. & Lewis, M. (1985). *Practical Techniques for Language Teaching.* Language Teaching Publications.
   Holden, S. (ed.) (1979). *Teacher Training.* Modern English Publications.
   Hubbard, P., Jones, H., Thornton, B. & Wheeler, R. (1983). *A Training Course for the Teaching of English as a Foreign Language.* Oxford University Press.
   White, R. V. (1982). *The English Teacher's Handbook: A Short Guide to English Language Teaching.* Nelson.
2. Further reading on **warm-ups**:
   Buzan, T. (1974, revised and extended edition first published 1982). *Use Your Head.* BBC Publications.
   Woodward, T. 'Warm-ups, Breaks and Fillers' a regular column in 'The ETAS Newsletter', English Teachers' Association of Switzerland.
3. Further reading on **history of language teaching approaches and methods**:
   Kelly, L. G. (1976). *Twenty-five Centuries of Language Teaching.* Newbury House.
   McArthur, T. (1983). *A Foundation Course for Language Teachers.* Cambridge University Press.
   Strevens, P. (1977). *New Orientations in the Teaching of English.* Oxford University Press.
4. I am grateful to John Morgan for the idea of feeding new techniques to trainees who in turn feed them into the group.

6 No name

This chapter will be done 'backwards'. That is, I'll lay out a training session in steps and then afterwards I'll ask you what you think the aims and processes were. Here's the training session.

The fourteen steps of a training session plan

1. a) The trainer gives trainees a copy of the same ink blotch each. Here is an example blotch.

Figure 12   Ink blotch

(Rotate the page if you're more of a vertical or left-to-right type and this blotch is, to you, going the wrong way!)
The trainer asks trainees to note down, individually, five things the ink blotch suggests to them. Then all suggestions are written up on a board. People comment if they want.

b) The trainer flashes up an illustration like this:

and asks trainees, individually, to write a sentence describing what they see.

The different descriptions are read out.

2. The trainer flashes up a large card for two or three seconds, like this:

> PARIS IN THE
>
> THE SPRING

Some trainees will see this as 'Paris in the spring'.

3. The trainer plays a tape of someone talking or singing. The trainees listen, think and then sketch, in words, what they feel the person would look like and be like[1].

4. The trainer shows the following illustration of a young and old woman:

Figure 13 Young woman / old woman

The trainer asks the trainees which they see, if they can see both, and then asks them to switch between the two visions – as fast as possible!

5. (For this exercise[2], a positive atmosphere of trust is required.) The trainer asks each trainee to fill in the following form:

   a) Three things someone would tend to notice about my physical appearance when they first met me:
     i)
     ii)
     iii)

   b) Three things someone would tend to notice about my personality after they'd known me for a while:
     i)
     ii)
     iii)

Next, the trainees go into pairs, keep silent and look at each other for a few minutes. They fill in this form:

   c) Three things I noticed about my partner's physical appearance:
     i)
     ii)
     iii)

   d) Three things I think might be true about my partner's personality:
     i)
     ii)
     iii)

Pairs then explain to each other what they've written, pool impressions and await surprises or reassuring confirmation!

6. Play the trainees a sound or video tape of themselves. Give them a chance to discuss what they feel about the person on the tape (themselves).

7. The trainer writes up a text in a language unknown to anyone in the group and tells them it's a poem. The trainer asks the trainees if it's a good one[3].

8. The trainer asks trainees to think back to their own school days, to the teacher they most liked or disliked. What can they remember about this teacher's voice, gestures, clothes, manner, what the teacher taught them, the subject matter? Which is most remembered, the teacher, the context or the content?

9. One trainee in the centre of a circle is the 'teacher'. All the others are 'students'. The trainer stands where the teacher can't see flashcards held up with words on them like: 'Bored', 'Feeling fidgety', 'Can't understand', 'Tired', etc. The students act out the words on the card as they feel they might in a classroom. The teacher has to guess what

is written on the card by watching the students' behaviour and body language.

10. The trainer shows an extract of a film showing a language teacher at work in a classroom. Some trainees are not told what to watch for, others are asked to watch for very different things, e.g. the energy curve of one student throughout the lesson, patterns of interaction between students and teacher, the teacher's gestures and some are asked to guess the aim of the lesson.

11. The trainees are asked to discuss the video mentioned above as if the teacher were present in the group. They are asked to justify all the comments made, by reference to actual instances in the lesson.

12. The trainees are shown a lesson plan of half of what they saw and are asked to match what they saw to what was planned. They then devise different ways of doing the second half of the lesson so that it still fits the teacher's overall aim.

13. The trainees are shown observation checklists, interaction analysis sheets and classroom placement diagrams.

14. The trainees make a diagram showing the seating arrangement of the session and mark on it the positions of the trainer and trainees up to this point. If you've used Steps 1–13 so far, then trainees will need to make several drawings since people will have moved round several times.

DISCUSSION

You have just read through a plan of someone else's session without really knowing what was going on or why. This is usually bewildering and may well have involved you in a lot of guessing, predicting and readjusting at each step in order to know what the session was supposed to be about. By now, though, you could probably guess what the name of the session was.

What point do you think was being made through each of the session steps? You might like to take time to go through each step and jot down what you think the purpose of it was.

When I planned the session I thought it could be called 'Getting ready for lesson observation', or, more abstractly, 'Perception'. The points I was trying to make through each of the steps were:

1. People can see the same thing and think different things.
2. We can be misled by what we think we see.
3. We have fast, strong impressions based on what we see and hear.
4. Once we've seen or thought one thing, it's hard to see or think another, no matter how plausible an interpretation the second might be.

5. We have ideas about who we are. These are not necessarily matched by other people's ideas of who we are.
6. If we could see or hear ourselves from the outside, we might have different ideas about ourselves. Other people can give us this view sometimes.
7. It's hard to judge things if you're not party to the inner logic of what you're seeing.
8. Students spend time looking at teachers. They remember them, not necessarily for the things the teacher would want to be remembered for.
9. Teachers differ in the extent to which they can judge how someone is feeling.
10. There are lots of things to watch in a lesson apart from the teacher.
11. There are courtesies to be followed in giving feedback.
12. What we end up doing in a lesson is sometimes different from what we set out to do. There are many different ways of getting from A to B.
13. There are ways of making what you think and see more objective. Is that true?
14. Trainees need practice in the skills of observation.

I imagine that your proposed title for the session and your ideas of what lay behind each step were different from mine. I imagine too that now you could be thinking, 'I'd never run a session like that. All those different bitty little steps.' To my mind, this is the problem of observation. First of all, can we as trainers see what the participants saw? Can we grasp the inner logic from the participants' point of view? And how can we change the natural feeling of 'I would've . . . ', 'I wouldn't have . . . ' into helpful feedback that goes beyond the response of the taxi driver's when asked the way to somewhere: 'Well,' he said, 'I wouldn't really start from here!' But I am *here*. How do I get *there*?

You have just been through an experience that I sometimes put trainees through when I'm running a session that aims to prepare for lesson observation. Sometimes I show a video of a teacher at work in a classroom, where the teacher never makes clear what the aims of the lesson are. Sometimes I run a session similar to the one you've just read through and I give no title or explanation of any of the activities. I do it to show that if you don't happen to share the teacher's knowledge of what the point is, you may feel pretty confused about what is going on (or even manipulated). Observers can feel confused in other teachers' classes if they've arrived late, asked no questions or been given no replies, and, more importantly, students can feel this way in language classes. After all, teachers rarely give them a copy of the lesson plan!

People who are in classes and who are not party to the aims, reasons and explanations for what's going on, for whatever reason, are likely to make their own judgements of the whole event, as I'm sure you did at the start of this chapter, and to come away with their own understandings of what the whole point was. This may be no bad thing, but it's likely to be a little confusing. Unless session leaders are clear, other people in the room may feel as if they're on a magic carpet ride and act accordingly by looking at the view or admiring the carpet.

If observers don't bother to try and grasp the teacher's logic or to sense what the teacher and students are sharing, then they are just gatecrashers at someone else's party – unwanted troublemakers at an otherwise pleasant event.

Don't worry if you didn't understand what the session was about or why I was throwing you in at the deep end. Content (in this case ink, crosses, Paris, pictures, personalities and poems) is very distracting. We all tend to be blinded by content. Students, when asked what they learned at school that day, are very likely to remember interesting flashes of parrots and desert islands rather than the main learning point the teacher was trying to illustrate. Main themes, main learning ideas, and process ideas have to be made conscious and overt. I feel that it is only fair to work on making them overt, for we all tend to be attracted and distracted by odd bits of content.

If we continue to work backwards, you could now:
1. Attempt to locate some references that would help you to do a session entitled 'Preparing for observation'.
2. Make a list of points that trainees should remember in order to be popular observers.
3. Make a mind map or diagram showing where you think observation fits into a teacher training course.
4. Brainstorm the topic of lesson observation to make a review diagram rather than the usual preview or overview diagram.

I have done the second and the fourth, just to provide a point of difference for you to contrast your own ideas with. Here is the second.

Points trainees should remember in order to be popular observers!
1. Ask the teacher politely if observation would be possible. Accept 'no' for an answer, if necessary.
2. Arrive early.
3. Get as much information on the class, teacher and lesson as possible without harassing the teacher.
4. Have a clear idea of what you're looking for before you start.
5. Find out the teacher's policy on your writing things down, joining in pair and group work, leaving before the end, etc.
6. Sit where you're put. If you're given a choice, sit where you can see students' faces and reactions.
7. Keep your demeanour pleasant throughout no matter what happens!
8. Be natural. If students ask why you're there, tell them. Otherwise they may think you're from the immigration office.

9. Don't share your notes or feelings on the teacher with the students or the teacher's colleagues.
10. Thank the teacher afterwards. Ask questions if time allows. If the teacher wants feedback state positive points as well as negative. (In fact more positive than negative.)
11. Think about what you've seen.
12. Keep a relationship going with the teacher and students no matter what happened in the class.
13. Make sure you allow the same teacher to sit in on you sometime. Suggest or offer this.

Here's a reVIEW diagram with a pair of eyes in the middle, for the fourth point above. There are two tasks left to do . . . !

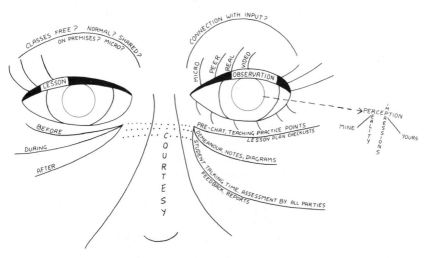

Figure 14   A lesson observation mind map

1. Thanks to Elayne Philips for this idea.
2. I learnt this idea from Judy Baker.
3. I learnt this idea from Yafa Kleiner who told me she learnt it from her trainer.

7 Being a beginner and starting again

On most training courses there is a session or two devoted to letting the trainees experience a language lesson in a little-known language like Rwandan, Tamil or Cherokee. It is rarely sound or video taped. Trainees are expected to be able to remember the thoughts and feelings they had during the time they took on the role of language students, and discuss these when they have returned to the role of trainee. They are usually helped to remember by a little Socratic midwifery, often in the form of a handout with some questions on, something like these:

1. Did you read the new language first or hear it or write it?
2. Did you experience a fear of forgetting?
3. Were you allowed to remain silent?
4. What do you think you were saying?
5. How were errors screened out / dealt with?
6. Were any single words given out of context?
7. Did you have times when you were waiting to be asked or dreading being asked?
8. How much practice did you have? How much practice did the teacher have?
9. Did the teacher talk about the language?
10. How was the classtime broken up into different phases?
11. How do you know if you made any progress?
12. Did you notice differences between your rate of progress and that of other learners? How did you feel about this?
13. Did the teacher show encouragement, praise or irritation? How did you feel about this?
14. Do you think you could've done the homework?
15. Did the teacher speak at normal speed?
16. Were you able to discern the individual sounds of words? Were you able to tell where word boundaries were?
17. Were there any sounds that you couldn't pronounce even though you heard them clearly?
18. Did you learn anything new or surprising about the target language apart from the language itself? What about gestures? How people deal with each other? Anything else?

> 19. What was your general impression of the new language? How did it sound? Any moral to be drawn from this?
> 20. How typical do you think this language lesson was?

Whilst often quite good fun and certainly thought-provoking, some trainees will be blocked from good experience by thoughts such as these: 'I don't want to learn Cherokee', 'I don't teach beginners', 'What a lovely language – will we get regular Cherokee lessons?' 'I'm not a beginner of the languages I'm most interested in. In fact, in most spheres of my life I'm more of an intermediate – not too bad at things, but no genius!'

Other trainers, trying to get away from the artificiality of these one-off or two-off language lessons will run language lessons as a regular component of the course or will arrange for parallel language courses to be available at a convenient time. To capitalise on the impressions received by the trainee-cum-language learner different sorts of questionnaire types or observation/participation sheets can be drawn up. Some examples follow.

ENTHUSIASM SHEET

Mark in on the graph below how involved or enthusiastic or interested you feel about the language lesson at ten-minute intervals. Above your rating make a note of any factors (for example, temperature, hunger, fatigue, behaviour of your neighbour, type of exercise, mode of working, e.g. groups, pairs, whole class, topic under discussion, etc.) that you feel may be responsible for your degree of enthusiasm.

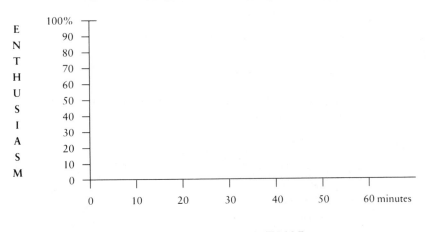

LESSON TIME

69

Being a beginner and starting again

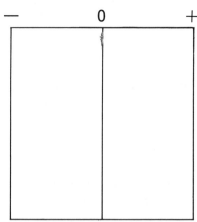

My teacher is friendly.
I understand what I'm to do.
I have a feeling of progress.
I get on with the others.
I have time to reflect.
I am challenged.

Mark with an X on the scale how you feel generally in your language learning lessons, then try to think why it is you feel that way. You can add other remarks to those on the left above, to reflect other elements of the lesson that you are interested in.

SENTENCE COMPLETIONS: BEFORE THE LESSON

Complete the following sentences before the language learning lesson:

I really hope I'll learn ....
I expect to feel ....
I hope my teacher ....
The other students will ....
As for homework ....

You can add some more unfinished sentences.

SENTENCE COMPLETIONS: AFTER THE LESSON

After you've had the language learning lesson, complete the following sentences:

I was surprised that ....
I felt ....
I learned ....
My teacher ....
The other students ....
The homework ....

There may be more unfinished sentences you'd like to add.

QUESTION AND ANSWER SHEET

Sometimes, when you're in a classroom learning something, you feel like asking the teacher questions, even if rhetorically, or you feel something so strongly that you want to make a comment. You can do this by filling in the following form during the lesson and giving it to the teacher after the lesson so she can answer your questions in writing when she has time.

Student's name .... Date ....

Teacher's name .... Time ....

Student's question/comment ....

....

Teacher's reply ....

....

Student's question/comment ....

....

Teacher's reply ....

....

Student's question/comment ....

....

Teacher's reply ....

....

Other remarks ....

....

....

If language teachers are willing to take part in this question and answer exercise (Deller, 1987) they can write their answers or comments in the space provided on the form. This form would work well in the situation outlined earlier where language lessons are laid on parallel to the teacher training course. If this is the case, the language teacher could be encouraged to be open to methodological questions and, in turn, would receive very valuable feedback on the forms from the students. I adapted this idea from Sheelagh Deller who drew up a form when she was observing trainees on an RSA preparatory certificate course. On her form the questions are asked by the trainer and the trainees are required to answer in the empty spaces on the form. The form, duly completed, is used as a basis for trainer-to-trainee feedback. Here it could be used for student-to-teacher feedback or as a basis for discussions on methodology in the training classroom.

Some trainers use the one-off foreign language lesson as a way of demonstrating an alternative method of teaching foreign languages. Thus, the main point is to help trainees discover something about, for example, the Silent Way, by having a Silent Way teacher come in and teach a foreign language to the group in the Silent Way. One problem with this is that it implicitly affects discussion of what level a method is appropriate for. It often seems that the trainees who think they could learn a language using the Silent Way say, 'Yes, it's a really good method for teaching beginners.' Other trainees say, 'I could never learn a language that way, so I doubt if anybody else could!'

Those wanting to get beyond foreign language learning to general learning may set out to help trainees to grasp a simple skill that can be learnt, at least to some extent, at one go. Examples of such skills might be: card tricks, making water lilies of paper, tying macramé knots, juggling with two or three balls, or understanding the workings of the combustion engine from a child's book. The trainer can make sure that each trainee or group of trainees learns in a different way, for example, from printed instructions, from a cardboard model, from a lecture, from an expert who continually intervenes and so on. Learning experiences can then be contrasted and discussed in an attempt to highlight points such as learning styles being highly individual and different teaching styles having different effects on different people.

Another idea in a similar vein is to ask trainees to make up a new (non-sense) language, describe it and teach it to others. Some trainees find this wonderfully interesting, and others find the idea unattractive and are unwilling to spend much time on it. Making up a language requires a certain kind of thinking, and it doesn't appeal to everyone.

My intention is not to criticise all these ideas. I've used most of them myself and probably will go on using some of them. But in the interests of congruence or consistency, I'd like to get back to the basics and discuss what we are trying to do with this kind of session. The stated intention of the beginner's lesson in a little-known language is often 'to help the trainees remember what it's like to be a language learner or a beginner again'. Perhaps we should look at these intentions a little more closely.

Do the trainees need to know how it feels to be a beginner? Are they beginning anything? Are their students beginning anything? If the answer to these questions is 'no' then perhaps we should change the intention to 'How it feels to be a pre-intermediate' or even 'Thinking about learning', which has obvious relevance both for the students the trainees will teach and for the trainees themselves on the training course. Might trainees think they know how learning takes place? For them? How do people learn anyway? Do you, as a trainer know? For yourself? For others?

This fairly radical kind of enquiry may take a long time. All the better if it leads to our dismantling totally, or at least into serial parts, sessions that have been taken as fairly traditional on training courses and thus have gone unquestioned. If what we are aiming at is for trainees to get in tune with how it feels to suffer from a reduction in expressiveness, or to struggle with a necessity through long periods of low or no motivation, or to combat the feeling that new, strange things are ridiculous or repugnant, or that knowing something theoretically is totally different from feeling it as you walk and talk, then can we really expect that one hour of Welsh or Rwandan will somehow take care of all that?

In Chapter 4 I suggested some steps for producing a loop-input session. Step 1 was 'Arrive at a topic for a session', Step 2 was 'Brainstorm what you know about the subject'. I hope this chapter has shown that these steps are not always easy. You might like to look at a publication called *How Do I Learn?* (Belbin et al., 1981). This is basically a report of an experimental programme designed to introduce young people and their teachers to the many ways of learning. The manual contains examples of teaching materials designed to make students realise that everyone can and does learn, that they learn in order to do different things, that there are a variety of ways of learning and that some ways of learning suit some individuals better than others. Another helpful book here is Tony Buzan's *Use Your Head* (1974). It can open up new ways of studying for students, trainees and teachers just as it opened up mind maps for me as a method of thinking, previewing, reviewing, overviewing and note taking.

Is your course about learning, about how students learn languages and how trainees learn teaching and how trainers learn training? If so, then a desire to loop that into the content and process of your course will lead you way past one foreign language lesson. It may well lead you to scrap that particular session and start again, with clearer intentions and activities more in tune with your intentions. It may mean that *you* start again, at the beginning.

8 Partial loops and drills (a partial loop)

I'm sure many people have had the experience of attending a course where a teacher, lecturer or trainer uses one or two particular input techniques to the exclusion of most others. Some teachers love using problem solving in groups, some do mini-lectures that turn out to be maxi-lectures, and others love student presentations. Originally, the technique probably constituted a real extension to their teaching repertoire, a real change and a bit of excitement. Three years on, and the reasons for the technique, the skill of setting it up or capitalising on it properly have perhaps been forgotten and the techniques are now worn, familiar routines that the teacher can slip on like a pair of old slippers. They feel comfortable and unthreatening.

To avoid the overuse of the particular technique explained in this book, I'd like to stress that loop input is just another tool to be used for getting information across. I don't do loop-input sessions all the time, nor just for the sake of it, but only when they add to the intelligence or neatness of a session. I use them when I feel they will increase the effectiveness of the session. I will say more about the evaluation of effectiveness in Part Two. Here I will mention just a few considerations.

Trainers and trainees know the conventions of the training classroom. For example, if trainees walk into a raked lecture theatre, they will pick their way to seats that suit their reactions to the situation. Many will choose seats in the middle section, a few will go to the very back and one or two might go to the front. There will be preferences for left or right, end of row or middle of row. I doubt if any trainee will go to the lectern or podium and sit there! Time is saved by people knowing what they want to do in the lecture situation. The trainer who has to use the lecture theatre for participatory group work or who hates facing empty front rows will know the time it takes to move people from their preferences or habits. Sometimes this rearranging time is time well spent. Sometimes the time is simply taken from the session, depending on what the point of the session is. Where possible, trainers often pre-arrange rooms to suit their own styles. In this sense we can say that we all know rooms. We know what to predict from different arrangements. We recognise our mood changes as we walk, for example, from large to small rooms or from dark to light rooms. We know that middle-sized rooms with rows and rows of chairs and a desk at the front are classrooms, a room with chairs arranged in a circle is a group discussion room, tables in a banquet shape are conference rooms and a huge auditorium with a few ancient chairs in it seems designed to create a thunderous theatrical entrance for latecomers (Leveton, 1977).

Trainees who are used to being flexible about where they sit and who they work with, and used to venturing remarks or asking questions without being called on by name, will be easy to work with, unless you expect them to sit passively through long talks. Trainees soon get used to what normally happens. A new trainer going in to a well-established group used to 'their own' trainer might have a feeling similar to that of writing with someone else's fountain pen or putting someone else's child to bed. One consideration then, when deciding whether to use a loop-input session or not, is whether the time spent getting trainees to work in a new way is time you want to spend, or not.

Another consideration is whether trainees will be flexible enough to suspend operations on one task, start another, and then another, and then return to the first task. Is the experience gained worth the possibility of confusion? An example here might help.

I'll imagine my trainees are teachers in a college in Japan where they are required by the administration to take the attendance register every hour regardless of whether they have changed rooms or groups, or not. Imagine that 35 trainees in a training classroom are asking for ways to liven up this tedious roll-call procedure. I could decide to loop the whole business of 'ideas to use while calling roll' into the training session by:

1. Listing all the trainees' names alphabetically.
2. Thinking up some register ideas, for example:
   a) Calling names at random while people are busy during a writing phase, and asking a different little question each time so as to give practice in spontaneous answers.

   Teacher: Chieko! Here?
   Chieko: Yes!
   Teacher: Akiko! OK?
   Akiko: OK!
   Teacher: Reiko! Doing anything special tonight?
   Reiko: Not really.
   Teacher: Kumiko! Finished?
   Kumiko: Not yet.

   b) Asking people to call each other's names and add a little phrase each time.

   Teacher: Jean! Are you here?
   Jean: Yes. I know you're here, Paul.
   Paul: Yes! I can see you, Marie.
   Marie: OK. José isn't here.
   Teacher: No, but what about Regula?

c) Stopping every 60 minutes during the three-hour training session and calling all the names on the list but using a different game idea each hour.

I could do it as in (c), but then I merely invite into the training classroom the problems the trainees face in the language classroom, i.e. a feeling of being policed every hour, an interruption of the task at hand, a loss of time, and an insistence that every member of the group takes part. I also add the extra problem of trainees trying to remember *why* we are doing this (trainee thinks: 'Oh yes! That's input. She's calling roll now not because she has to do it but to show me a new way of doing it. Now . . . what's the new way?') and *which person* they are assuming at any moment in the hour ('Is she calling me, the trainee, or me, the language student?').

Looping the ideas into the fabric of the session so thoroughly would, in this case, make the session more complicated. The experience gained is less than the bother caused. It would be simpler to make a little slot sometime where roll-call ideas were tried out with a few names from a list and time taken to discuss adaptations to each idea.

If these are times when I would not use a full loop, when are the times when I would?

- When I want an idea to resound in a trainee through several senses, so that experience, text, words and feelings chime together leaving the trainee with echoes in her ears that will continue to be heard for some time after the session is over.
- With trainees who can appreciate a joke, a pun, a double entendre.
- With trainees who like to think and to move and who enjoy a synthesis of the two.
- For trainees who drive for consistency. For those who want to experience things but are bored with straight EFL textbook content. For trainees in a hurry, who want everything at once.
- For me, for moods when I am relaxed and full of energy. For moods when I need the mental exercise of seeing how simple, neat and clean a loop I can make. For the joy of seeing the 'Oh! I see!' looks on people's faces. For the times when people say (as G did in the CLL session) 'well . . . we *are* doing it actually!'

All loops or no loop?

The choice is not simply 'all loops or no loop'. There are partial loops and loops at different levels. I'll give you an example of what I mean.

Drills or controlled oral practice: a partial loop

Before concentrating on how we can effect a partial loop in a session on controlled oral practice, we need to take a closer look at the content. A mind map on drills follows. The arrows flying in from the top right are a reminder that the content area will need to be set into a wider perspective on the course.

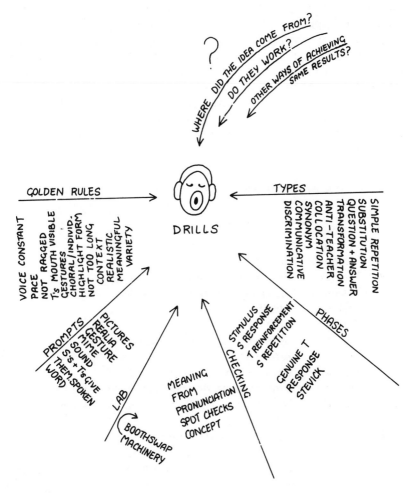

Figure 15   A drills mind map

In a session, or part-session on drills, you might like to play the teacher, drilling the class in English so the trainees can feel what it's like to be a student doing a drill. The trainees could, alternatively, do some drills in a language laboratory in a language foreign to them. Part of a session on behaviourism, mechanical practice, the disadvantages of drills, or whatever angle you happen to be interested in, could be run as a loop. Trainees can experience and make drills of a self-descriptive kind. Drills were, of course, invented or designed for language practice, so the ones below are in fact a spoof on language drills. They do, however, give trainees the feeling of what this kind of chanting feels like to conduct and pronounce, as well as containing some pointers and information. In the cases below, the content of each drill is about the type of drill. This may lead trainees to remember them better than normal language students remember language drills!

Trainees experience different kinds of drills

TO ACQUAINT TRAINEES WITH BASIC FORMATS

Trainer: This is a drill. Repeat after me. This is a drill.
Trainees: This is a drill.
Trainer: This is a simple repetition drill. Everyone!
Trainees: This is a simple repetition drill.
Trainer: Substitution.
Trainees: Substitution.
Trainer: (*looks cross and holds hands in 'complete sentence' gesture*)
Trainees: This is a simple substitution drill.
Trainer: Progressive. (*hand signals for choral repeat*)
Trainees: This is a simple progressive substitution drill.
Trainer: More difficult.
Trainees: (*produce what they can*)
Trainer: This last one is . . . an even more . . .
Trainees: This last one is a . . . (*mumble*) progressive . . . even more . . . ?

Hopefully a degree of chaos has been introduced and this can be discussed. The text of the drill above and the one below can be handed out on paper to trainees at some point so that they have a reminder of how simple repetition and substitution drills work.

TO GET ACROSS SOME IMPORTANT POINTS ON HANDLING DRILLS

Trainer: Drills – shouldn't – be – too – slow. Repeat. (*said slowly*)
Trainees: Drills – shouldn't – be – too – slow.

Trainer:	Or too ragged. (*gives no hand signal or indication of who/when to start*)
Trainees:	Or too ragged. (*raggedly*)
Trainer:	Drills shouldn't be too complicated or difficult to remember especially when students are tired. (*said very fast*)
Trainees:	(*say what they can or laugh*)
Trainer:	Too boring. (*intoned with hand gesture for 'whole sentence'*)
Trainees:	Drills shouldn't be boring. (*intoned*)
Trainer:	Or mechanical. (*robot-like*)
Trainees:	Or mechanical.
Trainer:	Is this one? (*fast, natural – to show how a sudden concept check or comprehension check can wake people up*)

To make drills more interesting and more human, Earl Stevick (1976) suggests adding three extra steps to follow the ones that most people use. The steps are:

a) Students give sentences from the drill in any order and without cues. This immediate and uncued free recall may enhance future free recall.
b) Students suggest sentences which are grammatically similar to those in the drill, but which contain different vocabulary. Here the student draws partly on rehearsal material but has some free choice.
c) Students suggest sentences similar to the ones that have gone before but which will draw reactions of surprise, interest, laughter, etc. from the teacher or classmates.

To demonstrate these extra three phases, trainees can be asked (a) to recall any sentences they can from the drills they've just been doing. So, for example, the basic pattern in the above drill is 'Xs shouldn't be too Y.' The next step then is (b) to make up a sentence with a similar structure, but with different lexis. An example here might be 'Dogs shouldn't be too fat.' The next step is (c) to make up sentences similar to the ones in the drill but with content that will surprise or please someone in the room, for example, 'Trainees shouldn't borrow too many books without giving them back, Angela!'

To help trainees with substitution drills, which are quite difficult for both trainees and students to handle, my suggestion is to take any drill from an intermediate coursebook, drill it fast and see how well the trainees cope. Then ask them to imagine how students would cope and how they could be helped to cope.

To demonstrate that cues or prompts can be varied by the teacher, the trainer can bring in a variety of prompts and try out the following stimulus response drill.

The trainer's basic model sentence is, for example, 'A picture can serve as a cue or a prompt.' The trainer holds up a picture as a prompt for this sentence, e.g. a picture of a cup. The substitutions for the model sentence can be, for example, a flashcard with a word on it, a real object, the teacher's voice, a mime or another picture. Each substitution is prompted by itself. Thus, after the model sentence has been given, a sentence such as 'A flashcard with a word on it can serve as a cue or a prompt' can be prompted by showing a flashcard with a word on it. Other sentences can be prompted, e.g. 'A real object can serve as a cue or a prompt', 'The teacher's voice can serve as a cue or a prompt', 'A mime can serve as a cue or a prompt', and each time the sentence is cued by the appropriate prompt, i.e. a real object, the teacher's voice or a mime.

If the flashcard has the words 'cup of tea' on it or if the real object shown is a cup and saucer, then many trainees will start saying 'Cues or prompts can be a cup of tea' because they will be confusing what they see and the generalisation behind it. Their minds will have trouble coping with the two things at once. There's a moral in this and it bears discussing! Is the trainee performance improved when the prompts are worked through once before the drill or when going through the drill for the second time?

To demonstrate that some drills are nonsense, just look through some coursebook drill exercises until you find one that is particularly inane and then drill it until trainees scream, for example, 'The cat is sitting.'

The teacher
The teacher's husband
Stand
The dog
I
Walking
You

To allow trainees to feel what it might be like to be forced to say things they don't mean, try:

Trainer: Do you like ice cream? Answer using *yes*.
Trainee: Yes, I do.
Trainer: Do you like coffee? No.
Trainee: No, I don't.

Follow this with examples chosen to go against trainees' normal likes and dislikes, for example, Mikhail Gorbachev *(no)*, sex *(no)*, whiskers on kittens *(no)*, *freezing rain (yes)*, drills *(yes)*, doing what you're told *(yes)*, saying what I force you to say *(yes)*[1].

Trainees practise handling drills themselves

At this point I'd like to bring in the term *self-descriptivity*. The sentence 'This sentence has seven words in it' is self-descriptive. That is, if you count the words in the sentence you find that there are indeed seven. The word 'pentasyllabic' is also self-descriptive. Some of the drills in the section above are self-descriptive too.

Trainees can make up self-descriptive drills. First of all, you'll need to work with them to produce a list of *Important things to remember when drilling your students*. A list such as the following, would do (the points are not in order of importance).

1. Speak at normal speed and keep your intonation and stress constant. If you can't, use tapes.
2. Keep a good steady pace.
3. Get everyone starting together and loudly.
4. Teacher's mouth should be on view.
5. Use gestures to control rhythm and pitch.
6. Dot around the class. Do some choral, pair, individual, half class and group drills.
7. Use eyes and gestures as well as names.
8. Highlight the form, stress and information with hands and fingers.
9. Response can be a word, a smile, or a real appropriate response.
10. Don't go on for too long.
11. Allow freedom in non-structural details.
12. The information in a drill can always be useful rather than inane. Drills can be meaningful in fact.
13. How much power should the teacher have?
14. How much power should the students have?
15. Students can give the prompts.

You may want to change or add to points on this list if you decide to use it. Whatever the list looks like, the idea is that trainees choose a point from it, make up a self-descriptive drill to exemplify it and then try it out on some other trainees. Here are some examples of drills produced by trainees.

- For Point 1, a trainee said 'Keep intonation constant' several times, with different intonation, looked irritated and then turned on a tape that said 'If you can't, use a tape!' over and over again in the same way.

- For Point 7, a trainee did a choral drill followed by individual drills using eyes and gestures instead of names to indicate when other trainees should speak. The sentence used as the model for the drill was 'I'm not using your name!'
- For Point 12, a trainee drilled 'There's a staff meeting at 7 p.m. on Thursday.'
- For Point 13, a trainee did a simple substitution drill with the model sentence 'Teachers are great!' with 'terrific', 'intelligent', 'underpaid' and 'overworked' as prompts.
- For Point 14, a trainee did a negative reaction drill using 'Teachers are great, terrific . . . ' etc. The trainee response was 'Oh no, they aren't! They're stupid, boring, intrusive . . . ' etc.

The point of doing these exercises is that they combine fun with peer-teaching and in the next session you can check which of the important points have actually been remembered by trainees.

Alternatively, you could try just one exercise to check if trainees can actually control and conduct drills properly. Ask them to stand in a circle. Each has a slip of paper with an utterance and a letter on it. If their letter is A, they leap out first and drill the utterance on their slip of paper (chorally, individually, in pairs or groups). When it's said to their satisfaction they go back into the circle and person B comes out to be the teacher. This exercise, too, can be partially looped. For example, the penultimate slip of paper can contain the utterance 'I'm absolutely sick of drills', and the last one can contain the utterance 'Me, too! Let's go for coffee!'

There are all sorts of things that you, the trainer, can be doing while the trainees are busy with the circle game. This is a perfect time for a spot of informal observation.

Last words

At any time before, during or after a session, different choices are available. A sensitive and thoughtful teacher or trainer will be aware of the variety and will make different choices at different times, for different reasons. The choice can be made to loop a whole session, not to loop at all, to loop parts of sessions, or to encourage trainees to loop as well. The technique can work at different levels and for different people.

1. Thanks to Tim Hahn for this 'power drill'.

9 The use of models

Showing someone how to do something is a natural thing to do, whether you are a parent, friend, sibling or teacher. If *you* know how to juggle or ride a bike or stake delphiniums, it seems so normal that you should show someone who doesn't know how to do these things – that they should copy you – until they can 'do it right', that is, your way. You give a model and the others follow. We've all given them and followed them all our lives. I have a memory of my uncle standing in cold, choppy water in the sea at Exmouth trying to teach me how to swim. His hands were held in prayer fashion as he showed me the start of the breast stroke. I don't remember when I actually started swimming myself, but I'm sure the feeling of being afloat and swimming was utterly different from the model given, from the sight of the hands held in prayer fashion. Still, I started swimming and, once started, my muscles developed memories of their own. It was the feeling that I sought again, the feeling of swimming, not the sight of someone else explaining. And yet, somehow the demonstration had helped.

The advantages of following models like these are that they are usually clear and definite. Followers know what is expected of them. They do not have to think too much, they just have to do it 'like that', or become 'like that'. The disadvantages of models are that we may copy without understanding, or copy without realising we are copying, or copy something which is imperfect in itself. We can certainly copy without believing and then change back to our old behaviour as soon as our model-giver is out of sight. (At Exmouth, this meant a return to the dog-paddle!) Our old pre-copying behaviour was perhaps the result of following a model too, but it had been part of us for so long that we no longer questioned it or considered that it came from 'outside'. New copying implies some sort of wiping out of the old, rather than a grafting on or remixing. Copying may seem stale and no fun at all to our creative side. The models might, too, be appropriate to the model-giver but not to the receiver. Modelled behaviour can become obsolete when the situation changes. Can modelled behaviour be recognised as obsolete and thrown away, or will it be aspired to and part of us forever? Can it have general value or does it just help us with specific cases?

Models in teacher training

Whatever the questions we might have, we use the giving and following of models in teacher training and language teaching all the time. We talk about providing good phonological models and of approximating texts. Any kind of specification of exit requirements for trainees on a course, exam-based especially, will tend to mould quite drastically the behaviour of trainees who want the certificate, at least until they've got it!

I feel very mixed about the business of models myself. I loved my own trainer, especially her accepting attitude to everyone in the room with her (that is, her students and trainee observers). I improved my own behaviour, in my own eyes, by modelling it very deliberately on hers, in this respect. But when I had my own teacher trainees I played the 'anti-model' game by making deliberate mistakes, encouraging criticism, feedback and adaptation so that trainees should not take me as gospel. I tried to remove myself from the centre too, monitoring in low-profile ways and trying to facilitate and manage discovery task work. I was deliberately thrown back into the centre, time and time again, by trainees who wouldn't play in a team with no captain. And then when I saw trainees doing things I had suggested, I had to admit I felt pleased. The ideas were quite good. Maybe I wasn't too bad as a model after all. Trainers wanting to be low profile, trainees wanting a definite model, bad behaviour modelled, good behaviour modelled . . . these are complex issues creating a complicated alchemy between them. However you and your trainees are going to handle the question of leading and following, modelling, mirroring, doubling or pacing, here is an ultra-conservative idea for dealing with one aspect of it.

Writing models

Just as students have to learn how to write letters, postcards and other texts in English, so many trainees will want to write dialogues and short texts for students as well as improve their letter, memo or poster writing for their own personal, trainee or teacher purposes. For the training course itself they may well need to write lesson plans, assignments, exam questions and projects in order to gain their qualification. Let's imagine you are working towards a particular end product, for example, an exam answer with a certain style, and your trainees cannot yet produce the required end product. You will probably decide to do some guiding and shaping. If you want trainees to have experience producing, adapting or evaluating writing models, then you can use writing models yourself when you help trainees in their written work. Having experienced the advantages and disadvantages of following writing models, they'll know better how their students feel.

You could (a) let them have a go at some written work first and then tell them where they went 'right' or 'wrong' later, or (b) provide them with a model to start with and then let them approximate it.

You might find that method (a) either builds up frustration or a real desire/need to learn. Method (b) might save time in one sense but involve less personal commitment and so mean less well remembered material in the long run (in real time).

You can let trainees experience different kinds of writing models where (i) the model does all the work and the trainee needs to think very little, (ii) the prompts or structure of the model are so badly written that trainees are led into making syntactic errors when changing parts of the text to write parallel texts, (iii) good structure is given but there is enough choice so trainees have to think hard.

Alternatively you can provide a written text and ask trainees to underline the parts that would make good prompts for someone wanting to write a parallel text, or you can provide nothing and ask trainees to construct a model with prompts. This takes us back to method (a) except that now the trainee is in a teacher role rather than a trainee role. We are back where we started – but not quite.

Writing exam answers

In Hubbard et al. (1983, p. 58) there is a section on teaching extensive reading in which there is a passage on extensive reading written in the form of a successful essay on the subject for an RSA DOTE (Diploma for Overseas Teachers of English) exam, as if by a trainee. The passage is reproduced here:

> Students are given guidance for intensive reading, but not for extensive reading. How would you help students to read extensively in English?
> Why do you think extensive reading should play an important part in the foreign language learning process?

Extensive reading should play an important part in the foreign language learning process for several reasons. Firstly, it is an activity that can be carried out by the student on his own, outside the classroom. Furthermore, it may be the only way a student can keep in contact with English after he has completed his course.

With older students, a class magazine library often proves very popular and the teacher can encourage the students to subscribe to magazines themselves.

Although it is true that the students will not read unless they are interested, the teacher can help the students to acquire the specific skills they are going to need for extensive reading. One such skill is the ability to infer the meaning of unknown words and structures. Students can be taught certain techniques for inferring meaning; for instance, they should consider whether the unknown word is a noun or a verb by its position in the sentence; whether (if it is a noun) it is singular or plural, countable or uncountable; whether it is similar to any known words; whether it may be a derivative of a known word. Students should also be made familiar with suffixes and prefixes and their significance, and whenever they learn a new word, they should be made aware of its derivatives.

Even with this help it is going to be impossible for the students to understand every single word in a reader and it is important that the students should be willing to tolerate less than one hundred per cent comprehension. The teacher can show the students how it is possible to understand the storyline of a book, even when there are quite a lot of unknown words. If students are given reading practice using passages a little more difficult than their level, which contain a few unfamiliar words and structures, they are made aware that they can understand the general meaning of the text, without complete comprehension of vocabulary and structures.

Sometimes, despite all the training he has had, a student may find it impossible to guess the meaning of a vital word in the text. In this case, he should be able to look it up in the dictionary. A useful skill the teacher can help students to acquire is the ability to use a dictionary quickly and efficiently. A lot of helpful ideas for exercises of this nature can be found in the workbooks which accompany many EFL learners' dictionaries.

Students are not going to read for pleasure if they read so slowly that they have no chance to get interested in the content of what they are reading. We have already mentioned that students should not be slowed down by words and structures they don't know, but it is also helpful to give the students practice in reading quickly. One exercise the teacher can do is to give the students a time limit to read a text and ask them to provide a title for it, thus making them aware that they can understand the gist of something even when they read very quickly.

Above all, extensive reading should be reading for pleasure and not a chore. It is therefore not usually a good idea to set deadlines by telling students they should have read so many pages of a book by a certain time. If the teacher makes the students read, it will tend to reduce the enjoyment and satisfaction they would have got out of doing something for themselves. In conclusion, it must be remembered that forcing students to read defeats the object of the exercise and it is the duty of the teacher to introduce the reading programme in such a way that the students are interested in spite of themselves.

Thus an RSA DOTE trainee reading the book gets double their money's worth on this section, for not only are they receiving input on extensive reading but they are also seeing the sort of style, length and content that would be acceptable in their final examination. Since the trainee is asked on p. 58 of the Hubbard book to read about reading, there is the start of a little loop here, but the text is about extensive reading whereas the trainee is asked to read the text intensively in order to answer the pre- and post-reading questions attached to it.

Perhaps we can borrow the idea of giving course input and information about exam answers in the same passage. If we wrote an acceptable answer to the kind of exit exam question our trainees will be faced with (for example, 'Discuss the advantages and disadvantages of constructing writing models for your students to help them write postcards and letters in English') we could make sure that the text contained all sorts of useful features for an exam answer, for example, (a) the repetition of the title in the answer ('The advantages of constructing writing models are . . . '), (b) the use of listing devices ('First', 'Secondly', 'Also', 'As well as', etc.), (c) the use of exam phrases ('Undoubtedly the main advantage / reason / kind of . . . ', 'Another advantage / method / reason is . . .', 'One way of . . . . . . ing is to . . . ', etc.).

A first reading of the text-cum-exam answer would give a basic cognitive understanding of the advantages and disadvantages of constructing writing models. This is basic course input. Trainees could then be asked to underline the parts of the text that could be used in another exam essay and to write their name at the top.

Each trainee underlines what they think are useful parts. These underlined parts can then act as a kind of guide or model for another trainee who takes them and tries to use them to write another exam answer. The guide or model phrases can be used by the trainee to write an answer to any exam question of the 'advantages and disadvantages' type, whatever the topic. Results are then compared. There follows a discussion of what the real advantages and disadvantages of following colleagues' models were and these reactions can be compared with the content of the original essay.

Once trainees have had practice in adapting texts for models and following models in this way, they could, if they found it useful, go on to provide lesson plan models for each other, thus breaking down the idea that there is one right way to write a lesson plan. If they find that following a tight model is too stultifying, they can be helped to use freer guidelines that offer more choice and creativity. Thus, at a time on the course when they are discussing freer practice for their students, they can be experiencing it themselves.

I don't think there can be a discussion of the provision of models for learners without a discussion of 'transfer', that is, the encouragement of 'generation', or using the model given, in new situations. I will deal with the question of transfer in a later chapter.

10 Role play

Some preliminary thoughts on role play are contained in the mind map which follows. In this chapter I won't deal with all these thoughts but will concentrate on a training session containing three main strands: methods of building towards a role play, different ways of giving out roles, and organising role plays.

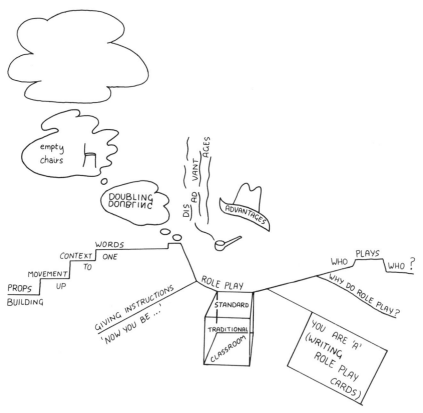

Figure 16   A role play mind map

Any trainers interested in teaching trainees how to build up a role play, how to give out roles and how to organise the role play itself, will need to know how to do those things themselves. Here are some ideas for each.

Ways of building up the situation, language, atmosphere and characters in a role play

- Choose a costume and/or prop and imagine the character to fit it/them.
- Work silently on the gestures and body language of the character.
- Imagine the place of the role play, then brainstorm associated words onto the blackboard, for example:

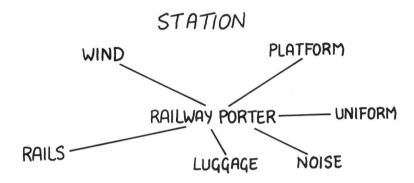

- Listen to someone discussing the place or time of the role play in some detail.
- Brainstorm snatches of dialogue suitable for the place and time.
- Watch a film or slides or look at pictures evoking the scene or situation.
- Watch a film, and copy the positions and movements of the main characters with the sound off after viewing the film.
- With the sound off, mime along with the film.
- With the sound on, speak along with the film.
- Play music or a tape of sounds that will evoke the atmosphere for the role play[1].

Different ways of giving out roles

- People choose the part they want to play.
- People choose a prop and make up the character to go with it.
- The names of roles, helpful information or dialogue suggestions are given out.
- The teacher asks a quiet person to play a 'loud' role.
- People sit in a circle. The first person starts a story with a few sentences, then stops. The next person continues by saying what they feel should be said at that point. Alternatively, one person can read the background story, stopping when characters are about to speak. This idea actually avoids giving out roles. Roles arise in the story and are 'given' to the person who happens to be next in the circle.

D

Organising groups of people before and during role play

- If there are two roles to prepare, the class can be divided into two large groups to prepare the content and character of a role. The two groups can have different stimuli chosen from ideas above to build up the role play.
- The teacher gives out role cards to individuals or pairs who work in a separate space in the room to prepare their role(s).
- Form concentric circles, with equal numbers inside and out. The people inside face out and the people outside face in, so everyone in one circle faces someone in the other circle. These pairs try out a dialogue for a while. At a pre-arranged signal the people in the inner circle move one person to the right. This results in a new partner to work with and people take good ideas from the first conversation into the second. This is then repeated.
- This is the same as above except that desks make up a U-shape and people sit opposite each other. When the signal is given, the inner people move one chair to the right and the person on one end of the U has to cross to an inner seat on the other end.
- Everyone stands up and mills around the room practising words and/or gestures for their role. At a pre-arranged signal they accost the person nearest to them and start a dialogue.

Other things to consider are the provision of ideas to groups that are stuck, switching roles, how many times people try out each role, correction policy, making a record of the role play, follow-up possibilities and so on.

To do a session on role play on your training course you could get people to talk about experiences they've had using drama, get a theatre person in just to loosen trainees up, give handouts from drama resource books or anything else you liked. Obviously, if you wanted to loop input part of your session, you could run a role play. You can build up to, organise and allot roles in any of the ways mentioned above and then all you need is some content for your role play. If content is to be useful to your trainees at the level of their own course needs, then doing a role play on 'The proposed new motorway' is not going to work. Here is an idea for a situation.

> Two teachers are sitting together in a staffroom. They have, unusually, time to talk. The idea of using role play in a lesson comes up. One of the teachers is totally opposed to it. The other is very pro. They do battle.

During the preparation for this role play, trainees will have to consider the advantages of using role play in order to put words into the mouths of their characters. The trainer can go round listening to what points are being made and can then decide if more need to be injected. Depending on your aim, homework could be: asking trainees to try to write out role cards in clear language (this is a difficult skill they will need to practise for their own classes), or to list the pros and cons of role play that they heard during the dialogue and to add any more they can think of or have read about. This full list of pros and cons will constitute a sort of handout which the trainees will have made for themselves. An example of this list of pros and cons done for homework follows (Woodward, 1986).

Advantages
Can use for diagnosis, test or review
Good for body language
Build up = psyching up to real language use
Have to negotiate with others
Props add reality
Fun
Cards easy to write
Unpredictable
T free to monitor
Shy students come out
Or can take shy roles

Disadvantages
Check comprehension of task?
Language input and correction – when?
Noisy, unpredictable, inhibiting
Cards difficult to write
T not really working
T can't hear everyone
Embarrassing
When do you stop?
Wrong number of people, e.g. threes when the role play is for a pair

Once you have received a list such as this, it will enable you to see what the trainees know and think about role play. It is, then, in a sense, a form of diagnosis (see the first point in the advantages column). You can then choose whether more discussion or input is needed or whether you can all move on.

Writing role cards for homework will practise one of the many skills involved in managing role play. Here is a list of some of the other practical skills involved.

Practical skills checklist

Trainees need to be able to do the following to manage role plays in their own classrooms.

- Decide if role play is to diagnose, test, practise or review.
- Know when role play is appropriate in a course or lesson.
- Use a variety of methods to build up, give roles and organise.
- Predict what language, gestures, etc. are likely to be needed.
- Explain clearly what students have to do.
- Start, stop and switch roles, and ensure that phases run smoothly.
- Check students' understanding without asking 'Do you understand?'
- Decide on appropriate correction and monitoring policy.
- Use a variety of relevant follow-up procedures.

Can you think of others? These ideas are very conservative.

More subtle variations on role plays

The use of role play in classrooms has begun to take on powerful dimensions. Here's an adaptation of an idea I have seen used[2].

The class divides into two halves sitting at either end of the room, facing each other across a gap. One person sits a little in front of her group. The arrangement looks like this:

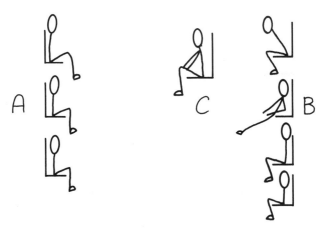

Group A asks C some questions. C doesn't answer, but B answers on C's behalf. The questions can relate to teaching and training if you want a tight loop. Thus someone in A might ask, 'Do you like your students?', and someone in B might reply, if they feel they know a little how C feels, 'Well, most of them, but I'm a bit scared of the aggressive teenage boys.' C can indicate by nodding or shaking her head or by other means if B has in fact come close to expressing her true feelings or if the answer was inaccurate. After all the questions and answers have finished, C is allowed to comment. Then someone else sits in the centre, this time in front of group A who try to answer on the new C's behalf when members of B ask questions.

For an extremely tight loop you could confine the subject of the questions to 'new departures from role play' but I think the loop would be so tight as to become a noose. But you could start there if you wanted to. Wherever you start, trainees will soon be asking what they want anyway. Trainers have a responsibility to initiate when required, but having structured an experience, it's important that they allow the momentum of the event and the trainees' energy to run.

Last words

In this chapter I have touched on some mainstream role play ideas and, towards the end, the slightly more unusual idea of answering questions for someone else. If this role switching exercise interests you, you might want to follow the idea back to its source, which is the *doubling* technique in psychodrama. In this fascinating technique, one person supports, interprets or contradicts another when standing behind them observing the way they are dealing with a situation[3]. For ideas on full-blown, sustained role plays or simulations, see Jones (1982).

Role plays can be very powerful emotionally on any kind of course, whether it's a language course or a teacher training course. Be prepared, then, for sparks of all sorts during and, more especially, after the 'staffroom' role play. An important thread, which I haven't dealt with in this chapter is 'decompression' or 'leading *out*' of a role play. I will avoid that and, instead, lead out of this chapter.

1. Thanks to Judy Baker for five of these ideas.
2. I first saw Rod Bolitho using an idea similar to this.
3. Further reading on **psychodrama**:
   Blatner, H. A. (1973). *Practical Applications of Psychodramatic Methods.* Springer Publishers.
   Leveton, E. (1977). *Psychodrama for the Timid Clinician.* Springer Publishers.

11 Student talking time

At some point on a training course, the question of student talking time (STT) and teacher talking time (TTT) and the proportion of each may need to be discussed. One way of setting up part or a whole session on STT is to give trainees topics to prepare a couple of weeks beforehand. The topics might include:

- Does STT depend on the level of the students?
- Does STT depend on the type or part of the lesson?
- Do students need a silent period or gestation time before starting to speak a language?
- Should STT in our lessons be increased?
- Why is TTT often high?
- Are all types of TTT the same and equally desirable or undesirable? Think of a teacher giving instructions, telling a story, explaining why they are tired, etc.
- How can some types of TTT be decreased: by planning and preparation of metalanguage, instruction giving, class atmosphere, correction policies, gestures, aids, different techniques at Presentation, Practice or Production stages, or by using the Production stage first as a diagnosis phase?
- What does the teacher do while the students talk?

It's a good idea to get at least two people working on each topic in case one of them doesn't turn up at the session. Appoint a chairperson who has a list of the points you think should be covered, a variety person whose job it is to organise one-minute breaks when necessary, and someone to take notes or tape record the main parts of the session. A reading list or some texts can be handed out well in advance of the session. You'll need to check exactly who can attend, otherwise the session will fall flat. The trainer's job during the session can be, with non-native trainees, to analyse their language strengths and weaknesses, and with native speakers to map out the paths of their social interaction during the session. If preferred, the trainer could write a diary entry on how she felt about not doing anything and how this related to her image of herself as a teacher and trainer. This could be made available to the trainees afterwards. Discussion after the session could include asking whether the trainer had had any less control of the session by not talking.

Interesting things have happened when I've planned sessions this way. Once, I watched while the chairperson attempted to hijack the discussion onto his favourite subject and failed because the other trainees had spent time preparing and wanted to use their material. I had intended to write a diary but got too involved watching the group deal with each other. I realised that strong machinations were going on in the group amongst the members. I hadn't suspected this before, and realised that I didn't really know the trainees very well at group level.

Last words

I haven't done a full mind map, though I've thought of an idea for one. In the centre there are two students talking to each other and the branches are speech bubbles coming out of their mouths. There are thought bubbles too, but I'm not sure what to write in them. What would you put in them?

Figure 17   A student talking time mind map

12 Vocabulary

The wealth of EFL terminology (Tomlinson, 1984) allows loop input to be a perfect vehicle for sessions on vocabulary teaching. Trainees will need to recognise the terms when reading and attending conferences and lectures, and to produce them in essays and articles. This is a problem for native and non-native trainees alike. They cannot learn all these terms at once and so the terminology component of a training course will have to be carefully planned so that new words are grouped, limited in number, demonstrated or explained, met and remet, reviewed, refined, stored, memorised, recalled and tested just as new words are in language courses. There is then a natural parallel between your trainees and the students they teach, although a major difference is that a high proportion of EFL words will be abstract and thus hard to explain by physical demonstration.

In this chapter, I will take just three areas of vocabulary teaching and learning – grouping, storage and review – and show how, by endeavouring to consider these three areas ourselves when exposing trainees to EFL jargon and by carefully drawing their attention to what you and they are doing, you can give your trainees ideas for teaching vocabulary.

Ways of grouping new words

BY SERIES

This refers to a series of actions that happen to occur consecutively in the real world. Thus 'starting a car' might go, 'First, I fasten my seat belt, then I put the key in the ignition, next I check the gear's in neutral.' Series games can be played as warm-ups, and at trainee level a series could be 'using an OHP'. 'First, I take some transparencies home, then I plan what I want to write on them, next I . . . ' The good thing about series grouping with trainees is that it revises words and ideas. Heated discussion can arise when people reverse the order of two items, for example in an 'introducing a new function' series, someone who starts with, 'First, I'll do a role play to see what students already know . . . ' might be challenged by someone who hasn't considered the deep-end approach. Similarly, someone who says, 'I'll play the tape first' might be challenged in a 'using a tape' series by those who feel that either the counter should be set at zero first or that the students should be given some context before they start listening.

BY SUBJECT OR FIELD

This can be used as a preview to see what people know, or as a review to see what they remember. An example of a field could be 'functions' and the field brainstorm made by trainees could look like this:

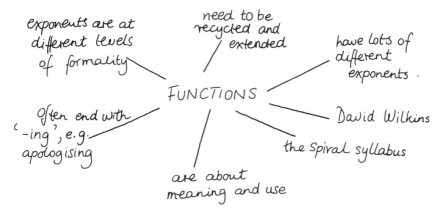

BY SUPERORDINATE AND HYPONYM

Grouping by superordinate and hyponym is useful not only for reviewing vocabulary but also for sketching the way a session might go or for reminding people of the broader perspective after the different points have been discussed. Different topics can be looked at, for example, mechanical aids, changes that happen at speed in phonology, or what teaching methods relate to what approaches.

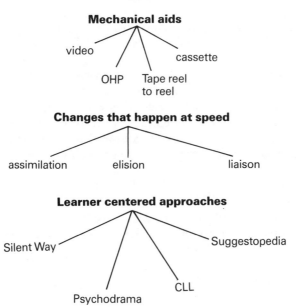

BY SYNONYMY

There are many terms in EFL that are paired by synonymy (e.g. cue/prompt, extensive/gist), near-synonymy (e.g. register/style, lexis/vocabulary), antonymy (e.g. synthetic/analytic, intensive/extensive), association (e.g. micro- and peer teaching), virtual converseness (student talking time / teacher talking time) and there are even examples of affixation (e.g. pre-questions, pre-vocabulary, in-reading). The words within EFL that demonstrate these semantic relationships can either be used as examples in any work you do based on principles of lexical organisation or used gradually over a number of sessions to preview, store or review terminology and ideas (Gairns and Redman, 1986).

Storage

By *storage* I mean what people do, physically, with new words once they've met them. Do they write them down in neat columns? Do they stick them around their shaving mirrors? You can encourage trainees to store words in different ways so that they are helped in their memorising and understanding as well as becoming familiar with these methods before recommending them (or not) to their students. One storage method was suggested on the 'record and review' sheet in the chapter on classroom management (page 55). There are further possibilities:

COLOUR

Terms can be divided into categories depending on whether they relate to teaching approach, teaching method or classroom tactics. Each category can be given a different colour, for example, blue, green or red. Words associated with teaching approaches (e.g. *cognitive*, *mentalist*) can be written in blue or on blue paper, words connected with teaching method (e.g. *Structural situation*, *Direct method*) can be stored on green paper, and so on. In order to allocate a word or colour, trainees will have to debate and understand the threefold classification, which is useful as a process. Some people have strong colour-visual memories and when recalling a word would tend to recall the colour and thus the category.

MEANING FEATURE GRIDS

If your trainees are confused as to what certain words mean in terms of classroom practice, you could make the meanings clear using a meaning feature grid like this.

	Can happen in the classroom	T more evident	Concentration on Accuracy	Concentration on Fluency	TTT↑	STT↑	Context provided	Instant correction	T monitors	Use of visual aids	Use of authentic material	Whole class	Pairs	Group work possible	Individual work possible	Concept questions
Presentation	✓	✓	✓		✓		✓	✓		✓	✓	✓				✓
Controlled practice	✓	✓	✓			✓	✓	✓	✓	✓	✓	✓	✓	✓	✓	✓
Free practice	✓			✓		✓	✓			✓	✓	✓	?	✓	✓	✓
Use	?/✓			✓		✓	✓			✓	✓	✓		✓	✓	✓

Figure 18   A meaning feature grid

This may dispel some common misconceptions or, alternatively, reveal the trainer's own biases at the same time as helping trainees to get used to dealing with grids. Trainees can also construct grids themselves.

INSIGHT PICTURES

The idea here is to write the word so that some element of the meaning is visible in the way the word is written. For example:

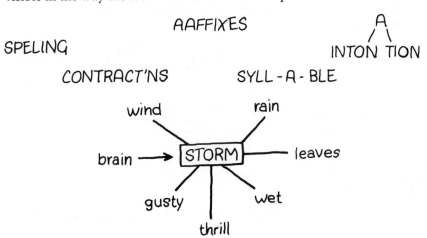

Vocabulary

MNEMONICS

Mnemonics can be used to help trainees remember such things as possible criteria for selection of items in a syllabus, for example:

'If You Can Emulate, Do!' (I F U C E D)
Interest
Frequency
Usability
Combinability
Expediency
Demonstrability

If the trainer can't think of a mnemonic, there's usually a trainee in the group who's good at them.

Of course, storage doesn't have to be in trainees' books. If you can use the walls of your classroom, you can store words in imaginative ways where they will enter the peripheral vision or absent-minded consciousness of a trainee gazing around in the middle of a lecturette or silent reflection time. Things often sink in better when you're not trying to force them in. If trainees find this out when they're learning, they're likely to try it out later when they're teaching.

Review

Any normal EFL vocabulary review game can be used with EFL terminology, like the following games:

MATCHING

Put each of the following words on a separate card and get trainees to match the pairs:

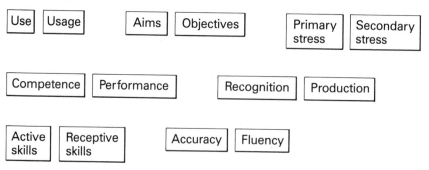

Trios exist too, for example, Presentation – Production – Practice, Form – Meaning – Use.

MEMORY MATCHING

This is like 'Matching', using similar paired cards. The cards are all laid face down on a table. Trainees can turn over any one card at a time, and then turn it back, trying to remember where the words are. When they turn over a card and think they can remember where the pair card is, they're allowed to turn that one over too. If they are successful they keep the pair. If they're wrong they miss a turn. The winner is the one with most pairs at the end of the game.

VOCABULARY REVIEW GAME

The words you want reviewed are written on cards and put in the centre of the table. This is the 'pack'. Trainees sit round the table in two rings with equal numbers in the inner and outer rings.

Trainees work in pairs, that is, one inner ring person works with the person behind her. One person from each pair, the one nearest the table, takes a card from the pack and the trainer starts timing. The pairs have two minutes to prepare: (a) a definition of the term on their card, and (b) a likely sentence containing the word used in its EFL sense. The trainer says 'stop'. The pairs take turns to present their definitions and sentences. If their definition is not watertight, they can be challenged, for example:

A: The Silent Way is a fringe method that has sprung from the human-istic approach.
B: Challenge! That could be CLL!
C: Challenge! A fringe method of what? Peeling potatoes?
D: Challenge! It didn't spring from an approach. It sprang from some-one's mind.

The trainer decides which challenges are justified, and correct challengers get a point. Watertight definitions get two points, and correct sentences one point. This game is adapted from Woodward (1985).

CLAPPING, CHANTING AND MILLING

Trainees choose words they like or dislike or have trouble spelling or remembering. They can either clap out the stress rhythm to other people and ask them to guess the word or 'walk the word' by stepping out with long strides on the accented syllables and short steps for unaccented syllables, or chant it forwards or backwards or in rhymes as they walk round the room. At any time they can ask about, comment on, or take over anybody else's word.

WORD ASSOCIATION

Trainees sit in a circle, and are given a word. Everyone gives their reactions to the word. For example, if 'cloze test' is given, reactions might be: 'total', 'computer', 'crosswords', 'white-out', 'text', 'too difficult', 'template', 'nth', 'guessing', 'holes', 'is the spelling "s" or "z"?'

LAST LETTER, NEXT WORD

Again, the trainees are given a word, and the last letter of the word is called out. It is used to start another word, like this: 'behaviourism – M', 'mentalism – M', 'mnemonics – S', 'structure – E', 'elementary – Y', 'yes/no questions – S', 'suggestopedia', etc.

Practical skills checklist

Here is a checklist of steps that trainees might need to take in order to teach vocabulary well in their language classes. The steps are not in order nor are they complete.

- *Research* Find out where to go for information on words. Find out how to get the best out of monolingual dictionaries, thesauruses and lexicons, and understand their drawbacks. Find out what skills are involved in their use.
- *At the start of a course* Brainstorm semantic areas the class may need. Check the coursebook to see what lexis it contains, how it's dealt with, and if there's a glossary. Plan some diagnostic work to see what students know.
- *During the course* Decide how to group words; plan elicitation of what might be known, give a variety of explanations or get the students to explain. Decide how to deal with confusions, false friends and cognates, and how to indicate where one word stops and another begins, how much information to give on one word, what goes on the board or in their notebooks and how to check new words.

To recap

In this chapter I've touched briefly on three areas of vocabulary teaching and learning: grouping, storage and review. See the mind map opposite.

I've only put a few things on it, so you might like to fill out more of it. You could then choose a branch and make it the focus of a new mind map. On that map you would write out all the things you normally do with EFL classes and think how you could adapt these ideas to work with your training group. You will then have another set of practical ideas. For example, you might take the 'testing' sub-branch and start a mind map like the one on page 104.

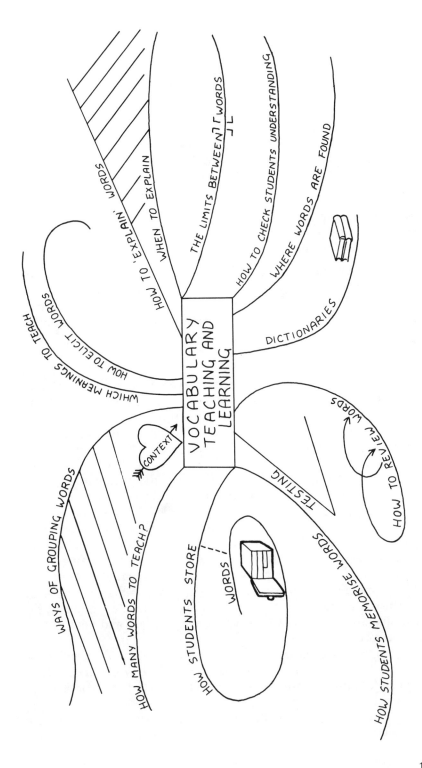

Figure 19   A vocabulary teaching and learning mind map

Vocabulary

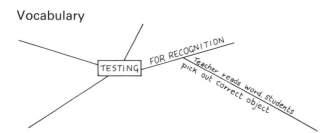

The first idea marked on the map is 'Teacher reads out a word, students pick out the correct object.' No sooner have you this one idea on paper than you might think of an adaptation of it for use in the training room. For example, the trainer says the word 'cloze' and the trainees have to choose between the following items on a sheet in front of them:

a) a text with no gaps   b) a text with no title
c) a text gapped for prepositions   d) a text gapped at every fifth word
e) a blank piece of paper

Discussion follows over which of these items correctly describes or defines the word 'cloze'.

The idea might work for you in your situation. If not, keep adding to the mind map. A new addition will trigger an adaptation that's right for your circumstances.

I can't, in all conscience, leave this chapter here, although some years ago I would have been happy to. Since then I've read Ashton-Warner's book, *Teacher* (1980) and Morgan and Rinvolucri's *Vocabulary* (1986) and have come to realise, slowly as a teacher and trainer, but more swiftly as a language learner, that words are hard to learn unless you want them, in a strong way, from inside yourself. Where you are when you meet them, and how you feel at the time, and what happens next are all somehow bound up with 'the word'. The word you want, the word you get, from whom, the way you turn it over in your head or write it down or carry it with you on a scrap of paper to a shop, the way it comes out of your mouth, how people react to it – they are all part and parcel of the word, for you, from then on. I learnt the Italian word for difficult, *difficile*, at night, in the dark, chatting to somebody. I got the stress wrong about seven times and was gently but firmly corrected each time even though we were in the middle of a conversation. Whenever I hear the word *difficile*, I am transported back to that summer's night. I see the outline of the woman against the window, I remember what I felt, and now I never forget the correct stress.

How can we give trainees a sense of this non-intellectual grappling for words they need when so many words in their EFL world are imposed from outside? How can we get away from the categories and labels that EFL gurus have already mapped out and help trainees to the categorisations of teaching experiences that interest them? For a few first tentative thoughts you might like to look at Woodward (1990).

13 Reading mazes

Just as when you walk into a real life maze you see several choices ahead of you and paths leading off in various directions, so in a reading maze you have a starting situation and some decisions to make. Some of the paths or solutions to the entry problem will turn out to be dead ends, some will lead you on for a while and others will take you, gradually, after more decisions, to an exit or good solution.

Reading mazes usually consist of situations and options written on cards. The group discusses the situation as it unfolds, arrives at a group consensus on which paths to take, and moves on. If the texts are well written, the situations interesting, the decisions realistic and the exit solutions satisfying, then the work will go well. The trick is to find a subject and set of choices that groups can identify with or become interested in.

With a group of trainees I had once, I wanted them to gain experiences of mazes by doing some. I also wanted them to be able to adapt and write mazes themselves, and to get out into the open some of the worries that individuals had been quietly expressing about the course, the final exam, the workload, and so on.

The maze I wrote, which could no doubt be improved, follows. The trainees' discussion was cathartic, not least because they found out that I had written the maze for them before I had even met them. They were astonished to find out that their fears and concerns could be so accurately predicted and were therefore perhaps shared by other trainees on other exam courses!

ENTRY TO THE MAZE

You're a busy teacher in a Swiss school. You've been teaching for fifteen years and you don't feel as if you've changed much in the last ten. You're tired and rather bored with your job. Your choices are:

a) Leave the teaching profession (see Card 1).
b) Take an RSA (DOTE) course (see Card 2).
c) Go on as you are (see Card 3).

1.

Who's going to employ a tired, middle-aged ex-teacher? Unless you've got a private income, I suggest you think again!

EXIT OR RETURN

2.

You start on the RSA (DOTE) course, but what with the travelling, the Thursday nights and the homework, you find it's really much more work than you'd imagined. Your choices are:
a) Talk to the tutors (see Card 4).
b) Drop out (see Card 5).
c) Sigh and keep going (see Card 6).

3.

Well, you'll just get more and more bored, frustrated with your classes and boring to those around you. Do you really want to age that fast?

EXIT OR RETURN

4.

The tutors are sympathetic and try not to overload you, but basically they just tell you to keep going.

GO BACK TO CARD 2

5.

So, you're a quitter are you? Well, then, you're back at the entry to the maze except that now you feel as if you've failed at something too. Wouldn't you like to think again?

EXIT OR RETURN

6.

You keep going but after a while you have the feeling that everybody else is doing better than you. Your choices are:
a) Keep quiet about it (see Card 7).
b) Tell the tutors (see Card 8).
c) Talk to the other students about it (see Card 9).

7.

You suffer in silence but things don't get any better. You're driven mad with jealousy and despair. What are you going to do?

RETURN?

8.

The tutors are very encouraging and keep telling you that you're doing all right, but you don't really believe them. You still feel bad.

RETURN?

9.

You're amazed to find that a lot of the other students feel exactly the same way as you. You talk about it, feel reassured, and decide to do more group work.

MOVE TO CARD 10

10.

You keep going on the course and try to keep up. You meet a lot of new ideas. Your choices are:

a) Try all the ideas out on your students exactly as they were taught to you on the course (see Card 11).

b) Tell your colleagues at work about the ideas at every opportunity you get (see Card 12).

c) Not try anything new (see Card 13).

d) Take the ideas you like, adapt them to fit your situation, try them out and adapt them again if necessary (see Card 14).

11.

A lot of the ideas don't seem to work as well in your classes as they did on the course. You've forgotten quite why you're doing them and your class is stunned anyway by the sudden bombardment of strange ideas. Confusion. Lack of confidence.

DEAD END

12.

Your colleagues at work become bored and defensive with and at your enthusiastic ramblings about 'DOTE – this' and 'RSA – that'. You find yourself increasingly isolated in the staffroom and amongst your colleagues. The head of department becomes wary of you.

DEAD END

13.

Well, you've stayed at the entry to the maze really, haven't you? Plus . . . it's doubtful if you'll get through the exam!

DEAD END

14.

You gain confidence gradually as you adopt and adapt more and more ideas. Your class gains confidence as they find they can communicate more and more successfully in English. Things are looking up.

MOVE TO CARD 15

15.

Your techniques improve. Your language improves. Your classes improve. But then the RSA exam looms up before you! Your feelings are:

a) 'My God, I hope I pass' (see Card 16).
b) 'My God, I'm sure I'll fail' (see Card 17).
c) 'Well . . . whether I pass or fail I'll have learned something anyway' (see Card 18).

16.

Then you'll have another piece of paper in your pocket, which is good. Perhaps more important is what you feel you have personally gained as a result of the course.

EXIT

17.

Then you won't have that piece of paper in your pocket. But perhaps you'll feel that you've learnt a lot for yourself that will help your work as a teacher.

EXIT

18.
You finish the course. Your career has been refreshed. You think you might be able to make it through the next few years with increased interest.

EXIT

Although I had written the maze before the course started, I held on to it until a time in the course when it seemed appropriate to use it to defuse some tensions. It was written for a group, but different entry situations could equally well be devised for individuals within a group. Or again, different entry cards could be written or set for smaller sub-groups within a class, like these:

You have very little time as a teacher, since you have 26 lessons a week at four different levels and in three different languages. None of your classes are parallel so you can't double-up on your preparation. Your boss has just asked you to:
a) Accept a trainee teacher in your class.
b) Attend an in-service training course.
c) Take on a senior teacher role with no decrease in teaching load.

You're just finishing a training course. Although some of the ideas on the course were impractical and farfetched, there are still quite a few you'd like to implement back at school. Next week you face the task of trying to sort out the new ideas and fitting in with your old colleagues again. Some of them are a little wary of you on your first day back. Read the next card for some of the options open to you.

You could write different mazes for different trainees, or ask groups to complete maze choices and solutions for each other, or individuals to write 'worst case' entry situations for themselves.

You might like to consider basing a maze on your trainees' current concerns or let them show you what their concerns are by the way they write their mazes. Whatever entry situation or maze is written or chosen, working with reading mazes takes some special skills. These are listed in the following checklist.

Practical skills checklist

Trainees wanting to use reading mazes with their classes will need to be able to:

- Find or write appropriate mazes for a group (see Berer and Rinvolucri, 1981, and Farthing, 1981).
- Try out mazes with friends and colleagues first to see if the exits are satisfactory.
- Get language students to write mazes.
- Make sure all the cards are present, legible, numbered, in order, and that there are enough complete sets for the group.
- Explain what a maze is and how to do one (e.g. keeping track of numbers and avoiding reading ahead).
- Monitor the activity and decide on an appropriate correction policy.
- Decide what to do about new words that come up on the cards (e.g. whether dictionaries will be available or prior explanation will be given).
- Predict the language that will be needed:
  - a) for the group to get itself organised;
  - b) to check if the group is ready to listen to a new card being read out or to read on for themselves;
  - c) to elicit suggestions on a course of action;
  - d) to persuade or disagree with others in the group;
  - e) to move on to a new card.
- Predict how much of this language is known, whether it should be pre-taught or whether to use the maze for diagnosis.
- Handle early and late finishing groups.
- Handle the end discussion on the subject of the maze, its relevance to the students, its authenticity, what the groups did and how they felt about their exits.
- Deal with the follow-up (e.g. reading skills, the vocabulary, the inter-action language, the content of the subject, whether to change the options or solutions of the maze, or do another one, perhaps written by individual students.

14 Teaching listening

You might like to draw up your own mind map for teaching listening skills before you start this chapter.

How you run your session on teaching listening will, of course, depend on what you want to get across. Your trainees may primarily need help in learning to manipulate a tape recorder from the wrong side without looking at it, or perhaps they would like to discuss the issue of authentic material or authentic tasks at elementary level. I have given sessions on jigsaw listening and on basic methodological models for running listening classes. Sessions on what people listen to in normal everyday life are easy to handle because people do have everyday lives.

Perhaps you'd like to do a session on the different ways that listening comprehension can be checked without using comprehension questions. The loop is clear. The trainees can listen to a tape or tapes on the subject of checking comprehension of listening. In order to check that trainees have understood the tape you check their comprehension in some of the ways suggested on the tape, for example, using a grid, drawing diagrams, filling in gaps on a chart and so on.

Ideas for a session on the differences between listening and reading

Perhaps you'd like to do part of a session on the main differences between speech and writing. In terms of input styles here, you could do a mini-lecturette, do a group brainstorm of the differences people can think of, or ask them to do some reading and suggest they come back the next week with the main points summarised on a poster. If you'd like to loop the content of the session because you want a change in input procedures or because you think looping is the best way to carry this point, you could prepare a handout entitled 'The main differences between speech and writing' and put half the trainees in one room or give them time to go home and read it. The other half of the group would have to stay near you. You could lecture, answer questions or have a conversation, as you liked, on the subject 'The main differences between speech and writing'. After that, many options are open to you. You can get one trainee in group A to phone one in group B, or give them all an essay to write on the subject, or ask the ones who read the handout to talk and the ones who listened to write. Some main points are bound to emerge about the length of time it takes to absorb information through different channels, where and in whose company you can read or listen, the style, density of information and so on.

So far in the book there have been ideas on warm-ups, one-minute breaks, tasks, classroom management ideas, review and record sheets, homework, tapes and texts that would all resonate with the theme of listening and would provide process mirrors for the content you wish to display. Thinking in terms of loop input will probably have started you making both pre-scripted and authentic dialogue tapes on the subject 'Should tapes be pre-scripted? What happens if they are?' Or perhaps you are playing with the idea of writing 40 'revenge questions' for the end of the session so that trainees can cross out the comprehension questions they don't want to answer. Perhaps you're thinking of making tapes or giving lecturettes on 'prediction exercises' where you suddenly stop and ask trainees to predict what comes next. Or you'll include sentences in the lecture that have new words in, possibly nonsense phrases like 'retaliatory listening', to demonstrate what happens to people's concentration on the flow of talk once they've heard something they don't understand.

The guided note-taking sheet on the next two pages might be useful as an accompaniment to a talk about listening materials and whether they should be pre-scripted or contain features of natural speech, what material is available commercially, and what problems there are in storing taped listening material and preparing it for use in the classroom.

Lecture on listening materials – sample worksheet

Fill in the gaps in this guided note-taking sheet.

1. The lecturer discusses pre-scripted, authentic and .... listening materials.

2. Pre-scripted tapes have both advantages and disadvantages.

Advantages	Disadvantages
Can include vocabulary and structures that teacher wants students to have practice in.	People reading from scripts tend to alter their stress and intonation patterns unnaturally.
....	....
....	....
....	....

3. Authentic taped material has both advantages and disadvantages.

Advantages	Disadvantages
They are a cheap, readily available resource from radio, friends, etc.	Their syllable per minute rate may be extremely high.
....	....
....	....
....	....

4. The third type of listening material .... also has advantages and disadvantages.

Advantages	Disadvantages
....	....
....	....
....	....

5. What sort of tapes available commercially are mentioned in the talk?
    a) ....
    b) ....
    c) ....
    d) ....
    e) ....

6. What is the best way to go about gathering non-commercial taped material?

7. What important factors in storage of taped material are mentioned on the tape?
Labelling

....

....

....

....

..:...

....

8. What do you, as a teacher, need to do to prepare taped material for use in class?

:...

....

....

....

....

....

9. From the talk you will be able to fill in some points under each question. After the talk, try to find some more points under each question. Do this by using any of the following: discussion with colleagues, reading of the references given in the session, reflection on your own teaching experience, checking the teaching materials in your staffroom.

Follow-up   The guided note-taking sheet can be partly filled in by listening to a tape or to a lecturette, but can also be finished off by adding in extra information gained from other sources after the session.

If you would like to demonstrate the idea of in-listening questions, important for establishing how much of given material has been understood before moving on to new material, you could try the following.

Simply stop after key points in your lecture and set problems, ask questions, ask trainees to tell you what your last few words were, note the differences between what you have just said and an argument flashed up on the OHP, and so on. For a tight loop the lecture would, in part, be about 'in-listening tasks'. The idea of in-listening questions can, however, be introduced during a lecture on any subject. For example, in a lecture on 'Learning theories', some halts would be made and questions asked and answered. The technique can then be referred to at a later date when the topic of in-listening questions comes up. If in-listening questions are being asked during a lecture on in-listening tasks, people are obliged to work on two levels at once. They are listening to a lecture and gaining content from it. They are also watching and taking part in complementary process at the same time, and gaining content from that.

It's possible to keep the two levels straight in your brain while you're lecturing. If you think of how many parallel times we can handle in everyday conversation I think you'll be convinced. Here's an example from a lecturer:

'Now, I'd like to talk about the period in history that I mentioned in the lecture last week. It was after the inspector left. Do you remember? Now what period were we talking about? That's right. The late eighteenth century.'

We've got about five parallel times here. There is the general time in which the lecture is set when people are sitting listening to the lecturer. The opening 'Now' refers to the flow of time in the discourse. There's a lecture last week, a moment when an inspector left the lecture hall and a period in history. A student has calmly kept five parallel times in her head and come up with the one the lecturer wants. We perform feats like this every day, so asking trainees to keep their minds on two things at once, though in a slightly different area, that of process and content, is nothing new to them. They will already have been keeping a few brain cells on the content of your lecture and many others on how funny your hairstyle is, the hole in their pocket, what time lunch is, the shopping list they're writing, and so on. Trainees are probably more flexible in this respect than trainers are!

15 Transfer

Your trainees may have been brought up on the 'three Ps' model that is sometimes expressed by a triangle diagram:

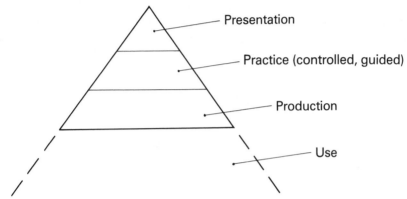

Figure 20   A 'three Ps' triangle

and sometimes expressed by a continuum or scale:

Figure 21   The communication continuum

In the communication continuum, *input* can be taken to mean times when the teacher selects a piece of language, creates a context for it and presents it to students. At first the students simply demonstrate comprehension of the concept behind the target language item and there is no element of choice or risk. The teacher intervenes every time a mistake is made in the target item. *Output* can be taken to mean times when students have a desire, purpose or reason to communicate and they choose from a variety of options. They take risks and experiment and there is no teacher intervention or control over materials.

Both models rest on the belief that bits of language can be isolated, fed in and practised, and that these bits will later become part of the students' repertoire, transferred and used in situations other than those in which they were presented. If teaching or training is built upon either of these two models, then all discussions of, for example, how furniture is arranged, where people are in the room, the size of visual aids, the proportion of teacher talk to student talk, types of correction, fluency emphasis, lesson steps, planning, instruction giving, pairing and grouping, timing, balance, variety, where people start talking, and many other issues, will be influenced by the key questions, 'What part of the triangle are we in?', 'What stage of the continuum are we on?' and 'What point in the predictable learning cycle are we at?'

Once trainees have become thoroughly conversant with one teaching model such as the 'three Ps' model, and are used to seeing the model expressed diagrammatically by an upright triangle, it will be possible to encourage them to think about different ways of looking at learning simply by showing them different diagrammatic expressions representing other teaching models. For example:

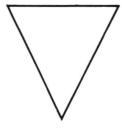

Figure 22   The deep-end approach

The following shapes will help them to adapt and change the sequences of teaching steps they already know:

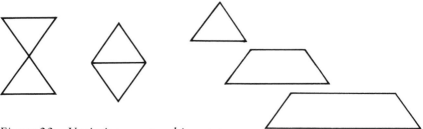

Figure 23   Variations on teaching steps

Another way of encouraging trainees to think about learning is to discuss the question of transfer. The underlying assumption of much teaching and training is that transfer takes place, that is, when people are exposed to new patterns, they understand them, grasp the generalisation behind them and introduce them into their own behaviour, not only in the special state of the classroom, but into appropriate contexts in the real world.

Many teachers, after spending half an hour in the language laboratory drilling 'When did she go?', 'She went there yesterday', 'When did he go?',

'He went there yesterday', and then hearing students saying to each other as they leave the lab 'Have you been there?', 'Yes, I've been there yesterday!', may wonder if transfer ever does actually occur. You may want to get at this difficulty, this irritation the teacher sometimes feels, this incredulity that students could be so dim, and turn it into learning. One way of getting this across is by using a kind of loop. The trainees would be invited to a session on transfer, or if you prefer 'guided to free practice', and the session might go something like this:

1. The trainees are alerted to the importance of weaning students off model sentences and linguistic guidelines by the gradual removal of linguistic support.

2. The trainees take on the role of students and learn a short dialogue such as:

   A: I've got a terrible headache.
   B: Oh, dear!
   A: Have you got an Aspirin?
   B: No, I haven't but I've got a Disprin.
   A: Oh, good. Thanks.

3. Once comprehension has been checked, these transfer prompts are written on the board:

   A: A lot of work to do
      Word processor
   B: A typewriter

4. The trainees are asked to make a new dialogue similar to the old one, but with these new words. There'll be a bit of stumbling before the correct dialogue comes out. The problem can be discussed that the core structure of the dialogue has to be grasped before the transfer dialogue can be completed.

5. Next, give them some bad prompts, for example:

   A: Loads of visitors coming
      Any camp beds
   B: Sleeping bags

   Hopefully, when they try it out in pairs as mock students they'll have problems with 'a' before 'loads', 'an' and 'any', and missing 'some' or 'a few' before 'sleeping bags'. The point is that these sorts of changes are hard for students to make.

6. Next you can give trainees a base dialogue such as:

   A: Could you pass the salt, please?
   B: Er. Yes. OK.
   A: And the butter too?
   B: Sure.

   and ask them to write a set of transfer prompts. They are back now in the role of trainee. They can try out in pairs the transfer prompts they have written, alter them accordingly and swap them.

7. Next, they can choose a structure or function of their own to do and write both the base dialogue and the prompts.

8. When they've completed this task, they can look back over what they have done as trainees during the session and will see that they themselves have experienced some guided to freer work.

9. If you want to consolidate the confidence gained so far you could give a short text such as:

   I've got a friend. She lives in the USA. She's a teacher and likes her job. I don't see her very often.

   and as a whole class exercise ask trainees to suggest transfer prompts such as:

   sister   Brighton   doctor   not   visit

10. Next, tell them that you'll teach them a technique called 'paralleling'. Draw this on the board (Spencer, 1967):

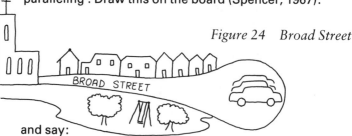

Figure 24   Broad Street

and say:

   Broad Street is a mile long. It starts at the church and ends at the car park. There are houses along one side of it and a park on the other.

   By pointing at the map to jog their memories, and by working gradually, the group will be able to piece together and repeat the text orally and correctly.

11. Next, trainees write the text down.

12. Once it's checked you read out a parallel text such as:

    Spicer Street is three miles long. It starts at the car park and ends at the railway station. There's a supermarket on one side of the street and a theatre on the other.

13. This time trainees draw the diagram as they listen.

14. They then talk about their diagram, approximating the spoken text. They can use their first text to help them with the basic format and structures.

15. Explain to the trainees that they've now been exposed to the paralleling technique. Ask them to work alone for a while to produce a similar exercise that they could use with their own students. Don't help them much. As trainees start to work, you will see that most of them will be producing diagrams and texts about roads, towns and geographical features. They will be showing the understandable and inevitable tendency to follow closely any model that has been given by a teacher.

16. Once they have all finished their streets, etc. draw their attention to the fact that most of them have kept closely to the model. Raise the possibility that the same basic idea could have been used to describe cars, machines, people, houses or processes, for example:

    In the spring all the trees go green. The leaves come out and the woodlands look young.

    In the autumn . . .

17. Discuss why it was so hard for them to transfer, to see the general pattern through the particular expression shown to them, and to create wider uses of the same idea. Then draw them back to the start of the session. What insights have been gained?

E

Much of our training and teaching is model-based, and thus the issue of transfer is absolutely central. How does an idea or a piece of target language become available to someone? How do they interact with it, accept or reject it, and come to feel that they 'own' it so that they can use it in their own way? Mere copying is relatively easy, but creative use is something else. Talking about the issue of transfer is one thing, but becoming irritated when it doesn't happen is another. Experiencing the inevitable tendency to follow a model very closely and then waking up to the generative possibilities that the model actually allows may help the penny to drop.

The work in this chapter is experiential: the trainees experience the difficulty of transfer. The content of the session has not, however, been fused with the process. The content of the mini-dialogues and the paralleling exercises is about aspirins and sleeping bags, streets, and stations. This session is not a loop, therefore.

Can you think of making a looped session about transfer? In other words, can you take the model that has been offered to you in these chapters and apply it to a new situation – without help? If so, then transfer has taken place.

16 Evaluation

Evaluation and feedback on courses can be anonymous, signed, written, spoken, done at home or in class about any facet of a course, by teacher or student. It can be filling in long questionnaires formally or swift informal impressions in the shape of a coloured diagram, with the teacher present or not. The results can be carefully analysed by computer or torn up in front of the class (once read!). The process can lead to frustration or catharsis, and it can take place too often or not at all. It's often left out of courses, or left to the very end, but it can be done just when you've begun to get well into a subject.

You might want to stop here for a moment to try to find a loop for sharing ideas on evaluation and feedback.

But if you can't wait, I'll tell you what my idea for a loop is. Whenever you want to have feedback from the trainees on aspects of the training course you are running, use some of the feedback techniques that you were planning to tell trainees about for use with language students. That way, you get feedback on the teacher training course, the trainees have plenty of chances to tell you how they feel about the course, and everybody gets to experience some different techniques.

Some informal evaluation formats follow. I'm sure you will know of many other ideas.

A POSSIBLE EVALUATION FORM

I liked:

_____

I didn't like:

_____

I suggest:

A SCALE-BASED EVALUATION FORM

FEEDBACK

A

The room was
unpleasant _____ pleasant

We made it
better _____ worse

• • • • • • • •

B

The main tutor was
organised _____ disorganised
friendly _____ unfriendly
audible _____ inaudible
lively _____ boring
demanding _____ undemanding

The amount of correction was
too much _____ about right _____ too little

The pace was
too fast _____ about right _____ too slow

The amount of consultation was
too much _____ about right _____ too little

The aims were
clear _____ mysterious

• • • • • • • •

C

My classmates were
friendly _____ unfriendly
same level _____ different level
good mixture of nationalities _____ not good
supportive in pair work _____ not supportive

• • • • • • • •

D

My own contribution in
punctuality ⎫
homework ⎪
stamina ⎬ was _____
oral classwork ⎪
attitude to learning ⎭

        GOOD   **BAD**

● ● ● ● ● ● ● ●

E

A coursebook would have been a good / bad idea

● ● ● ● ● ● ● ●

F

Contents of the course

	more than enough	enough	not enough
Listening			
Speaking			
Reading			
Writing			
Accuracy			
Fluency			
Grammar			
Vocabulary			

● ● ● ● ● ● ● ●

G

My overall impression was
favourable _____ unfavourable

Other comments:

GRAFFITI WALL

For this you will need a page of 'bricks' in a 'wall' so that trainees can write their comments, graffiti-style across them (Lavery, 1985).

Figure 25   The writing on the wall

JAPANESE TEMPLE TREE

Bring in a branch of a tree stuck in a pot. Trainees write their thoughts on long slips of paper, fold them and then twist them around the branches of the tree, just like temple prayers. They can write their thoughts in terms of wishes. If they are Japanese, you can ask them what happens next!

Figure 26   Japanese temple tree

CONSECUTIVE SLIPS

People write three separate remarks about the course or an aspect of the course on three separate pieces of paper and put them in a box in the centre of the room. The papers are all stirred up and then people pick out three papers from the box. Make sure nobody has picked out their own paper again. Somebody starts by reading out the comment written on the piece of paper they have picked out. Other people listen. If someone listening feels that the comment is similar in topic and mood to any of those on their pieces of paper, then they read out their related comment.

Thus, if the first comment which is read out relates to, say, the resource library, then other people will start to read out any comments they have that relate to the resource library or to resources in general. When that topic is exhausted, someone else reads out a fresh comment on a new topic. There may be a few comments left at the end that do not relate to anything anyone has so far read out. They are simply read out last[1].

POSTER EVALUATION

Individuals or groups make posters or mind maps expressing what are for them the most important things about the course. These are pinned up on the wall and trainees stroll around reading them. If necessary, the individual or one person from the group can stand by a poster to explain it.

CONSEQUENCES EVALUATION

Each trainee receives a large piece of paper and at the top writes down one question about the course that they would like to have answered. Papers are then circulated one person to the left. On receiving a piece of paper with a question at the top, people write a comment or an answer to it. The papers continue to circulate, a person at a time, until each question has a large number of answers or comments written below it. The trainer can join in with this exercise. Nobody's name needs to appear. The papers can be read out, photocopied or pinned up.

BLACKBOARD CONSEQUENCES EVALUATION

This idea is similar to the one above except that silent dialogues take place on the blackboard. People come up and write what they like: questions and comments. It is not anonymous and open discussion can follow.

NOISY EVALUATION

Trainees make a tape of noises that express how they feel about the course, for example, 'phonology' – sound of a yawn, 'applied linguistics' – sound of a raspberry, 'drama' – sound of a scream. The tapes are played in open session, and laughter is guaranteed.

GOALS/ACHIEVEMENTS EVALUATION

The trainee is given time at the start of the lesson, day, week or course to make a note of some personal goals for the time to come. After the period is over they are given time to think about whether the goals were reached and why or why not. Discussion is possible at both ends.

PINS ON THE CHART EVALUATION

The trainer puts one list of possible topics and one list of possible input methods up on the wall at the start of a course. Each trainee is given a set of drawing pins (coloured ones look nicer) and can stick them by the topics (for example, phonology) and input methods (for example, lecture) that they favour. If they wish to stick all their pins on one item, they can. The pins and lists stay up throughout the course. The trainer needs to have a different colour so that she can mark each topic and input as 'done' as the course progresses. As trainees find out more about the topics and methods and what they mean on this particular course, they can move their pins around. Maybe at the start of the course 'teaching literature' on the topic list has only two pins by it. After an enjoyable session on the subject, more people might put some pins by it to try and get a second session on the same subject. Conversely, after a particularly boring lecture, all the pins may be removed from the 'lecture' item on the input methods list and moved to the 'buzz group' or 'trainee presentation' items.

Here is a mind map of some of the issues that evaluation raises.

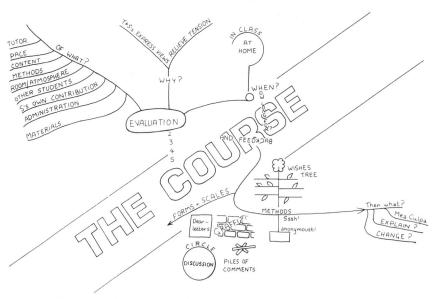

Figure 27   An evaluation mind map

1. I first experienced this idea with John Morgan and Mario Rinvolucri.

17 The last chapter in Part One

Despite being on the various levels of *The stack* (Figure 1) quite often, I still don't really know how people learn or change (two words for the same thing?). I have a hunch though that it has something to do with the following processes:

1. Understanding what you do in your present practice.
2. Making some mental models or representations of your present state and of the desired states.
3. Playing around with the models or representations.
4. Transferring information from them.
5. Changing (which involves will and a desire for different gains).
6. Freeing yourself to make new models or no models at all.

I'll endeavour to explain what I mean by these steps.

In order to understand what your present practice is, or what you do, you have to become aware of what you do and, in order to compare and contrast, become aware of what other people do. This can happen in many ways – by reflection, receiving insults and compliments, by watching others, talking to people, reading, experiencing things, moving from one situation to another, finding out what's difficult and what's easy for you. This will lead inevitably to a certain preoccupation with self, with minutiae and motivation, and though it is usually intensely interesting to the person doing it, it often appears obsessive and tedious to others.

Some cognitive scientists believe that external processes are translated into internal representations which can be in word, symbol or number form. These representations are fitted into already existing models, thus constituting a recombination of old (and new) functions, or they can exist as separate new models. They are not necessarily complex or accurate but are just some sort of simulation which can arrive at new positions and then be translated into external processes again.

As Johnson-Laird says in *Mental Models* (1983), 'Reasoned argument alone is seldom responsible for a permanent change in behaviour.' There must be understanding and reasoning and the desire to change. There must also be an ability to relate what is going on outside with what is going on inside the person.

Can people really make and use mental models? Are we capable of it? Let's think of some mental models we all use all the time.

There's metaphor for example. W. Alston (1964) takes a metaphor from the poem 'The sweet small clumsy feet of April' and discusses it. He says that there's no sense of 'feet' that would allow us, normally, to speak of the 'feet of a month' and yet e. e. cummings, the poet, is not introducing new senses of the word 'feet'. The uses are parasitic on the established ones. It's a certain kind of extension. Thus, he says that metaphor is a sort of figurative use in which the extension is on the basis of similarity. 'One is not simply using the term in one sense, but is saying something different though related and working through the established sense in order to do it.' It's a double operation.

The fact is that we are all capable of making metaphors, understanding them and getting use out of them. Perhaps I should try to set up a new metaphor to see if: (a) I can set it up, (b) people can understand it, (c) it has some similarities to the thing it describes and so is a form of model, and (d) it can lead us to new thoughts or to unusual, amusing, poetic or interesting thoughts. I think I'll try a new metaphor for the content/process distinction. Let's say that the content of a training session is a precious stone or jewel! It is set in a holder or band of metal, which is the process. The glue that joins the jewel to its setting is metalanguage.

If the content of a session is excellent, it's worth a lot – it's a diamond. But the content could also be waffle or paste, and not worth setting. A diamond (wonderful content) could just sit in your pocket wrapped in cloth so that nobody would see it or share it. Or it could have a simple, elegant setting that makes it wearable, shareable. There has to be some glue otherwise there's no connection between the diamond and setting. The stone will simply fall out and there will be two disconnected things. On the other hand, if there's too much glue (metalanguage) it'll cover part of the stone, it'll be too obtrusive and distract attention from the stone. It'll look and feel tacky.

Well, I think you've probably had enough of that metaphor! But, although it wasn't brilliant or sparkling, it did just about hold together. The interesting thing is that we are able to abstract some features from the teacher training session and allow them to be compared to some features of a ring. We can keep elements from the two realities in our minds at the same time and play with them, going back and forth between the two simplified models in our thoughts to see if we can get anything productive out of the comparison.

Lakoff and Johnson (1980) claim that our normal conceptual system is metaphorically structured. They believe that people understand their experiences by organising them conceptually, using metaphors. They would ask not whether we are capable of making and using metaphoric models, but whether we would be capable of stopping ourselves from using them. Let's take the example of 'argument as war'. In the English language, expressions such as 'He attacked the weak point in my argument', 'I won the argument', 'She wiped him out', 'It was a real slap in the face' show up the predominance of this metaphor. If we try to change the 'argument as war' metaphor to an 'argument as dance' metaphor we'll see how hard it is: 'She opened her argument with a few gentle steps.' It doesn't work. 'He danced circles around her.' It worked, but we're back to war again! It is hard to dance and argue at the same time in our culture, but I don't think there's any doubt that we are capable of using metaphoric models.

We are all capable, too, of 'chunking'. When we first start to drive a car, we have to think of every separate movement individually. 'Changing gear' doesn't really exist as a unitary concept or 'chunk' of behaviour. At an early stage of learner-driving (that is, at the 'Don't rush me, I'm thinking' stage) there are, rather, a succession of steps that one has to fight to get into the right order – check the rear-view mirror, listen to the engine sound, depress the clutch, pull the lever down from the middle-top (= third), slide it to the left and then down to the bottom-left (= second), foot off the clutch, now listen to the engine howl, hang on while you're thrown violently forward, check rear-view mirror (where did he come from?), sweat, pray, done it!!

A few months later, changing gear happens somewhere between your hands and your feet while you are 'driving' (= new chunk) and 'listening to the radio'. Or perhaps the changing of the gears happens between your ears, and it's your feet that are listening to the radio. It's all so smooth now it's hard to know what's doing what. It's in your body memory. But how did it get there? Possibly some simplified model of driving or changing gears now exists in your mind.

Coming back to teaching, it is the case that experienced teachers remember more of a lesson than inexperienced teachers, perhaps because they can chunk. 'Rather than leaving the beginning teacher to develop expert schemata through practice and error over time . . . teacher education might design courses and methods aimed at aiding the development of beginning teachers' schemata for classroom teaching and learning' (Peterson and Comeaux, 1987).

It's possible that some people tend to construct internal models whereas others don't. Perhaps some people tend to construct more complex models than others.

Johnson-Laird (1983) quotes evidence that individual differences in reasoning ability are related to the ability to form integrated models of the premises at issue. Good readers are more likely than average readers to make implicit references in order to build up mental models of stories. Models, like chunks, seem to take up little mental space and be easier to remember than fragmented information.

I also have a hunch that people who don't want to or can't seem to change are those who have one rigid model that has become, to them, sanctified and unchangeable.

If it is the case that people learn, change or reason better when they are helped to build and adjust mental models, then helping them to do this may be one of our responsibilities as trainers.

What should people make models of? Well, models are possible, of course, within data and within theories, but when it comes to making models of behavioural change, then perhaps we should consult those who are especially interested in this area – the therapists and the neuro-linguistic programmers in our culture. What would it mean, to make a model of our behaviour now and of the desired behaviour?

The neuro-linguistic programmers (NLP)[1] might say that it would mean studying or calling to mind the breathing, gestures, facial expression, skin colour, eye movement and emotions of certain times, i.e. times when good or bad, routine or different events were experienced strongly and clearly. It would mean, too, working with other people in simulations so that you could be helped to spot, understand, and change these things. There is a special terminology in this field just as there is in our own field. Thus, if interested, we will have to learn about 'doubling' and 'pacing' and so on.

If you stand in front of a mirror and lift your right hand, your mirror image will lift the hand on that side too. This is 'mirroring'. If you stand opposite a friend and ask her to do what you do, then raise your right hand, she will raise her right hand too. This is 'opposites'. If your friend turns round so you face her back, you can watch what she does and do the same. This is 'following'. If you're side by side and one of you tries to breathe, move or walk at the same speed as the other, this is 'pacing'. Once you've achieved unison, this is 'overlap'. Then when the one who originally decided to follow the other's pace starts changing the pace, this is 'leading'.

These terms and actions may seem far away from the world of EFL, and yet if we think of observing trainees teaching, what is our own role? Is it not to find out what trainees can do already, fit in with that, and then open out some new options for them to consider? In other words, to follow, to pace, to overlap, to mirror, and then to lead or be led.

Let us think too of what microteaching is. Yes, it's a scaled-down teaching encounter, but also a simulation, perhaps, or an acting-in which allows for freezing frames, action replay, consultation, support and retrial to occur. If we feel we know what observation and microteaching 'are', if our mental model of them is too fixed and rigid, we may miss the chance to see them as parallels to situations in other areas or disciplines, whether these be learning to drive a car, psychodrama therapy, or the training of medical practitioners (Aeberhard, 1988). If we do allow parallels to be drawn, we can learn from other fields by incorporating new functions from their models into our own model of what observation and microteaching are.

Of all the different models you could use when training teachers, loop input is just one. Loop input is, in a sense, a metaphor: some of the existing connotations in the word 'student' are applied to something that does not normally have that surface meaning, i.e. a trainee. Parts of a student's experience are blended experimentally with parts of a trainee's needs. A thread is wound from one bobbin to another.

Loop input is also, perhaps, a kind of simulation or acting-in. Loops are very natural things. Once you start seeing them, you see them everywhere.

> 'I'm not shouting!' bellowed the man next door.
>
> 'Stop using that bloody, filthy language!' said the woman at dinner.
>
> A young trainee wrote on the board, by mistake, the word 'ERRER' for the word 'ERROR'.
>
> I saw a man commuting from Cambridge to London. He was reading a book called *How to commute and survive*. Is it only a loop if he survives? Oh, loops, loops! A plague of loops!

Of course, as Johnson-Laird says (1983), 'A model's usefulness is not enhanced by extending it beyond a certain level.' It is just a tool. Let's return for a moment to the driver who has successfully chunked most driving manoeuvres and now hardly thinks at all of the individual motions involved in, say, changing gears. If this person were to try to think hard about what she was doing when she changed gears, or attempted to explain what she was doing to a learner sitting in the pasenger seat, the chances are that her effectiveness in performing the manoeuvre would drop. She would change gears more slowly and might, momentarily, have some difficulty actually remembering what she normally does. In other words, sticking to, or going back to, a model that has been surpassed is uneconomic.

Models are sometimes criticised by people for not doing things that they were never built to do. We are by nature greedy. It's the natural tendency of human beings, when faced with someone juggling with three balls, to ask, 'Can you do it with four?' It's also human nature, and stupid, to criticise a model wave-making machine for not being wet. It is a confusion.

Another major option for encoding information in the brain, apart from propositional representations, is the use of images. The fact that loop input is seen and done will help here, but I often use diagrams such as *The stack* (Figure 1) to map the way in and out of exercises for participants.

Pointing to a line in *The stack* (Figure 1) when you say, 'OK, can we return to this level now, the level of teacher trainee, so that we can discuss what we've just done' can speed up the mental change of gear and avoid confusion. It is an aid to decoding the experience. It also helps people not to get stuck at the wrong level.

Most of the time we walk around feeling like people, but sometimes, for example when we have a terrible cold, we walk around feeling like a nose on legs. This is inevitable, but it would be silly to feel like this after the cold had gone. As Johnson-Laird points out (1983), after more serious illnesses we often do find it difficult to return to the level of a whole person and tend to remain rather obsessed for a while with the particular organ that went wrong. Getting stuck at a level inappropriate for the current situation can be disadvantageous, so we have to help trainees to come back to themselves. Whether we do this by telling people we're moving from level to level, pointing to lines in a diagram, or wearing different hats or masks, will depend on trainer style but it needs to be done and time should be allowed for it.

I'd like to move on to the question of transferring information from models. Krumm (1973) states:

> 'If the teaching goal of modern language teaching is the students' ability to communicate, then it holds especially true that the teacher should hold himself back in the face of the student. One could therefore ask whether a teacher training which is always necessarily teacher-centred is the right training form or whether it would be more advisable to include some form of "classroom simulation" where the teacher is the reacting partner.'

Is it easier to transfer information after you've experienced it through a simulation, or is the simulation, because so many senses are involved, even more spell-binding, even more context-bound?

I would now like to quote from Bandler and Grinder's *Frogs into Princes* (1979) because I think they answer this point exactly.

> 'If you change the form, you change the outcome at least as well as if you work with the content... It's a lot easier to change form, and the change is more persuasive.'

In another part of the book the authors say:

> 'People have almost no consciousness of any meta-levels if you distract them with content.'

You will have your own ideas of how change takes place. Perhaps we should ask whether we have the right to try to change people. But that question reflects, I think, a belief that on training courses only trainers 'do things' to trainees. That is, of course, a nonsense. Change will happen just by people being in a room together and it can happen, or not, to anyone in the room.

Trainers are perhaps in the business, not of changing people but of adding choices and options to their trainees' repertoire (see Stevick, 1986). If so, then the trainer's responsibility is to make sure she has choices herself. So, she has to practise new scales and play old scales in new ways. When she has plenty of techniques at her fingertips, then she can select the right one for the right moment, depending on how the group is feeling, what point in the course it is, etc.

On some courses it will feel difficult and time-consuming to give trainees power. For example, on exam courses the content expected from trainees will be fairly circumscribed. Process will be circumscribed to some extent too, as, for example, on many RSA courses where trainees have to prove they can organise their thoughts into lesson plan or essay form. If people on training courses are to be sensitised to the importance of process as well as content, however, they should have the chance to experiment with different kinds of process. Could homework take the form of a tape, a poster, dialogues between debating trainees, or diagrams? Could trainees give the trainer a dictation? If you, as a trainer open up the possibility of different homework formats then your homework correction and evaluation methods will have to evolve to match. It's hard to mark a tape!

I feel it would be an interesting and essential component of any training course that states process to be important, to open up part of class time, and some homework time, for trainees to present content in a way that they feel suits the situation. If it's all right for the trainer to use a foreign language lesson to get a point across, is it all right for a trainee to submit a self-access unit on beginner's Swahili for homework? If it's a good idea for a trainer to loop a session, couldn't a trainee be given the chance to loop a reaction? If we see trainees as empty vessels to be filled, then the content will belong to the trainer and be passed over little by little to the trainee throughout the course until the trainee is 'full'. Questions of how to transmit the content will then only be asked of the trainer. But if it's believed that trainees also have content, that which is in them already, which they express in questions and comments in sessions or to their neighbours in asides, in group work, in homework, in projects, in their classes, in their microteaching, in their very presence in a room, then they will be busy experimenting with ways of expressing it. This natural instinct could be encouraged! If course time and the right to choose a method of expression is handed over to trainees, then some might choose to mirror back to you forms you have used yourself.

An exercise which I've used worked like this[2].

Trainees are given some books, articles, and teaching 'recipes' to choose from. They pick out a teaching idea either for themselves (something they would like to try out in a language classroom) or an activity which they think might suit someone else in the room. That deals with the content. Next, they think out how they are going to 'give' this idea to others. They could talk about it or demonstrate it or do anything they like to get the idea across. Given this sort of framework someone might choose to loop an idea.

The important thing is that trainees have time, help and encouragement to play with different styles of getting things across. That is something trainers need too.

POSTSCRIPT

Sometimes after a loop-input session for teacher trainers, trainers come up and ask:

'Supposing I do this . . . and then I do that . . . and then they do X and Y . . . is that a loop?'

Usually, I can answer 'Yes' or 'No', but if the answer's 'No' I can't always say, fast, what it is, if it's not a loop.

It's possible that the activity referred to might be:

a statement
a repetition, a redundancy
underlining, doubling
self-descriptivity
a mirror image, a reversal, an opposite
a circle, a shift in level, a spiral
an echo
recursion, nesting, a set of Russian dolls, identical objects one inside the
    other
a metaphor
a parallel
a tangent, an alignment
a round, a fugue

If it is a loop, then it could be a partial, total, tight, loose, low-level, tangled, deep or shallow one.

Finding the language to talk about what I was doing in the training classroom took about a year. First, I drew lines in stacks and then circles and then Möbius strips. Then I found metaphors like *The stack* (Figure 1), the loop and the deep sea diver with bends (page 8). Then came individual words like 'consistency', 'congruence' and 'alignment'. Finally, came the most helpful metaphor of all. I should have known it would be – the metaphor (page 130). It is the most helpful because it unites reason and imagination (Lakoff and Johnson, 1980). Reason takes care of the categorisation of experience and the selection of some features and not others, the inference perhaps. Imagination comes in the selection of the productive metaphor, the ability to see one thing in terms of another.

Because loop input is experiential but with content relevant to trainee need, it bridges the gap between objective fact and subjective intuition. It also gives a set of metaphors that can help people, in the midst of flux, to communicate, partially, their shared and unshared experiences. Provided that metaphors are applied consistently but also changed and shifted often, they can give insight and understanding until outgrown.

1. Further reading on **neuro-linguistic programming**:

   Bandler, R. & Grinder, J. (1975/6). *The Structure of Magic* Vols. 1 & 2. Science and Behaviour Books.

   Bandler, R & Grinder, J. (1979). *Frogs into Princes*. Real People Press.

   Cleveland, B. (1984). *Master Teaching Techniques*. The Connecting Link Press.

   Dilts, R. B., Grinder, J., Bandler, R. & Delozier, J. (1979). *Neuro-Linguistic Programming* Vol. 1. L. Cameron – Bandler Meta Publications.

   (Information on all these books may be obtained from: Changes Bookshop, 242 Belsize Road, London NW6.)

2. Thanks to Mario Rinvolucri who first developed this idea.

Introduction to Part Two

In the first part of this book, after some initial defining of terms, I plunged straight into a demonstration and explanation of one set of strategies for use in input sessions on teacher training courses. The set of strategies was called *loop input* and was applied to different sorts of content and different types of classroom management issues. References within the text tended to be fairly informal and made to other people's ideas, materials, methodologies, or to personal encounters.

This preface is intended to count as a kind of government health warning to Part Two, to prepare you for something different. In the first chapter (Chapter 18) I will take a step outside the training classroom. We'll go outside for a breather so that we can discuss such matters as how we classify and define teacher training events, and what the advantages and disadvantages are of putting order into events. The talk will be less about the fine details of practice and more about mental schemata inside the trainer's head. It will be a little more intellectual in tone, but not over-academic.

In Chapter 19, I'll discuss two kinds of external reality in teacher training. First of all, I'll discuss everyday matters such as rooms and light fittings, the roles of caretakers and janitors, the availability of cupboards and keys, and how these everyday matters can help or hinder a course. Secondly, I'll discuss the opinions and preconceptions in heads other than the trainer's. These parameters will be expressed in different ways, and will strengthen the plea for a process of categorising rather than for the formation and conservation of fixed categories.

In Chapter 20, the juggling starts. I will play at balancing parameters with process options, variable with variable, in a spirit of harmony or challenge to see if it's possible and to see if it's fun.

In Chapter 21, the issue of evaluation will be discussed. First thoughts will be entertained, the definition of 'evaluation' made broader and an evaluation model discussed which will enable working trainers to evaluate for themselves and with their trainees the value of the process work they are doing.

18 Ways of thinking and talking about training

Introduction

Teaching and teacher training are both complex events. They bring together, in a cluster, an enormous number of features such as people, places, times, materials, content, processes, course types, and aims. These features meet and jostle in a spontaneous kaleidoscope coloured by the past histories, present speculations, and future possibilities of all the features at the event.

Many people, when faced with such complexity, attempt quite naturally to put a little order into it. One way of doing this is to divide up the complex experience into chunks or blocks or categories and then to name these chunks. This attempt to separate out key elements, to isolate them and to name them is in fact, 'an illustration of the dominant research paradigm, derived from Descartes, which advises dividing something up the better to study it' (Evans, 1988). We will all, however, tend to do the dividing up and naming in different ways.

In Part One of this book teacher training events were divided up, by me, into the categories of *content* and *process* and the roles of student, teacher, trainee and trainer were defined.

I worked with the process and content categories because the question of *how* to do things was the first one I really grappled with when I became a teacher trainer. I noticed that if I set a session off in one way, people's eyes would glaze over and they would fall asleep. If I encouraged things to set off another way, the room would be full of animated people moving about and laughing. I was interested in the difference. Roles were important to me too. I switched from student to trainee to trainer and back again often and it seemed to me an important thing to outline. So I divided things up and labelled them in these particular ways because it made sense to me. One person's category divisions and the names and reasons for their categories will rarely suit another person right down to the ground, however. It is quite possible that my category divisions do not fit with your distillation of experience. The idea of putting non-native and native-speaking trainee teachers into one group, for example, may go against your own way of allotting people to groups. Alternatively, rather than the particular category division, perhaps the language in the naming or labelling or the categories causes problems for you. The word *trainee* has a pre-service feel for some people and the term *process option* is too unfamiliar for some people to accept.

Whatever your feelings about the particular categorisation and labelling of different parts of the teacher training event in Part One, we do now, if you started with Part One, have over 100 pages of shared experience. It is as if at the beginning of a teachers' workshop we purposely went through some activities together in order to have something to refer back to, discuss, and to compare and contrast other work with. If you have not read Part One, but are starting the book here, don't worry. It'll make sense your way too.

In this chapter, I'd like to look at some other possible ways of imposing order on the complex event of teacher training. I'll try to show how different categories bring with them different mental images, expectations and insights. I'll discuss the advantages and disadvantages of forming fixed categories and I'll put in a quick plea for categoris<u>ing</u> as an *active process* rather than categoris<u>ation</u> leading to *fixed categories*. I'll look back at loop input after that to see which of the category labels could be applied to it.

DIFFERENT WAYS OF CATEGORISING TRAINING

First alternative classification: a three-tiered model for placing ideas

There are many different types of ideas around in teacher training today. For example, there are ideas in practical journals on how to run feedback sessions, books on the design of long-term teacher training courses overseas, and discussions at conferences of the general aims of teacher training. It can be hard for someone just starting off in a job as a teacher trainer to see what connection these ideas have to each other or to their own teaching and training thoughts and practices. One helpful scheme, developed for teaching, but applicable to teacher training and development, divides all the ideas into three levels: approach, method, and tactics. A full account of each term follows, but briefly, by *approach*, I mean the beliefs people hold about teaching, learning and training, and the discussions they might have about overall aims, strategies and policies. By *tactics* I mean activities, exercises, and moment-to-moment decisions made in the training room. *Method* occurs somewhere between the two as an inter-relation of thoughts and beliefs on one hand and the fine detail of a particular session on the other. The level of *method* encompasses decisions about selection and sequencing of content, objectives, materials and roles. I will now discuss each term more fully.

The level of approach

At this level we encounter theories and beliefs about teacher training, often in the form of questions such as: What is a good teacher? Is it possible to ascertain what a good teacher is? Is a good teacher someone with depth and charisma or someone with skills? What exactly are skills?

In the realm of language teaching, Widdowson has defined the terms *training* and *education*: 'training tends to convergence and a reliance on established technique, whereas education tends towards divergence and a readiness to break from the confinement of prescribed practices' (Widdowson, 1983).

Prabhu[1] made a general distinction between two perspectives on language education. One is that it *equips* learners in specific ways with knowledge, skills, or patterns of behaviour that they will need later to be useful and productive. The second view of language education is that it gives learners the opportunity and support necessary to realise their *own* potential. This view considers that later demands on the learner are likely to be varied and unpredictable and thus learning has to *enable* the learner to cope with divergence and ongoing change. Although Prabhu feels that any activity will be a mixture of these two views, he feels that different kinds of pressure – from institutions of formal education, from government, and other sources – are at present weighting curricula for both language learners and teachers in training towards *equipping procedures*.

Widdowson's distinction between *education* and *training* and Prabhu's distinction between *equipping* and *enabling* procedures, both borrowed from the field of language teaching, can be applied to language teacher training to give us the questions: Is it training or education that language teachers require? Is it equipping or enabling procedures that are needed? Prabhu feels that only true *enabling procedures* in teacher training encourage professional activism and increase the teacher's ability to interpret experiences and to relate perceptions to practical problems.

This kind of debate on fundamental aims and purposes is encountered in the three-tiered model at the level of *approach*.

The *education / training* and *equipping / enabling* distinctions start us off on a discussion of the types of goals which are appropriate in teacher training and to what degree it is possible or wise to specify these goals. The goals of any one individual may select will depend very much on their concept of a 'good teacher'. And what is thought to constitute a good teacher may vary depending on your generation, the country you come from, your own personal experience of teachers, and your view of what is possible in teaching and in learning. Who should be allowed to decide what good teachers are? Should it be the teachers? Or should learners, schools, inspectors, or individual governments be able to decide?

So, within the level of *approach* fall questions of the type of goal appropriate in teacher training, discussions of what a good teacher is, and of who should have the right to decide on these two issues. Discussion of the political and social role of the teacher comes within this level too. Should teachers pass on the values of the society in which they live, as the values seem to be at the moment, or should they act as the progressive conscience of the society, readying the next generation for new structures and ideas? In countries where values are changing fast, where should the teacher stand, for or against change? Should a British or Chilean or South African teacher educate for a conservation of the status quo or for radical change? Should teachers simply transmit the values with which they were imbued or should they work for radical overhaul of these values? Through discussion of these issues we can consider what constitutes a good teacher and what training goals are worthwhile or necessary.

Strategic concerns occur at the level of *approach*, too. An example here is whether teacher training should take place in schools and be done by practising teachers or in completely separate institutions, such as teacher training departments of colleges or universities. Are separate training colleges likely to be behind or ahead of the work in the classroom? Should training be done by those who no longer teach normal classes regularly? Should teachers for a certain country be trained within that country or can they be flown in from outside? Who should be allowed to be a teacher? Are all the sexes, colours, ages, religions and beliefs present in a community represented in its teaching force? At every level?

As well as discussion about the aims of training courses, the role of teachers, and the position of training centres, the level of *approach* encompasses assumptions and beliefs about the philosophy and psychology of teaching, learning and training. In other words, how *do* people learn to be teachers? Do they learn by watching someone and copying, by having theoretical input first and then applying it to practice, by trying something out in class first and then reading theory about it later? Is it better to avoid risks and mistakes at all costs or are risk taking and mistake making vital to progress? Does learning to be a teacher involve change from something not very good to something better? Or does it involve affirmation, support, and the building of confidence in what someone is already doing?

In the three-tiered model all these discussions – political, social, philosophical, psychological and strategic – fall within the level of *approach*.

The level of method

This is the level at which the specification and inter-relation of theory and practice take place. In simpler language, this is where what you think and believe start to influence your course design and course planning. For example, if you believe that a good teacher is one who can perform certain acts skillfully, then constituent skills will be included as syllabus components in your course. Examples of constituent skills might be: writing clearly on the blackboard, making and using appropriate visual aids, recognising when learners do not understand, spotting discipline problems brewing, handling mechanical aids smoothly in the face of power cuts, keeping students working while you write on the board, etc. If, alternatively, or, in addition, you feel that a good teacher is one who can act as a researcher and plan, execute and evaluate experiments in the classroom, your syllabus may include components on action research, collecting classroom data, keeping teaching diaries, recording classroom interaction, and so on. In other words, your assumptions and beliefs at the level of *approach* will tend to inform your decisions on the selection of content (e.g. constituent skills), the general objectives (e.g. exactly what skills are to be taught) and specific objectives (e.g. what types of visual aids are to be made and handled for what purposes).

Assumptions about teaching, training and learning can affect the sequencing of course components too. Let us imagine that you feel that the 'performance element' of teaching has had too much attention in the past and that you feel that a good teacher is one who is less concerned with her own performance than with listening to students and encouraging them to interact with each other. In that case, you might choose to start a course with discussion, input and teaching practice on the four skills rather than with a standard, lock-step grammar presentation and practice model.

A belief that people learn by working on small amounts of information little and often could lead you to organise the timetable so that there were many short ten to twenty minute slots each day rather than a pattern of longer one to two hour sessions.

If you believe that a sound knowledge of applied linguistics and cognitive psychology are essential for the long-term development of a good teacher, then these rather more field-centred subjects will be represented in the syllabus.

Thus, at the level of *method*, theory is translated into decisions about how much of what type of content to put in the syllabus, in what order, and for what purpose.

Also at this level are considerations of the trainee's role. If you feel that trainees are independent negotiators with experience and knowledge of their own, then you will choose processes and offer choices of process and material to reflect that view. Depending on your view of trainee role, you may invite trainees to monitor their own progress towards their own goals, or foster dependence upon trainer evaluation of how well they are approximating a trainer model, or find some half-way point between these two, possibly at different points in the course.

Discussion of the trainer's role comes in at this level, too. Is the trainer a model-setter, a catalyst for change, a diagnostician, a consultant, a knower of some things but not others, a therapist, a joint adventurer, or a fence-sitter?

The role of materials is important, too, in the level of *method*. Are materials necessary at all? Who makes them? Are they for self-study? Do they prohibit or encourage trainee interaction with others and with data-bases? Do they encourage risk taking or simply test? Do the materials allow for different rates and styles of learning? What happens to them after the course? Are they useful? Should they be made during the course by participants for use in their own classrooms or should they be stylishly prepared by the trainer beforehand to 'save trainee time'?

The level of *method* has been described as if major decisions about objectives, content, materials and roles are always informed by the assumptions and beliefs held at the level of *approach*. This inter-relationship can exist in a conscious, thought-out way as the beliefs and attitudes that we know we have and can describe are applied to decision making, or can just happen unconsciously without the decision maker openly stating beliefs and assumptions or even necessarily being aware of them. A disadvantage for a trainer inheriting a course for which decisions have already been made is that she may run the course along the lines already set down by a predecessor for some time, before realising that the course actually runs counter to her own beliefs and assumptions. On the other hand, an advantage of inheriting a course or attending one run along other people's lines is that it can be an excellent way of becom-ing aware in detail of what one's own beliefs and assumptions are.

The level of tactic

Differences in *approach* or *method* are likely to manifest themselves at the level of training classroom procedure in different types of activities, exer-cises and decisions from moment to moment in the training session. If a cluster of constituent skills has been listed in the syllabus, then this will show up in the arrangement of 'microteaching' sessions, and 'observation sheets' may have been produced. Both are evidence of the belief that 'good' teaching behaviour is observable and gradable.

In this way, a top-down influence can be seen to be working. There is not necessarily, however, a simple one-to-one correlation between a belief about training and an individual training room tactic. One tactic (e.g. a ball game used for learning names in the language classroom) can be used for many different reasons, for example, as light relief in the training room, as an example of using movement and sensation to aid learning, to provide practice in analysing the language of teacher instructions, or to give an example of how activities need to be adapted for large classes. One tactic can also be used in different ways by different trainers to get dif-ferent messages across. For example, a traditional lecture can be used to demonstrate concentration levels, to show that lectures can be interesting, participatory and fun, to please a particular participant who has asked for a lecture, or because the trainer always tends to use the lecture format.

As well as a possible top-down influence from the level of *approach*, through the level of *method* to the level of *tactic*, bottom-up influence is also possible. A trainer trying out a new tactic and finding it workable may find it changing her beliefs and attitudes. Equally possible is an influence outwards from the level of *method* in both directions, up and down. For example, a decision to let trainees have more time to themselves (because of trainer shortages during a flu epidemic) could lead to changes in classroom tactics (more self-study, more trainee-to-trainee task work and discussion) and, if it worked splendidly, this could then lead to a change in trainer assumptions about trainee role and the amount of contact time necessary on a course.

There has been plenty of discussion on what to call these three tiers, should you wish to divide training up into three sections in this way. For an investigation of alternative terms such as *design* (method) and *technique / procedure* (tactic) as used in approximately ten different sources, see Strain (1986). After a consideration of the terminology, references and goals of each set of terms and of the different slant given by researchers and teachers, Strain finishes by saying, 'It is surely not a question of which definition is better or the best, but rather what each has to contribute to the learning / teaching process to success in foreign and second language learning instruction.'

What this model looks like

Whichever term you use to denote the different tiers, the model above is likely to be expressed visually in one of the following ways:

1, Approach

2, Method

3, Tactic

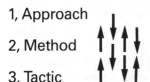

Figure 28   The approach, method, tactic hierarchy

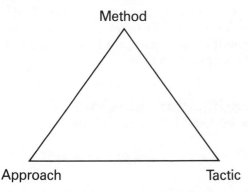

Figure 29   The approach, method, tactic pyramid

Underlying assumptions behind the model

Because of the use of the words *tier* and *level* in describing this model, it is likely that people will think of a hierarchy or stack with an order of generality. *Approach* will tend to be seen on top and training classroom *tactic* (or procedure or technique) at the bottom. The numbers 1, 2 and 3 (Figure 28) reinforce this. As long as it is realised that all the influences can go in both directions, the person introduced to this method of categorisation will understand that while a new belief or theory might lead a trainer to try out different things in the training classroom, it can equally well be the case that something that works in a training session can lead to adaptations in beliefs about learning. A disadvantage to this schematisation of the model might be the tendency (a) to forget the arrows and so think of this model as top-down only, and (b) to infer that the three different levels mean three different jobs, for example, that level one belongs to the theorist in a university, level two to the syllabus designer in the ministry of education, and level three to the trainer.

Bolitho (1988) has also expressed worries about the implications of stacked, hierarchical models such as the one above. Discussing Brumfit and Rossner's 'decision pyramid' (1982) which also has a number of layers descending, Bolitho says, 'The implications are worrying for several reasons: (1) the pyramid model is hierarchical, and it implies the closing off of avenues, (2) even if the implied dynamic of the model is "bottom-up", it is all too easy to see it as "top-down" (most hierarchies work this way), (3) it therefore devalues teaching as a lower order activity.' For a fuller discussion of top-down versus bottom-up approaches to teacher education, see Maley (1987) and Bowers (1989a).

By placing the three-tiered scheme on a page in consecutive paragraphs or diagrammatically in a stack, and given the fact that 'top' and the number 'one' tend, in our culture, to denote the most important, dominant or first chronologically, the model carries strong assumptions and associations. Layout of paragraphs, numbering and visual metaphors, even of the simplest sort, thus carry strong messages which can affect our thinking and feeling without our necessarily being aware of this. Whilst helping us to order events and information in simple, powerful ways, then, metaphors can be dangerous if we are not aware of the full range of assumptions and associations they bring with them.

Second alternative classification: bi-polar scales for clarifying attitudes to teacher education

Another way of imposing some order on teacher education is by using bi-polar scales, for example:

| training _____ | education |

Figure 30   The training – education scale

See Widdowson (1983). Or, more recently:

| teacher training _____ | teacher development |

Figure 31   The teacher training – teacher development scale

Around each end of a scale a number of associations, connected tendencies or generalisations grow up. Thus, for Figure 31 we could end up with something like this:

teacher training _____ **teacher development**

compulsory _____ voluntary

competency based _____ holistic

short term _____ long term

one-off _____ ongoing

temporary _____ continual

external agenda _____ internal agenda

skill/technique and _____ awareness based, angled
    knowledge based   towards personal growth
    and the development of
    attitudes/insights.

compulsory for entry _____ non-compulsory
    to the profession

top-down _____ bottom-up

product/certificate _____ process weighted
    weighted

means you can get a _____ means you can stay
    job   interested in your job

done with experts _____ done with peers

Figure 32   Teacher training – teacher development associations

This is similar to a diagram by Davis[2].

147

Underlying assumptions behind the model

With bi-polar scales something has to be on the left and something has to be on the right. Is left dominant? We do belong to a left-to-right reading culture and the dominant or most important elements do tend to come on the left in phrases like, 'men and women', 'boys and girls', 'Mr and Mrs', 'bread and butter', 'fish and chips'. But then we do say, 'Ladies and gentlemen'. When using bi-polar scales, it might be worth experimenting with what comes on the left and what comes on the right.

To return to teacher training, the bi-polar scales in Figure 32 make visual a philosophic debate about the slant of work with and by teachers ('by' and 'with'?). The debate thus fits into the *approach* level of the three-tiered model above and includes implications for the *method* level.

There are advantages to using scales and clines to organise ideas. First, they can help us to see things less dogmatically, less black and white, less in separate boxes, and more as mixtures and blends. They can encourage a gradually evolving and changing view of many valid points spread out along the middle of a scale from one end or extreme to the other. There are disadvantages to the use of scales and clines too, though, apart from the possible 'left is dominant' problem mentioned above. The mid-points of scales can tend to get de-emphasised and the poles re-emphasised so that ideas and attitudes are gradually crystallised into two opposite and extreme positions. Even this crystallisation *can* help us to see our own practice anew and to reflect on its assumptions, but a greater tendency is perhaps for the poles to become detached from each other, separated, and for one pole to be labelled 'better' than the other. When this happens, teachers and trainers are dumped into guilty corners or feel 'holier than thou' and the arguments start!

Perhaps one way around the problems associated with bi-polar scales would be to use a visual image which is less polarised and polarising. The yin-yang symbol would be useful here.

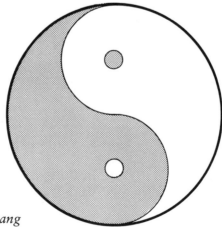

Figure 33   Yin-yang

The idea of balancing scales can be used as an organising principle at levels below that of *approach* (to use language from the three-tiered model). It can be used, for example, to check variety in materials and in forming theories, in trainer and trainee centredness, content blocks or classroom groupings. For example, trainers could have by them, as they plan their weekly training programme, a page of balancing scales such as these:

theoretical input ――――――――――――― teaching practice

peer teaching ――――――――――――― real teaching

pre-lesson help ――――――――――――― post-lesson help

plenary work ――――――――――――― small group work

trainer comment ――― peer comment ――― individual trainee comment

Figure 34   Balancing scales

By checking against the page of scales, they can adjust their training programme to suit their aims. In this way, the scale is seen as implying that balance and variety are good. If all the ticks were close to the poles or to one pole, the trainer would probably feel something was wrong.

Another way of broadening out the use of scales and clines, apart from using a number of them parallel to each other as above, is to use them horizontally and vertically as multi-dimensional clines, like this one for work on correction policies[3]:

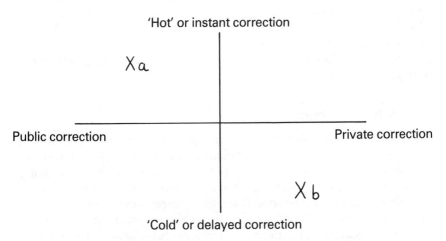

Figure 35   Correction clines

Teachers can be asked how they normally correct students and then to plot these methods onto the space between the intersecting clines as shown in Figure 35. 'X a' represents a teacher interrupting a student and using their voice to correct in front of others in the class. 'X b' represents a teacher contacting a student privately after class and giving them a note to read about some errors they made in class. If, after plotting onto the clines, most techniques are seen to be in a cluster, there can be a discussion of why this is, whether it's a good thing, and what other techniques exist that could be plotted onto a different area of the clines. So this kind of 'target practice' can be used at the level of *tactic* to review correction strategies, establish the tendencies in one's own strategies, and push one towards trying out techniques outside one's own normal range.

Bi-polar scales seem to bring with them some interesting assumptions. If the *poles* of the scales are emphasised, there is a tendency for middle ground to disappear and for an evaluative weighting to attach itself to one particular pole. If the *middle ground* is kept in, then there can be a tendency to assume that it is more correct than the extremes. Using scales in more than one dimension can get around some of these problems.

Scales do seem to have rather insidious tendencies of their own, but for all that they tend to highlight discussion of attitudes, insights and strategies in a particularly focussed way.

Third alternative classification: individual techniques and technique sequences

Within the level of *tactic* there is another extremely simple and much used basis for systematising training events and activities. Trainers often talk about 'short intensive courses' or 'two hour workshops' and one of the main questions asked by a trainer before a session or course is 'How long have I got?' or 'How much time will I have with the group?' We can classify ideas in teacher training according to whether they are individual techniques, or technique sequences joined together to create programmes of longer duration.

Individual techniques

Individual techniques can be used, reused, combined and recombined with more than one piece or type of material within a course of almost any type or length. Individual techniques are the components of a training session and they fall within the level of *tactic* in the three-tiered model. An example here is the brainstorm. This technique can be used at the start, in the middle or at the end of a session. It can be combined with other techniques such as the lecture, individual work or class discussion, to provide a variety of focus and type of activity.

Technique sequences

Technique sequences are ways that a trainer, mentally, visually or practically links ideas into a coherent frame for a programme of at least one hour. The linking can be by content theme, process theme, classroom management, or anything else. Sequences can correspond to the type of course organisation implied in the level of *method* in the three-tiered model, although they are on a shorter time scale. They are the matrix into which individual tactics and activities are placed.

Underlying assumptions behind the model

The idea of this linking together, smooth blending or matrix binding individual items together within a couple of hours' training is the special insight gained from using this particular category label. In language teaching the bridges from one sentence to another (the study of discourse) have been neglected until recently. Perhaps there has been a similar neglect in teacher training of the bridges from one training activity to another.

Individual techniques and sequences of techniques are ways of organising input and time from the trainer's point of view. A trainer with a three-hour workshop ahead of her may well prepare a session plan with slots for individual training ideas written on it together with estimated times and some notes on the transitions possible between the ideas. Many trainers use the idea of length of time and number of techniques as a way of organising input. It does not discount the idea of trainee participation since some of the slots may read 'trainee question time', 'silent reflection time' or 'trainees discuss results of discovery tasks'. It does, however, show up the initiating or performance role of the trainer, just as a timed lesson plan shows up the initiating and performance role of a language teacher. Selection of individual techniques and the planning of sequences by the trainer has both advantages and disadvantages. It can indicate a trainer's concern for variety and balance, and it can also give trainers confidence, allowing them to feel well prepared and on top of things. A drawback though, just as in teaching, is that it may lead the trainer to press on with the plan despite hints of a different mood or different desires or needs amongst the trainees. It may make it more difficult for a trainer to be sensitive to signals and offerings from the group.

Fourth alternative classification: course models and course metaphors

Course models and metaphors are the expression of training aims and beliefs about teaching, learning and training, in the form of metaphors, images or equations, and are applied to whole courses.

Everyone who runs a course has, either consciously or unconsciously, some set of beliefs guiding their decision making. This was noted before in the discussion of the level of *approach* in the three-tiered model. The difference between the level of *approach* in the three-tiered model and the category of *course model* here is that the set of beliefs referred to is encapsulated or simplified here into a particular image or expression which then creates a sense of congruence throughout the course in decisions about methods, tactics, sequences, and so forth.

Let's take an example first. I ran a course a while ago based on the model of a substitution table. A substitution table is a mixture of 'fix and flow'. Here's one:

This		a series of columns.
This table		a substitution table.
This diagram	is	a transformation table.
What's in this figure		something with structure.
This substitution table		something with variable parts.
		about substitution tables.

Figure 36   The substitution table substitution table

In the substitution table above there is a fixed column for the first phrase in the sentence, a fixed column for the verb, and a fixed column for the last phrase in the sentence. There are some interchangeable parts too, slotted in vertically within each column, which can create variety when reading from left to right. Any item within the left column can combine with the verb and with any item in the right column to make a sentence. So, if you read from left to right, you can make many different sentences and they will all be correct. The substitution table is then, to repeat, a mixture of 'fix and flow'.

It was this mixture of 'must' and 'maybe', this blend of 'fix and flow' that attracted me to the use of the substitution table as a metaphor for a training course. I'll explain why.

Anybody who is a teacher will know that there are certain constraints or 'musts' in their job. There are certain things that have to be done. Most teachers must, for example, get to class on time and start the class. They have to set and mark homework and plan lessons. They have to prepare students for exams and meet colleagues and parents sometimes. These are the parts of their job that they can't change. These are the fixed parts of their personal substitution tables. These fixed duties can be expressed diagrammatically by putting them at the head of the fixed columns of a substitution table, like this:

Teacher has to:			
plan lessons	*start classes*	*mark homework*	*etc.*

Figure 37   Substitution table – teacher headings

Many people choose to become teachers, however, because there *is* some choice and variety in the job. It's true that as a teacher you have to plan lessons, but there isn't usually anybody breathing down your neck telling you whether you should do it on yellow paper, on card, as a diagram or as linear notes. Similarly, under the other headings, teachers can usually start classes any way they like: by saying hello, writing on the board, telling an anecdote, or by saying 'Open your books at page 32.' We can plot these variable parts onto the substitution table within the fixed columns, like this:

Teacher has to:			
plan lessons	*start classes*	*mark homework*	*etc.*
but can do so:	*but can do so by:*	*but can do so by:*	

on cards
on paper
as linear notes
in mind map form
with other teachers
by negotiating with
   students to take
   into account
   their needs and
   preferences
	socialising
	taking the register
	doing a warm-up
	   activity
	reviewing past
	   work
		crossing out in red
		providing correc-
		   tions
		writing symbols in
		   the margin
		getting students
		   to correct others	

Figure 38   Full teacher substitution table

F

Thus, a teacher's job is a little like a substitution table. Some parts of the job are fixed and have to be done, but there are lots of variations on how the jobs can be done. Any combination of variables is possible as long as the jobs get done and in a reasonable time and order.

I used the substitution table idea as a framework for a teacher training course, going through the idea with course participants at the start of the course. This was done so that we could:

- Establish priorities (the headings of each teacher's personal columns).
- Build on trainees' prior knowledge (they filled in what they knew already).
- Dot about in the input without losing a sense of system and coherence (since having established the columns, variables can be slotted in and new columns can be started to the right or left or in the middle).
- Show how all combinations from left to right are possible, though some may combine particularly well and others may send mixed messages.
- Build up an even variety throughout the trainees' repertoire in the different column areas.
- Show that, generally, no one option is necessarily better than any other.
- Review or reinforce the use of substitution tables in the language classroom.

Underlying assumptions behind the model

Just as using the three-tiered model can set up assumptions of top-down hierarchy, or using bi-polar scales can tend to lump things into two camps, or using length as an organising criterion can lead trainers into controlling the use of all the time in the training session, so whatever metaphor you use as a course model brings with it certain assumptions, advantages and disadvantages.

The substitution table above assumes that there *are* fixed parts to a teacher's job and that having a variety of ways of doing things is not only possible but inherently good. Using a substitution table at the start of a course sets up the expectation that there will be lots of ideas under each category on the course and that any of these can be used in combination with any other. Teachers may not necessarily agree with these assumptions; they may come from schools where peer pressure, constant observation and a tight system do actually force them to do even tiny parts of their job in a certain way.

Other metaphors

In the broadest sense, we would say that the three-tiered model, the first example in Part Two of a way of categorising teacher training, is a kind of metaphor – a vertical metaphor involving a stacking of levels. The second example, the bi-polar scale or cline is also a metaphor – a horizontal one. Discrete items and sequences of items constitute another metaphor, and the substitution table is a metaphor taken from language teaching. Many other metaphors are used overtly or tacitly by trainers and trainees on training courses. Here are some more examples expressed in Figure 39, just for fun, in the form of a substitution table. (Regarding Figure 39 (c),* see Stenhouse, 1975, and Hopkins, 1985; see also Bowers, 1989a, and Calderhead, 1989.)

(a)	Learning Teaching Training	is	a shared endeavour. the striving for divergent interpret- ations of data.
(b)	The classroom	is	interactive. asymmetrical. symmetrical. differentiated. a social institution. a research laboratory.
(c)	The learner The trainee The trainer The teacher	is	a researcher*. an empty mug. a stuffed goose. a hungry person. a secret reader. a full jug. desperate to teach/learn.
(d)	The learner The teacher The trainer	works on	language data. classroom interaction data. herself.

Figure 39   The metaphors substitution table

Establishing a metaphor at the start of a training course can be useful for many reasons. First, it can make clear a trainer's assumptions about teaching, learning and training. It can provoke thought and start the course off with a clear image and a clear statement of what a course participant can expect from the course. As the course progresses, reference can be made back to the metaphor or image, which can create a sense of coherence. The establishment of a course metaphor can, in turn, lead to decisions being made about which types of process options to employ, what type of material to use, and so on, in order to set up a coherence, an echo, throughout the course within the spirit of the metaphor.

There are, of course, disadvantages to the use of one metaphor by the trainer. The metaphor chosen might not be a good one for all participants. It may not come alive or have meaning. Worse still, it may confuse or run counter to the course participants' own metaphors. A way around this could be the provision of a number of different metaphors contributed by participants and trainers.

Seet Beng Hean has written a very interesting article[4] on the use of metaphors on language teacher training courses. Examples such as 'the seesaw' (used to 'balance' theory and practice), the 'translation' of theory into practice (where the two are seen as two different languages), the 'horse and cart' (where theory has to come before practice) and other metaphors are discussed along with their implications.

THE ADVANTAGES AND DISADVANTAGES OF CATEGORISING TRAINING

The advantages

So far I have mentioned four different ways of imposing order on training ideas or attitudes: the three-tiered system of classification, the bi-polar scale, individual technique and technique sequences, and the metaphor or model that attempts to encapsulate the spirit of a course or part of a course, to set a tone or create an atmosphere. In Part One of the book a different kind of order again was imposed on training: two key elements were abstracted, content and process, and these alone were considered. Next, I would like to discuss the arguments for categorising training events.

There are many arguments in the literature on education for mentally organising reality. Baddeley (1982) writes, 'Organisation helps in two ways: it structures what is being learnt so that recalling a fragment of information is likely to make the rest accessible, and it relates newly learnt material to what has gone before, which means that the richer your existing knowledge structure, the easier it is to comprehend and remember new material.' Organisation of facts or material into higher level units than simply one item has sometimes been called 'chunking'. Another way of explaining chunking is to say that it is the marking of a number of small stages as one routine. It has both advantages and disadvantages: one advantage is an increase in speed of grasping the meaning of situations (see page 131 in Part One).

People do structure or chunk reality. We see faces in clouds, and animals in the flames in the fire grate. We structure reality in such definite ways that when we see a photo of a familiar object taken from an unfamiliar angle we may not be able to recognise it. Sometimes our structures are so useful that a word can be quite badly miss-spelllet and still be recognisable to us. We certainly structure reality in very different ways depending on our personal point of view. At a conference recently someone asked me what 'Sue from Cambridge' looked like. I said she was medium height with blondish hair. (I am tall with brown hair.) 'That's funny', said the enquirer, 'Someone else said she was tall and had brown hair.' I can only assume that his other informant had been short and blonde. Our mental constructions can be rich and delightful. This is the wonderfully positive attitude behind Stevick's work in his book on images and options (1986). He suggests that after reading a text containing a sentence such as 'She dived into the lake' students should be encouraged to share with each other the different mental images they will all have of the colour of the lake, the height of the dive, etc.

READER ACTIVITY

Let's try an exercise here, just to work with this idea a little further.

* * *

If I give you the numbers 363, 366, 369, 372, what number do you think comes next? You may think that it's 375. How do you know that? How would you feel if I told you that the next number is actually 879? (It's not, by the way, as you know well!)

Let's try another one. I'll give you some words and you try to explain their meaning to yourself as you meet them. Ready? OK: 'ball', 'pick up', 'drop'.

How are you doing? Right. I'll add a few more to the group to make it bigger: 'single', 'double', 'main', 'contrast'.

Are you getting anywhere? Or are you backtracking, having made a wrong assumption? Here are some more words. They belong to the same group as the previous seven: 'left', 'right', 'centre'.

Is it getting easier? If not, let me add these words: 'cast on', 'cast off', 'knit', 'needle', 'purl', 'plain'. Have all sixteen words suddenly gone to a different place in your brain?

* * *

This little detour is just to emphasise that we do tend to chunk or structure reality. If we didn't chunk at all, or if we chunked in extremely idiosyncratic ways, others would find us slow and irritating, or downright humorous. Let's return to more academic discussion.

Bruner and Postman (1949), debating the emphasis of structure in subject teaching, state that, 'Unless detail is placed into a structured pattern it is rapidly forgotten. The pattern allows reconstruction and regeneration.' Looking at all the ideas and attitudes in teacher training and sorting them into chunks, classes, tiers, scales, defined attitudes, metaphors or diagrams may then be an extremely useful way for us to come to grips with them, find out about them, and compare and contrast them with other realities and our own perceptions and practices. It enables us to interact mentally with the information and 'learn' what it may mean.

The disadvantages

Classifications can be counter-productive too, however. I have already touched on the dangers of the four different types of classifications. Categories can also become fixed and stuck, and are sometimes used long after they are in fact useful. We mentioned before the importance of people *interacting* with information. A similarly active engagement is evidenced in Neisser (1967) who writes, 'If cognition is constructive and the process of construction leaves traces behind, then *manipulation* of data should improve recall.'

If categories become fixed and known, as if engraved on tablets of stone, then little interaction or manipulation is possible. Finally, there is a tendency for pre-existing schemata to cause a distortion of new data or an inability to see new data as it really is. The well-known experiment, described in Bruner and Postman (1949), where people were asked to identify a series of playing cards, illustrates this point dramatically. Many of the cards, flashed for short periods, were quite normal. A few, however, were anomalous, for example, a *black* four of hearts. Even when allowed to gaze at the cards for 40 times longer than the average exposure necessary to recognise normal cards, some subjects never managed to adjust their mental categories enough to state exactly what they had seen. They would insist that they had seen either a red four of hearts or a black four of spades or clubs. Their mental classifications were so fixed that they could not see reality. What they saw was not possible for them.

My point here is that mental classification, division and naming, sorting and ordering, are extremely useful *as a process*. Every way that reality is classified brings with it interesting and useful insights. It is hard to prove, however, that one way is inherently better than any other. Certainly, if only one way is used, this way may not accord with external reality in the present and may also tend to block further insights in the future. Categories and classifications need to keep changing in structures as well as in detail. This is why I have referred to the *process of classifying* rather than the *formation of closed categories*. The process needs to continue. After we have grasped the structure, meaning and detail of one system, we need to keep trying out new forms of organisation and new classifications so that we can gain new insights rather than block them and so we may see more of reality.

HOW DOES LOOP INPUT FIT INTO THESE ALTERNATIVE CATEGORIES?

Loop input was defined in Part One as a vehicle for transmitting information, a way of conveying or eliciting skills, knowledge or information. As such, then, it would fit neatly into the *tactic* level of the three-tiered system. However, it also follows from a particular *approach*. That approach is that people learn by doing, that they enjoy the intellectual and physical parallels in loop input, and that a resonance is set up between content and process that helps learning to take place at a deeper level. This resonance is caused by input coming via several different senses. Another aspect of the approach is that trainers should try to be consistent in their medium and their message. Since loop input is also one way of organising the process design of a whole course (and Part One of this book), and since it involves consideration of what the trainees' and trainer's roles are as well as the role of materials, it seems to fit into the *method* level too.

Let's take the second idea in this chapter, the bi-polar scale moving from teacher training to teacher development. Loop input is a way of eliciting and transmitting ideas. It is a tool which could be chosen by a group of teachers working together in a teachers' centre on, say, dictation techniques. If used by teachers, for teachers, for their own purposes, loop input falls at the teacher development end of the scale. Alternatively, loop input could be used on an exam-orientated teachers' course by a trainer giving an input session. In this case, loop input falls at the teacher training end of the scale. Whether loop input is considered as an imposed trainer choice or as a holistic developmental tool depends largely on who uses it, why, and how.

Loop input can be used as a short idea for ten minutes of a session or as a way of sequencing and blending several different parts into a whole session (see Part One). It can also be used as a course model.

It seems, then, that different forms of classification can be applied to loop input and that it in turn can be slipped into or described by most categories mentioned so far. Here we have another feature of classification, that it is quite normal for a phenomenon to be equally at home in more than one category. Although we have a tendency to insist that each thing stays in one category, reality does have a way of moving categories as it changes or of being equally describable in terms of different systems. Perhaps instead of trying to pin loop input into one or other level or pole, we should look at a different kind of label that allows, and furthermore, describes, both similarity and difference.

The general concept of *recursion* is about nesting: little Russian dolls inside little Russian dolls, plots within plots, stories within stories, and so on. The 'pushing and popping' referred to in Chapter 1 are also a form of recursion, a task within a task. As Hofstadter states (1979), 'Recursion is based on the "same" thing happening on several different levels at once

159

but the events on different levels *aren't* exactly the same – rather, we find some invariant feature in them, despite many ways in which they differ.' In the Scott Kim illustration (Figure 5), once you have seen a small fragment of the drawing you can extrapolate the pattern to a huge spatial area. Given a small drawing of concentric circles, as in Figure 40, you could take any tiny part of this drawing, and using the information in it as a key, rediscover the pattern of the whole piece. A tiny fragment of any of the circles will give the key 'curve'; a complete ring inside or outside will give the key 'circle'; any pie-shaped wedge will give you the information necessary to reconstruct the concentric circles. A tiny fragment of any part of the information will, if copied, on any scale, produce a drawing which is the 'same' in some way as the original drawing.

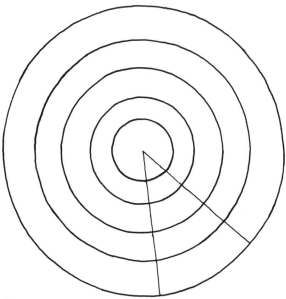

Figure 40   Concentric circles

The decision to capitalise on the parallels between language students and teacher students, between language classrooms and training classrooms (see page 7), to change levels from time to time, fuse content and process, and play on the light and dark spaces created by foreground and background (see page 15) are the essential rules, the key information in loop input that can be used again and again to create similarity-with-difference throughout teacher training events.

Each different way of dividing reality, classifying it and naming it, throws light onto reality. Different features are highlighted each time and our understanding grows and deepens. We must not be tempted to imagine, however, that reality itself is altered by our classifying or naming it our way, one way, or even many ways.

Summary

For readers who like brevity and clarity, may I offer the following nick-names and set of summary statements for Chapter 18. In this chapter I have touched on several things, though not necessarily in the following order.

INSIDE THE TRAINER'S HEAD, OR MENTAL SCHEMATA[5,6]

- Teacher training events are complex constellations of people, times, places, content, materials, aims, etc.
- When faced with complexity we can choose whether or not to order it mentally, verbally or visually. Even if we choose not to, our minds might start doing it naturally anyway.
- Both ordering and not ordering have their attendant advantages and disadvantages.
- I personally am in favour of ordering as an ever-renewing process rather than as a once and for all production of fixed categories.
- If you order the complexity of issues in teacher training there are many different ways of doing it.
- I've given some examples, e.g. a three-tiered system, a bi-polar scale system, individual techniques and technique sequences, and a use of metaphor. In Part One of the book another way was also given, namely the selection of one key element for discussion. Your ways may be different.
- Each different system has its own special assumptions, dangers and benefits.
- Different classifications can be placed on the same reality. You call something one thing, and I call it another. Reality will fit into your categories as well as into mine.
- Any one person may well have several partial classification systems existing at the same time. These systems may alternate in priority or superimpose on each other without the individual feeling any confusion or contradiction, in fact, sometimes without the individual even noticing.
- Some classifications seem to describe some aspects of reality more easily than others. Some classifications feel neater, simpler, more pleasing or more productive to one individual than other systems do.
- Loop input was created out of a mental classification that had concern for the categories of *content* and *process* and for the different roles present in language teacher training.

- Loop input can be described by or allocated to any or all of the example classification systems given in this chapter. It can also be described by the recursion metaphor.
- Loop input can be used on a course which has been described or classified in any of the ways discussed in this chapter.

1. Dr N. S. Prabhu, 'Language education: equipping or enabling', a paper given at the Regional Language Centre Seminar in Singapore in April 1987.
2. Paul Davis, 'What is TD and is it really different from TT?', an unpublished paper.
3. I learnt how to use multi-dimensional clines for work on correction policies in conversation with Penny Ur.
4. Dr Oliver Seet Beng Hean, 'False metaphors in pre-service language teacher education', a paper given at the Regional Language Centre Seminar in Singapore in April 1987.
5. Further reading on **mental schemata**:
    Aitchison, J. (1987). *Words in the Mind: An introduction to the mental lexicon*. Basil Blackwell.
    Baddeley, A. (1982). *Your Memory: A User's Guide*. Sidgwick and Jackson.
    Johnson-Laird, P. N. (1983). *Mental Models: Towards a cognitive science of language, inference and consciousness*. Cambridge University Press.
    Kuhn, T. S. (1962). *The Structure of Scientific Revolutions*. Chicago University Press.
    Lakoff, G. & Johnson, M. (1980). *The Metaphors We Live By*. Chicago University Press.
6. Further reading on **different models** for teacher training courses:
    Gordon, T. (1974). *Teacher Effectiveness Training*. Peter H. Wyden Publisher.
    O'Brian, T. (1981). The EROTI Model: A stimulating guide for teacher training. In *Focus on the Teacher: Communicative approaches to teacher training. ELT Documents 110*. The British Council.
    Rinvolucri, M. (1987). Course models in teacher training. In *Language and Literature*. The British Council 1987 Bologna Conference Report. Modern English Publications.

19 External parameters of teacher training courses

In Part One of this book I concentrated on one main way of classifying the teacher training event and on one particular process type. In Part Two (in Chapter 18) I discussed other ways that trainers might choose to classify or mentally organise teacher training. So far, then, we have looked at things very much from the trainer's point of view and from inside the trainer's head. It's now time to move out to other realities outside the trainer's head. In this chapter I would like to look at what I call *parameters*. These are the constituent elements in teacher training, such as numbers of people, rooms and materials. At first I thought of calling them 'constraints', but that does have a slightly negative ring to it as if trainees and trainers would be totally free to do what we liked if it wasn't for 'constraints' forcing us to do things we hate. *Parameter* is a more neutral term. Parameters act like the clefs, staves and bar lines that give shape and rhythm to music. They are the reality of our training lives and can make things interesting as well as impossible at times. They make thought and creative solutions necessary, and we all tend to view them in different ways.

An overview of parameters

Rather than presenting the parameters in plain list format, I'll try to find some more visually interesting ways. You've seen plenty of mind maps up to now in the book, so I'll use some different kinds of diagrams and mnemonics. This book is about interesting process and should also have some interesting processes within itself.

First, let's look at an overview of the types of parameters I'm talking about. The wheel diagram in Figure 41 sets out some of the main types of parameter. Thus, working from the outer ring inwards, we can see that there are the people (trainees, trainers and others, and contact possibility between them), the course (the type of course, course model, syllabus, history and future, materials and process options), the tangibles (rooms, desks and hardware), and the intangibles (the aims and beliefs of all the parties concerned). All these factors surround and shape the training. Another factor which bears on training is the evaluation or the measurement, informal or formal, personal or organisational, of the quality and quantity of the components.

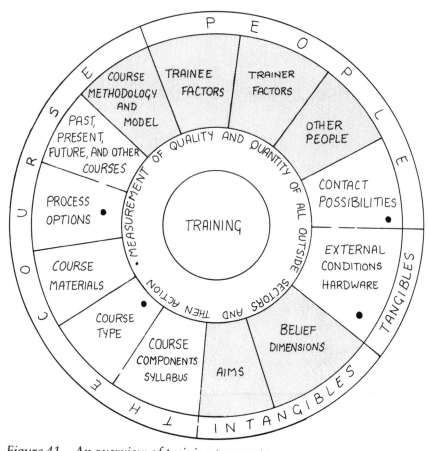

Figure 41   An overview of training parameters

Areas which have very strong relationships with each other, although placed in different sections, are shown by the use of similar shading, circles, etc.

Next, let's look at some individual parameters more closely. All these parameters serve to bring the training event into sharper focus. I'll describe each parameter in a little more detail in this chapter so that we can move on in the next chapter to the question of how we can respond to the parameters.

Individual parameters

THE TRAINEE

Every trainee is uniquely different from every other trainee. To present the trainee parameters visually may I then, tongue-in-cheek, use the crystal structure of a snowflake!

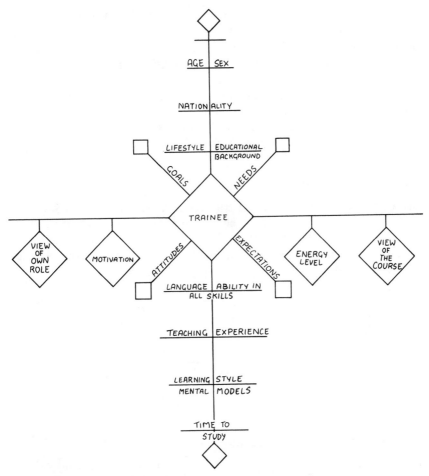

Figure 42   The trainee

THE GROUP

When trainees come together, you need to check if, together, they form a homogeneous or heterogenous group, and check too the ratio of trainees to trainers, the turnover of trainers and trainees, the size of the group, how many are attending voluntarily or compulsorily, and the basic chemistry of the group.

THE TRAINER

Trainers are every bit as unique and different from each other as trainees are. A trainer may be very familiar with the local context or may have flown in from another country. Trainers who have worked on a course for years may be working with those new to the course. Trainers can differ too in their commitment to the style of past courses or to the present course and its approach, methodology and tactics. Trainers can differ in individual training style as well as in age, background, qualifications and in all the ways that trainees or any group of people can differ from each other. It is as important to take into account the trainers' perceptions of themselves, their roles, their jobs and salaries, etc. as it is to take into account the trainees' perceptions of themselves, their roles on and off the course and their view of the amount they give in time, money and energy.

OTHER PEOPLE CONCERNED

Surrounding the main group of trainees and trainers are all the other people involved in the training event. Their silhouettes flicker around the event like shadows from a group photograph. They all have their own views and expectations of the event and can support or block proceedings in delicately different ways.

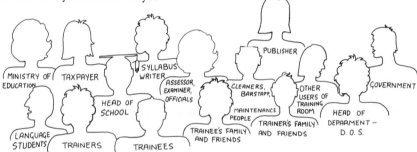

Figure 43   The group photograph

Let me give some examples of ways in which any one of these individuals can make or break a course: a gentle-hearted *director of studies*, in charge of interviewing candidates for the course and incapable, really, of failing anyone at interview, who allows onto your course all kinds of applicants who may later find they shouldn't be there. A *spouse*, who greets a course participant after a gruelling evening's input session with the right mixture of food, drink, privacy or chat, can turn a decision to drop out of a course into the realisation that other factors in life can balance stress and make it bearable. A *janitor*, who bursts into the middle of teaching practice at five minutes to five o'clock, insisting that everyone has to leave immediately so that he can lock up, can create the kind of havoc that leaves a bad taste in everyone's mouth. An *examiner*, who writes the exam questions carefully and thoughtfully, can, over a number of years, encourage a whole new positive slant to course work, teacher development and teacher training. Recently, I have seen some wonderful *language students* managing, with consummate grace and good humour, to train the teachers practising on them. During vocabulary presentation slots they would say with encouraging smiles, for example, 'Don't talk it to me – show, please.' or ' "Big" is not an explanation. Anything can be big to somebody!' With some language students you really don't need trainers.

EXTERNAL CONDITIONS

The quantity and quality of the following items can have a powerful shaping effect on a training event.

Physical space
Rooms (number, size and accessibility); lighting; noise; colour; furniture (fixed or movable, light or heavy).

Hardware
Charts and boards; audio and video recorders; OHPs and computers; reliable power supply; noticeboards and wall display space; books; keys and cupboards.

Support
Typing, photocopying and recording facilities; post and phone; filing and librarianship; cleaning; feeding and refreshing.

Finance
The cost of the course; the fee to the trainer; the charge to the trainee; money available for materials and parties. The cost of *not* doing the course; the cost of doing it a different way; the cost of supplementary training.

The big questions here are: Who has these things? How can you get them? Where do they come from? How can you transport and install them? How can you check what you've got before, during and after the course? Who has the power and authority to make decisions concerning them?

CONTACT BETWEEN TRAINEES AND TRAINERS

Traditionally, when we think of teacher training, we may tend to think of one or more trainers meeting groups of trainees in rooms for input sessions, or of one trainer supervising one practice teacher in a classroom. In reality, plenty of work can be done without trainers, with other trainees and with different sets of circumstances. Below I have listed just a few possibilities.

Who can meet who(m)?
Trainee(s) can meet trainee(s), trainer(s) can meet trainer(s), and trainee(s) can meet trainer(s) in any combination and number.

In what channel?
Face to face; by phone, letter, assignment or tape (sound or video); in class as a whole group; via diaries and lesson transcripts.

External parameters of teacher training courses

When?
Before, during or after work; on weekdays or at weekends; when people are fresh or at the end of term; when people are nervous before an exam or carefree after one; after a course has finished; some weeks after a workshop has been held.

For how long?
Any length of time between a few minutes and a residential course of some months.

How often?
Once and never again? – the case when an 'expert' flies in and flies out again. Many, many times each day? – the case of the apprentice who is team teaching with an experienced teacher.

Where?
In a coffee bar or corridor; in a home or hotel; in a purpose-built training centre; in a church hall; in an empty chemistry lab.

What's the reason for meeting?
Traditionally, perhaps, people have met in training to gain input, watch each other teach and give feedback on teaching. There are plenty of other possible reasons though. For example: to plan a lesson; to exchange thoughts on a lesson: to plan an assignment; to share the contents of diaries; to test input; to prepare materials; to practise an activity with colleagues; to discuss the provision of coffee in the break; to negotiate the next part of the course.

BELIEFS AND AIMS OF ALL THOSE INVOLVED IN TEACHER TRAINING

Every person involved in a teacher training course will have a different view of the aim of the course and different beliefs about the outcome, the role of input, the role of participants' own previous experience, and so on. Some of these differences are represented on the clines in Figure 44.

aims pre-defined _____	aims undefined
expected outcome _____	free outcome
trainer centred _____	trainee centred
trainer dependent _____	long-term trainee self-sufficiency
short-term objectives _____	long-term objectives
input/information based _____	output/performance based
education _____	training
equipping _____	enabling

train and teach _____	test and test
transmission based _____	conflict orientated
data/text based _____	experience based
judgemental, assessed _____	not-judgemental, not assessed
trainee as an empty mug _____ or *tabula rasa*	trainee as thinking person with own ideas and experience
trainer as a full jug _____ or writer on the board	trainer as a catalyst, counsellor, colleague
abstract syllabus _____	locally relevant syllabus
totally detailed, fixed syllabus _____	modular, negotiated, core only, a flexible syllabus
theory _____	practice

Figure 44   The 'different view' clines

The different beliefs and views held by each and every person involved in a training–learning event will give them a certain angle on the training

Figure 45   Different views on the training event

event. In other words, it is not just the trainer who has preconceptions and expectations. All the people coming to the event will come with different views, from different perspectives, walking towards the event from different directions and seeing different scenery on the way.

COURSE COMPONENTS

One major question here is: WHAT do you and all the other people with a hand in the course wish to have included in it? The content of a course can be described in terms of large chunks, such as 'Background theory' and 'Methodology', or in the form of the labels or names that might be given to individual slots on a timetable. As an external assessor it is my privilege to have access to a large number of timetables written out by different training centres for the same type of pre-service course. It is extremely interesting to see how different centres label their timetable slots and to see what different centres feel should be included in and excluded from their courses. I have listed below, in a deliberately unsystematic way, a selection of the content blocks I have seen included on timetables for four-week intensive pre-service training courses. The list is dense and unprioritised for a reason. As soon as I start to group the timetable slots into sections or put them into an order from first to last, I start to impose my own training traditions onto the material.

Reader activity

* * *

As an alternative to this, perhaps as you read through the list you might like to make a mental note of which of the content blocks you would or would not include on a short pre-service course, what order you would put the content blocks into, what extra content blocks your own trainees might wish to add to the list and how you relate the content blocks to each other and into sections.

past learning and teaching experiences	parallel language learning
storytelling	the difference between teach-
vocabulary	ing children and adults
history of methodological changes	phonology
teacher talking time	language analysis
the rules of this course	classroom management
the tools of the trade	tutorials
study skills	board work
what there is to teach	teaching practice
feedback	methodologies
structuring lessons	lesson planning
student case studies	the four skills
different levels of learner	introducing new language

controlled and freer practice	review
concept questions	group liaison time
visual stimuli	mechanical aids practice
drawing practice	textbooks
personalisation	linguistics
integrated skills	the use of readers
how can I change?	self-access work
learner styles	games
literature	jazz chants
testing	songs
drama	video
CALL	exams
EFL / ESL	careers
one-to-one teaching	adapting terrible materials
course summary	mime

* * *

Once you, as a trainer, have gathered together your own list of what is wanted on a course, the next questions to think about will be: How much of each component? In what order? In what proportion and relationship to each other? How will they be linked and reviewed or recycled? If you tend to do this listing as a group of colleagues in discussion before or during a course, the chances are that someone in the group will have been sketching. People often resort to paper, pencil and sketches when it comes to indicating the main proportions and relationships between different types of course content. Some will start straight away with a traditional timetable like this one.

Mon.	Tues.	Wed.	Thurs.	Fri.

Figure 46   A traditional timetable

Others will step a little further back from this degree of concrete detail, in order to make general decisions first. See Figures 47–53, where each figure illustrates a different kind of selection and grouping decision.

171

External parameters of teacher training courses

a)

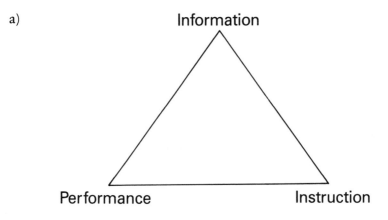

Information

Performance   Instruction

b)

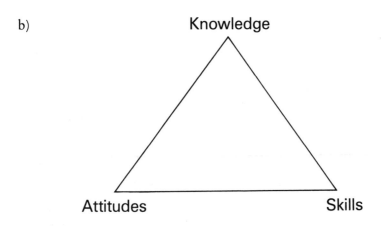

Knowledge

Attitudes   Skills

c)

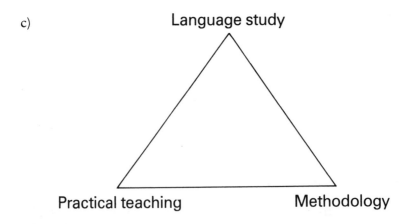

Language study

Practical teaching   Methodology

Figure 47   Triangle figures

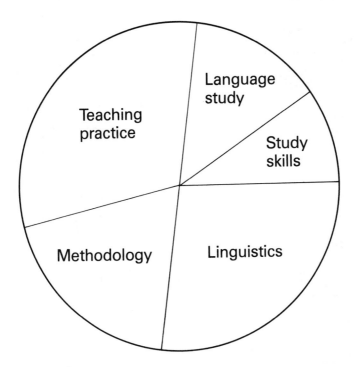

Figure 48   Pie chart

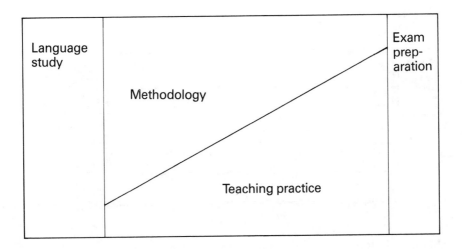

Figure 49   Proportional tanks

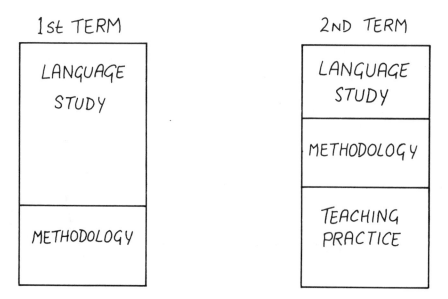

Figure 50   Blocks

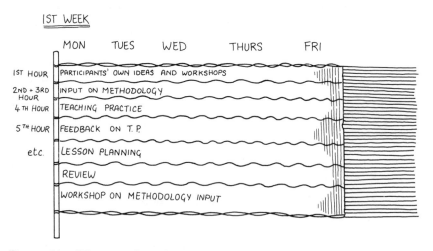

Figure 51   Weaving threads into a loom / course

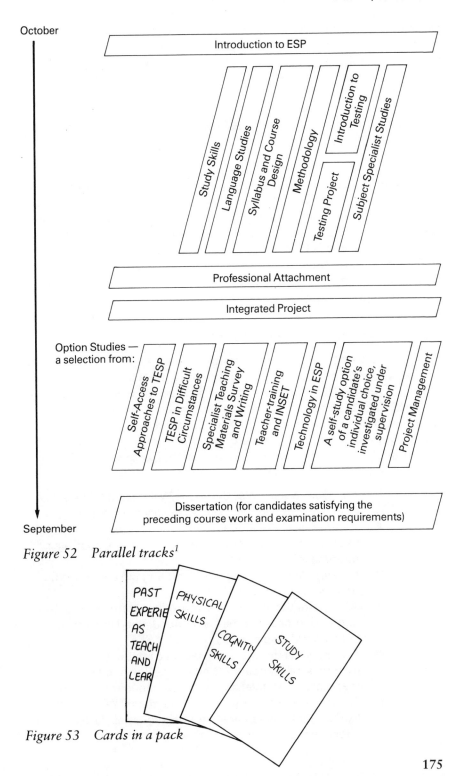

October

Introduction to ESP

Study Skills

Language Studies

Syllabus and Course Design

Methodology

Testing Project

Introduction to Testing

Subject Specialist Studies

Professional Attachment

Integrated Project

Option Studies —
a selection from:

Self-Access Approaches to TESP

TESP in Difficult Circumstances

Specialist Teaching Materials Survey and Writing

Teacher-training and INSET

Technology in ESP

A self-study option of a candidate's individual choice, investigated under supervision

Project Management

Dissertation (for candidates satisfying the preceding course work and examination requirements)

September

Figure 52   Parallel tracks[1]

PAST EXPERIE AS TEACH AND LEAR

PHYSICAL SKILLS

COGNITI SKILLS

STUDY SKILLS

Figure 53   Cards in a pack

175

During the discussion on content different people will be mentally 'seeing' the main course components in very different ways, and each way will represent a fresh insight. 'Threads', for example, will turn up here and there in the fabric of a course, whereas 'blocks' will be solid pieces at definite times. 'Cards' will each carry a definite message, but can be shuffled so that they turn up at different times. You might like to check your own view of course components against those above to see where the similarities and differences are.

Up to now in this chapter I have listed, in different ways, some of the parameters of a teacher training course. I have mentioned the trainees and trainers, the other people surrounding the course and how they can affect it, the external conditions, the type of contact possible between trainees and trainers, some training aims and beliefs, and some ways of expressing the proportions and relationships that different types of course content might have to each other. To gain a view of what other people see as constraints or parameters to training courses please see the short list of further reading[2].

Other features of the training course

I would like now to turn to other features of the training course itself. Casting aside the temptation to supply you with a mnemonic such as 'FIASCO' or 'TRIUMPH', I've plumped instead for the less interesting 'PARAMETERS' (Figure 54) as a way of prompting recall of some basic questions. Some people find mnemonics a useful way of remembering things (Bowers, 1989b). Mnemonics are also a type of process that I haven't used much in the book so far. You might like to see whether they work for you or for your trainees.

P *Previous* course? Was there one? Who did it? How was it done and has it left any kind of legacy or tradition?

A *Another* one? Will there be another one? What can you do to ensure that another course, if desirable, is possible and productive?

R *Reason* What is the reason for doing the course? Who ordered it and why?

A *Aims* Are the aims defined? Are they stated in input, output or process terms? Is output defined in terms of behavioural objectives?

M *Materials* Is the course based on a textbook? What materials exist already? Who will design and create new materials? Cost, availability, types, sequences, flexibility?

E *Exams* Are there any? Who wrote them? What are they like? Do they have a negative, positive or neutral backwash effect on the course?

T   *Type*   Is the course pre- or in-service? Initial or for experienced teachers? Part or full-time? Distance or contact based?

E   *Evaluation* of *effectiveness*   How will the effectiveness, quality and quantity of course participants, trainers, assessors, input, output, process, aims, materials, component balance, external conditions, etc. be evaluated? When will it be done? How, how often, and to what standard?

R   *Revision*   How much, how fast, and how often can you revise aspects of the course depending on the evaluation above?

S   *Spotlight*   What will you spotlight on the course that will make it special in some way? In other words, what are the special strengths in you and in your trainees that will add sparkle?

Figure 54   The PARAMETERS mnemonic

Discussion

One aim of this chapter has been to think about the external parameters surrounding a training course as a way of remembering that the mental models of trainers may well differ from the reality of external constraints. External realities in the training classroom exist in analytical detail – numbers of people, numbers of chairs, types of equipment and numbers of hours. There are also mental models and predispositions in heads other than the trainer's. There are, then, many variables both external and internal, apart from the trainer's mental image or personal fantasy about a course. As Prabhu said at an IATEFL conference, 'Wherever you look for variety and differentiation, you'll find it.'

Discussing a variety of different training parameters in this chapter and describing them one by one may possibly have two unfortunate effects. First, it may worry trainers and course organisers, by reminding them of all the things they have to think about (or, if they're already in the middle of a course, of all the things they haven't thought of). Secondly, by talking of variety and difference, we may obscure the similarities between training events happening in different situations. I think it's worth living with these possible disadvantages, however, in order to gain some strong advantages.

First of all, by considering parameters, rather than talking of constraints, we may be better disposed towards the shaping effect they have on a course and consider them an interesting design problem rather than a restriction or obligation. By considering parameters singly and adding some detail to each one consistently, we may start to see things we

177

hadn't noticed or give more attention to things that have never seemed important before.

Watching the way other people order or visualise parameters not only tells us a lot about them, but also makes clear to us our own tacit assumptions. Working with a trainer who sees 'threads', for example, whilst you see 'blocks' can be a broadening experience and lead you to try a course design that is new to you.

Even when we view external realities, we still tend to view them our way. First of all, what external realities do we actually see or notice? Which ones do we prioritise? And then, once we have chosen to concentrate on certain realities and not others, we inevitably map our own mental constructions on to them. This is natural and helps us to gain speed and understand large amounts of information, and also gives us a sense of creative control and pleasure. My plea here is, however, that we should try to become aware of our own tacit models, try to understand other peoples', and only use the models as long as they are useful and usable. When external variables rise up sharply and in significant enough numbers to force us to question our model, then my plea is that the model should be adapted, remade, or, if invalidated, dropped.

Summary

Here again, for readers who appreciate succinct summaries of arguments, are the main points of this chapter:

- There are other realities apart from the mental classification of events by trainers.
- All the people at an event will have a view on it. These views may well be different. Some people will see some things, others will see others, and different people will sequence, prioritise, organise and describe what they see in different ways.
- External parameters can include tangible things (like how many blackboards there are), intangible things (like what the aims of the course are), people factors (like trainee age and experience), and course factors (like how many hours of course time there are and whether the course has been run before or not).
- Both external and internal parameters can sometimes be referred to using diagrams, lists, questions, pictures, mnemonics and other methods (such as stories and parables) not used here.
- More variables could be discussed and all variables could be discussed in infinite detail and in different ways that show up the tacit assumptions of the person explaining.
- Despite the plethora of details and variables, there are similarities between training events and people's views.

- Trainers need mental models to cope with their jobs.
- Becoming aware of these (often tacit) models in yourself and others is enlightening.
- Models should be adjusted, broken down, rebuilt, exchanged, shared, or discarded when they cease to deal usefully with external variables or when they prevent us from seeing external variables that do not fit into our system or from seeing realities other than our own.

1. Thanks to The College of St Mark and St John Foundation, Plymouth, for the diagram.
2. Further reading on **course parameters or constraints**:
   Dunford House Seminar Report (1983). Design and implementation of teacher training programmes. Edited by Clive Holes, Tony O'Brien and Mike Vinter. The British Council.
   Dunford House Seminar Report (1984). Curriculum and syllabus design in ELT. Edited by Terry Toney. The British Council.
   Romiszowski, A. J. (1981). *Designing Instructional Systems: Decision making in course planning and curriculum design*. Kogan Page.
   Stenhouse, L. (1975). *An Introduction to Curriculum Research and Development*. Heinemann Educational.

20 Matching process to other training variables

Introduction

As outlined in Chapter 19, there are many variables in teacher training. They include all the many people at different levels of authority who can make a course possible (or impossible), and all the predispositions, aims, models and expectations these people carry in their heads. There are also the physical factors – the hardware and the financial and administrative setting of the work, the juggling of course components into the right balance to fit the course type, the course methodology and the materials. If you then add regular doses of evaluation and feedback, you have an interesting brew. Anyone who's set up a training workshop, seminar or course, will, from their own experience of wrestling with reality, be able to think of parameters that I have left out. We could spend time gathering and listing more, but the main point is simple – there are a lot! And we haven't even begun yet to list or discuss the different options that are available in the *process* of sessions. Brief mention was made in Chapter 18 of the fact that there are many options available for the transfer, elicitation, or sharing of information, experience, skills, opinions and knowledge in teacher training. In this chapter I would like to mention a few of these options and then to move on to a discussion of how these options and the parameters above can be adjusted to create harmony or challenge within a training programme.

A FEW PROCESS OPTIONS

I will briefly describe a few process options. There are hundreds of possible options for raising awareness, sharing input, consolidating work, learning from teachers at work and reacting to databases. The list below is by no means exhaustive[1].

The buzz group lecture

As its name implies, this option is a good one for those interested in creating variety in the standard lecture format. Before the lecture, the lecturer divides the content of the lecture into small chunks. At the start of the lecture, she talks for a few moments, so delivering the first chunk. Listeners, in small groups of from two to six people, then recapitulate what they have understood, and prepare questions and/or comments. The lecturer gathers in the questions and comments and can either deal with them immediately and directly or use them as the basis for the next part of the lecture. This involves the lecturer in mentally reorganising sections of the material, and in order to do this the lecturer needs to be both familiar and happy with the material.

This process of lecturer talk followed by listener buzz, question and comment is repeated with each section of the lecture. (For a fuller description of how to use the technique, see Woodward, 1987.) Bligh et al. (1975) have given a very clear diagrammatic representation of how buzz groups can be formed. Their diagrams look something like this:

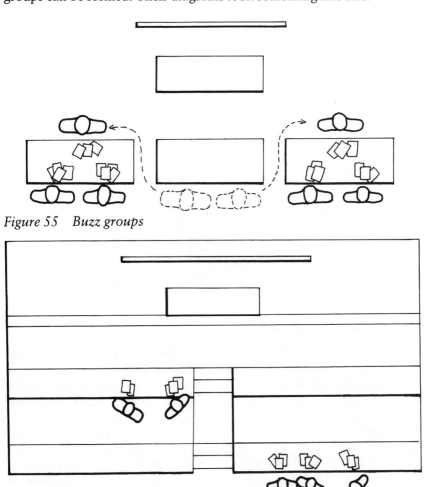

Figure 55   Buzz groups

Figure 56   Buzz groups in a formal lecture theatre

The brainstorm

This idea can be used at any time in a session as a way of gathering ideas quickly from all those present in the room. Group members offer a number of spontaneous suggestions in an intensive manner and in response to a stimulus or problem given by the lecturer. The suggestions are noted uncritically and in unlisted, random format, often on a blackboard or OHP. Here's an example of a brainstorm around the idea of 'How I feel about reading books'.

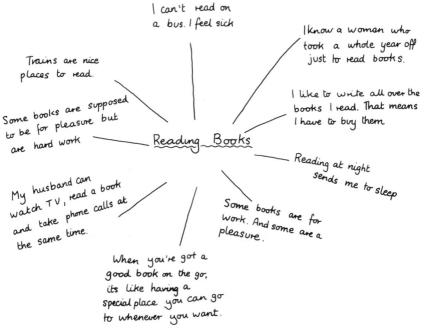

Figure 57 'How I feel about reading books' brainstorm

The starter question plenary

The starter question plenary is a good way of drawing on the experience of practising teachers in an informal, unthreatening way. The group sits in a circle and a question of interest is posed. Each person consecutively gives a response to this question. After each response other people are allowed to ask factual questions only. Judgemental or personal comments from others are not allowed. Once everyone has given an answer, all around the circle, and if ideas are drying up, the activity can stop or a new question can be posed. If people are still going strong, answers can be given all around the circle a second time. The activity works well with a question that relates strongly to people's practical experience. An example might be, 'What are the first things you do when you go into class?' Or 'How do *you* get students interested in boring texts?' (See Figure 58 and Woodward, 1988*b*.) It is a way for people to gain an insight into each other's classes without actually going in to observe.

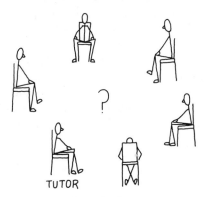

Figure 58   The starter question circle

The cross-pollination workshop

This idea works well as a way of moving ideas around the group during a participatory workshop. The participants are divided into groups and each group is given the same task. Once groups have settled well into the task, one member of each group is nominated as 'the runner' and is allowed to visit other groups to watch their work, discuss it, and then return with ideas to the home group. Runners can also discuss the work of their home group with other groups, so passing on ideas and possible solutions to problems.

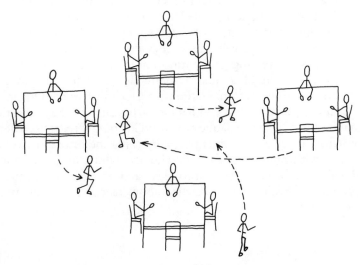

Figure 59   The cross-pollination workshop

Trainee task division

This idea is designed to foster group cooperation and trainee inter-dependence. A large and rather ambiguous task is given to trainees in plenary. The trainer is present at this stage but keeps a fairly low profile. The trainees discuss with each other what clarification, task division and task approach are necessary. They can ask the trainer for information and clarification at any point. They then decide how they are going to approach and divide the task. They continue, in session, to work on the task in any way they wish. The trainer can disappear at this point and come back when the tasks are finished or the time is up. This activity can be used for the group to plan and execute homework assignments cooperatively.

The changing room

This activity is a way of encouraging input from group members and fosters confidence in the passing on of ideas. From a pool of resources, such as recipe books, teaching magazines, videos or observations of other people teaching, trainees pick out one new teaching idea that appeals to them for whatever reason. They then try it out on other people in the group as if they were teachers in a class of learners. Everyone comments on whether the teaching idea is attractive or useful, needs adaptation or suits the trainees' style[2].

Questionnaires

Questionnaires can be used to discover facts, opinions and attitudes about language, learning and teaching. There is an interesting example in Hess (1987). Instead of taking a questionnaire and encouraging trainees to go straight out and use it, Hess suggests doing a lot of preliminary work. This work is on possible interview structures, on listening well, respecting privacy, creating good atmosphere, and so on. Participants work in groups to build a questionnaire designed to ask practising teachers about their work from materialistic, technical and philosophical points of view. Questions are divided into types such as: Fact questions, Opinion questions, Analytical questions and Probing questions. After the questionnaires have been commented on by peers and tutors, trainees are put in touch with practising teachers who are willing to grant an interview. Results are brought back into class and analysed by trainees in terms of what the trainees have learned about teaching as a job and the people who do it.

Interaction diagram

This idea is designed for use when observing teachers and helps the observer to concentrate on everyone in the room rather than just the teacher. The next time a trainee is required to observe someone teach they are asked to fill in an interaction diagram. The first step is to draw a seating plan. If the students are likely to move around during the lesson, observers write the names of the students onto the plan so that interactions between individuals can still be plotted onto the diagram regardless of where people are standing or sitting.

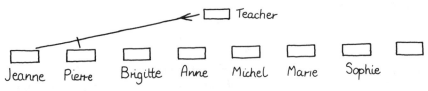

Figure 60   An interaction diagram

Lines are drawn between the names of people who speak to each other. In Figure 60 Jeanne and the teacher have spoken to each other, and this is shown by a line between them. Distinctions can be made between different types of interaction. A question addressed to someone can be represented by a little arrowhead (in Figure 60, the teacher has asked Jeanne a question). Answers can be indicated by a simple bar or slash on the line (Jeanne has responded to the teacher's question). Afterwards the diagram can be analysed for information such as the following: Who talks? Who doesn't talk? Who talks most? Who asks the questions? Who gives the responses? For more ideas on mapping different kinds of interaction, see Woodward (1989*a*).

Sound taping

Sound taping lessons gets trainees using real classroom data as a basis for thought and decisions. It also gives trainees a tool that they can use independently and when the course is over. A tape recorder is set up so that a trainee's teaching practice, or part of it, is recorded. The trainee takes the tape home and analyses it for any of the following: amounts of time devoted to teacher and student talk, amounts of meaningful versus meaningless language, teacher questions that encourage or discourage long student answers, amounts of silence, patronising language, and so forth. The trainee can listen, analyse, make notes, and select little snippets of tape that epitomise in some way points that surprise, intrigue or amuse her. At the next trainee/trainer feedback or discussion session, the trainee can present these edited highlights with comments to the trainer. This can form the basis for further discussion (see Woodward 1989*b*).

185

G

Wallwork posters

Posters act as bright, eye-catching summaries of thought and discussion. They are cheap and fun to make, and can be used both for preview and review work. After doing an assignment, watching a class or reading the same or different texts, trainees summarise what the main points were by making posters. The posters can be made on large sheets of paper, using coloured pens, magazine pictures, and so forth. All the posters are then pinned up on the wall and time is allowed for people to walk around, see each other's posters, and ask questions or comment (Sturtridge, 1987, and Marks, 1989).

Discussion of moral stories

In any job involving people, there are plenty of moral issues, that is, plenty of times when there are better or worse ways of deciding or acting. Bringing these issues up on training courses can be done in a relatively unjudgemental way by using moral stories. Trainees read a story containing some moral issues, where different characters take clear stances. They are then asked to rate in certain ways the moral behaviour of the characters. Discussion arises as people share their perceptions of the situation, its parallels in their own professional lives, and the way they tend to react to similar matters of conscience and morality in their own work (Lavery, 1988).

Classifying and categorising a database

In order to help trainees to interact with the vast amount of information there is in EFL, and to start to organise it mentally, the idea of classifying and categorising can be used. In this activity trainees work individually, in pairs or groups to sort lists of information into different categories. An example here might be for trainees to brainstorm a list of twenty possible audio-visual and mechanical aids and then sort them into two categories: 'useful in my own teaching situation' and 'difficult to use in my own teaching situation'. This activity works equally well if the trainees are asked to decide on their own categories and category headings and are simply given a guideline as to the number of categories required.

THE SORTS OF CHANGES PEOPLE CAN MAKE IN TRAINING

At every moment in teacher training, people are deciding whether or not to make adjustments to the parameters present. Trainees will wonder whether to shift position yet again in a hard chair or to keep still, whether to ask for something to be repeated or wait in the hope that things will become clear later on. Observers will wonder how to express a comment at the bottom of a feedback form. Workshop animators will wonder whether or not to intervene in a group that seems to have got stuck in its task work. Course planners may turn over the question of whether or not to introduce Krashen's work and, if so, when. We all make, and think about making, hundreds of adjustments and adaptations every day to make things simpler, more comfortable or more interesting.

One basic type of adaptation

In the area of adaptation and adjustment of variable to variable or parameter to parameter, I have become especially conscious of two types of adjustment. I'll call the first 'harmony'. This is where a decision is made, consciously or unconsciously, to blend like with like. To take an example from the language learning classroom: if a learner hates to see the colour red on the blackboard (I had a learner like this in a classroom once), then the teacher works in harmony with that feeling and tries to remember not to use red on the board. In another example, if students start asking questions like 'Why . . . ?', the teacher stops, thinks and tries to answer in some way that will appeal to this rational, cognitive enquiry. In this type of adjustment, by the teacher to the student, there is the desire for compatibility, for things to fit together smoothly, to match or to agree. From the learner's point of view, that is, if we take a learner choosing to harmonise with a teacher, it could mean smoothly following a model that has been presented.

A second basic type of adjustment

I'll call the second type of adjustment 'challenge'. This is where, again consciously or unconsciously, there is a desire to stretch people, to go outside a person's usual framework, and to challenge with new or different choices. In a lesson on polite requests, the teacher of that student who hated red could use red chalk deliberately as a way of provoking the student into using polite requests such as, '*Please* could you stop writing in red on the blackboard!' If a learner demands to know why the Present Perfect is not usually used with definite time expressions like *yesterday*, the learner can be given an answer such as, 'Why is the sky blue?' An answer such as this is non-rational. It deliberately runs counter to the student's request for a rational explanation. Another way of challenging the student's preferred mode of explanation is simply to present the student with more and more data showing that this use of the Present Perfect does not normally occur, whether or not we understand why. In this type of adjustment there is the understanding that challenge, opposition and incompatibility can lead to sparkle, energy, adventure or fun. Stepping from the language learning classroom back to the teacher training room we can often see too that fitting in to someone's desires, expectations or habits with cog-like exactness does not necessarily bring the most productive results. Challenge may possibly take longer, as trainees will need time to resist and/or settle to the unfamiliar.

So far, challenge has been presented from the point of view of the teacher or trainer's deliberate response to the learner/trainee. The trainer has decided quite deliberately to go outside the trainee's usual framework. However, it is also possible for the trainer to go against the trainee's expectations or preferences without actually meaning to. A trainer may have a manner, voice or set of strategies that are anathema to a trainee. Looking at challenge from the trainee's point of view, it is possible that the trainee sees something that she doesn't like and she can consciously decide to reject that learning. The trainee can decide to reject the model offered and either to avoid following the proffered model, do the opposite of the proffered model, or engage the trainer in debate on the model.

Reader activity

*   *   *

It might be an idea for you to stop at this point and think about your own learning experiences. Perhaps you've had some very pleasant ones or some very unpleasant ones. Why would you define one as pleasant and another as unpleasant? Does it have anything to do with harmony and challenge? In which situation did you learn most, learn best, learn deepest, learn what you expected to learn, or learn something different or better or worse than you expected?

You might like to think back to the last chapter where the parameters of teacher training events were explained by diagram, sketch, mnemonic, etc. Which method of illustration met an immediate response in you? Which illustration did you have to work hardest to understand?

*   *   *

SOME EXPERIMENTS PLOTTING PARAMETER WITH PARAMETER

Because there are so many parameters in teacher training and so many options to play with in terms of process, because different trainers and trainees will choose consciously or unconsciously to harmonise with or challenge what is in each other, and because we do not know in any case which of all these choices is truly effective, we can only experiment with all the parameters at this stage. After that we can only look and listen and check the results. One thing that does seem clear though is that it is unlikely that one single process option, whether the lecture or loop input, will be appropriate in all situations. It seems very likely that different decisions will need to be made at different times within a liberal training programme.

In order for different decisions to be made, two sorts of awareness are needed. First, the trainer has to be aware of her own repertoire of process options and her own training style, and has to have a desire to increase her repertoire. She has to have enough skill to manage process choices well and according to aims, and a desire to negotiate with others in the light of their choices. Secondly, the trainee has to be aware of her own learning style, of the trainer's process choices and the impact these choices have on her own learning; she has to be able to express and negotiate her own choices, and be aware of a repertoire of process types so that real choices are available.

Having said that it is possible to play with the parameters, let's take a couple of examples.

Experiment 1: Starting from trainee preference

Let's suppose that a particular group of trainees respond well to visual presentation. There is probably no way that we could prove that the visual channel was the dominant sensory channel at all times for all members of this group, but let's imagine that from past experience we know that things click more for this group when there has been visual support for ideas presented. Let's take, then, some training issues and see how they could be presented visually in training sessions in order to harmonise with the particular strengths or character of the group. This is what I mean by an 'experiment'; let's take a variable such as trainee preference and see how we can respond to it by changing the way we present training issues.

It is unlikely that every single piece of information on a course could be presented to the trainee group in pictorial, diagrammatic or schematic form, but once the awareness of this particular learner strength or style is there, it can act as an overlay onto content. Whenever a chance for visual presentation occurs, it can be grasped either for idea gathering (word roses, brainstorms and mind maps), summarising (posters and charts), or to pull ideas together at certain times on a course.

*Harmony with trainee preference is retained while working
with different training issues*

CLASSROOM MANAGEMENT

This is easy since rooms and people can be represented diagrammatically
and teacher movement, teacher-student interaction, and eye contact can
all be plotted onto diagrams using lines with different symbols on them
(see Figure 61).

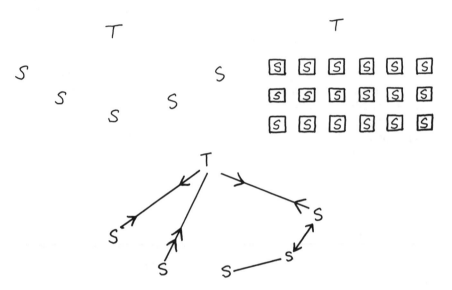

Figure 61   Seating diagrams

The position of individual students can easily be drawn with stick figures
(see Figure 62), and types of correction can be plotted on to axes (see
Figure 63), as described on pages 149–50.

Figure 62   Student positions

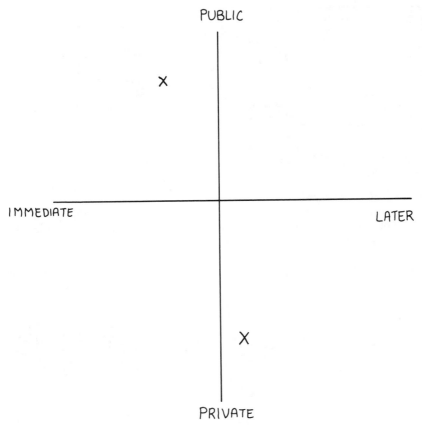

Figure 63   Correction axes

Timing can be represented by a clock face (see Figure 64), and aids can be represented by simple drawings or symbols (see Figure 65).

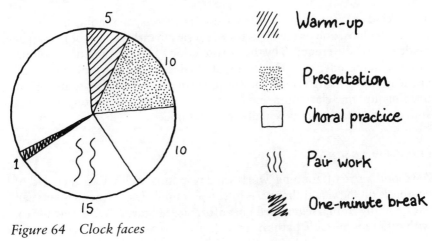

Figure 64   Clock faces

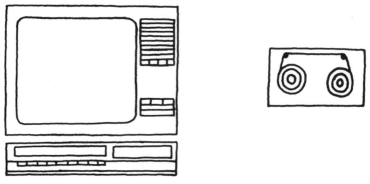

Figure 65   Teaching aids

Student concentration and mood can be plotted onto graphs or indicated visually in other ways (see Figure 66).

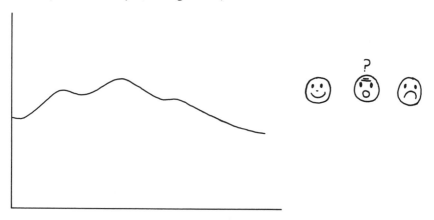

Figure 66   Student concentration graph

These kinds of visuals can be used in input sessions, on reading handouts, on lesson plans, and as the basis for observation tasks. Classrooms can be made to look different too by the introduction of objects, pictures, colour, flowers, materials, etc. This kind of dual strengthening of the visual element, (a) by using visuals such as those in the figures above, and (b) by livening up the classroom environment, can provide strong learning support for our group of visually strong trainees.

LESSON PLANNING

A second area of training work that responds well to an increase of emphasis on the visual channel is lesson planning. The format of plans can vary visually from a segmented linear form (see Figure 67) to a central box with different possible paths or exits (see Figure 68).

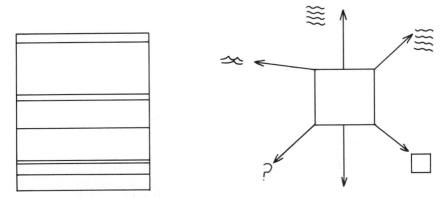

Figure 67   Linear lesson plan   Figure 68   Lesson plan exit box

Lesson plans can also be written on hand-held memo cards covered in brightly coloured headings and arrows, such as lecturers sometimes use instead of paper notes (see Figure 69).

Figure 69   Hand-held lesson cards

Trainees I have known have come up with interlocking circles as in Figure 70, and many other fancies depending on how they have visualised the progression of a lesson. (See also the options framework in Figure 81 for another lesson planning possibility.)

193

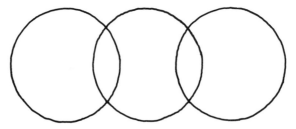

Figure 70   Circles lesson plan

Different trainees will want to prepare for their lessons and learn from their planning in many different ways. Trainees who respond well to visual stimuli will enjoy creating and reading different looking plans.

SYLLABUSES

During the course of a training programme trainees may well want to know the differences between different types of syllabus, i.e. those designed by structuralists, audio-linguists, notional functionalists and so on. After discussion of the way in which these types of syllabus differ from each other, the syllabuses can be represented visually and/or reviewed thus:

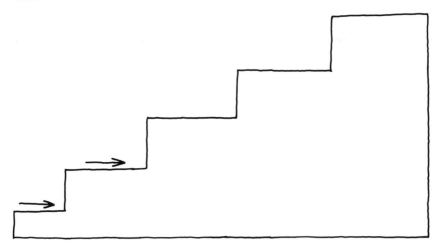

Figure 71   The structurally graded syllabus[3]

Figure 72   The spiral functional-notional syllabus

The idea of review and recycling the contents of any type of syllabus could be shown thus:

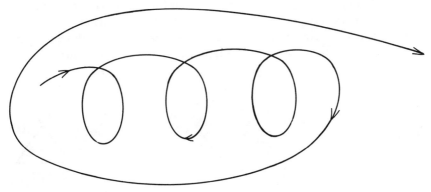

Figure 73   Review cycles

COURSE MODELS

The same kind of diagrammatic review or explanation can be done for course models. For example, the 'three Ps' model (see pages 117–18) can be expressed thus:

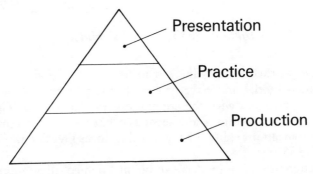

Figure 74   The 'three Ps' model

Trainees can relate the gradual introduction of new language followed by choral and invididual practice, pair work, open dialogues, role play and so on, to the diagram. At the top of the pyramid, there is teacher-centred accuracy work in plenary. In the middle band, students get lots of talking time, accuracy is still important, and tasks are very carefully set up, prompted and controlled. At the base of the pyramid, students are inter-acting more freely, the teacher is monitoring without intervening, and the concern is more for immediate fluency, with correction done later as feed-back with the whole group.

On courses which follow the 'three Ps' model, trainees can go back to the diagram after each input to see how the new information and tech-niques gained relate to the overall idea of moving from controlled to guided to free work. The picture of the pyramid with the different space proportions given to each band can act as a reminder or a review point since it schematises an immense amount of information very simply.

Once trainees have absorbed this basic triangle diagram, and know what it means in terms of lessons, stages and shapes, they can learn vari-ations quickly if the trainer simply adapts or alters the basic figure, thus:

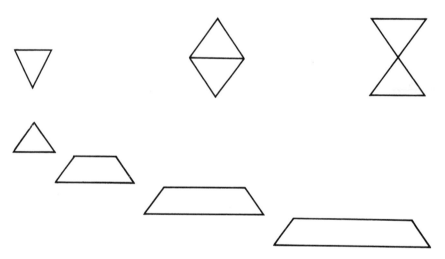

Figure 75   Variations on the 'three Ps' model

I have worked with trainees who have understood the main 'three Ps' pyramid model and have grown thoroughly familiar with Figure 74. When presented with the adaptations in visual form (Figure 75), they have realised within a few seconds what totally different lessons these would mean in reality. I have heard trainees literally gasp at the sight of Figure 75.

Different course models can be 'nicknamed' diagrammatically at the start of a course for ease of reference later on, as in Figure 76.

The jug and mug model

The deep-end model

The stuffed goose model

Figure 76   Course models

MODELS FOR LANGUAGE LESSONS

The common model for teaching the receptive skills in EFL is very often presented in textbooks diagrammatically (see Harmer, 1983).

197

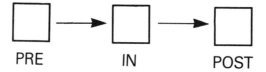

Figure 77   The skills model

The basic three-part skills model can be represented differently to suit trainees' visual preferences as in Figure 78.

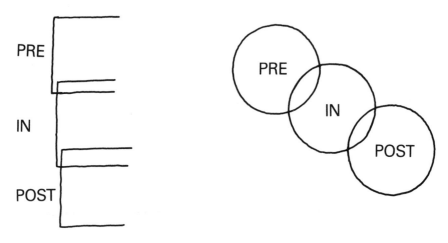

Figure 78   The skills model – visual variations

LANGUAGE AWARENESS

Trainees can be encouraged to learn about language and to present it to their own students with visual highlighting as in Figures 79 and 80.

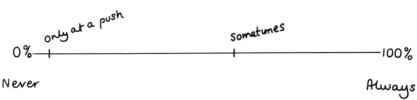

Figure 79   The certainty cline

Figure 80   Adjective steps

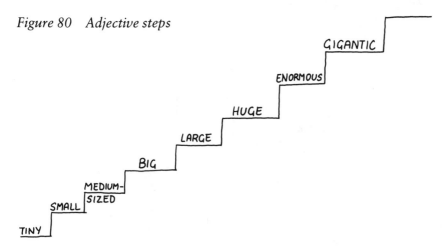

For many other ideas on how to present language awareness activities visually and schematically, see Bolitho and Tomlinson (1980), Underhill (1980), and Lindstromberg (1985).

FEEDBACK SESSIONS

So far I have tried to show how areas on a training course such as lesson planning, language awareness and input can be given visual highlighting for a group of visually strong trainees. Another area that can have a clear visual element is feedback on observed teaching. Feedback sessions can work from an options framework. I'll explain what I mean.

Every time a teacher walks into a classroom, a range of options opens up in front of her. She can say 'Hello' to the class, go straight to the board, talk to a student or do anything else that she fancies. Each option has its advantages and disadvantages. Going straight to the board to draw something may get everyone's attention in a quiet, undemanding way, but it may also make some students feel cheated of a greeting. Whichever option is chosen initially will in turn open up a further range of options. So, standing at the blackboard, drawing, a teacher can choose whether to draw silently, ask the students what they think is being drawn, or ask the students to come up and join in with the drawing. Any of these options has built-in advantages and disadvantages, and, in turn, opens up a new range of further options. Diagrammatically, this might look like Figure 81.

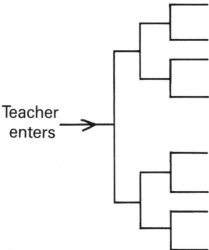

Figure 81   Teaching options

At any moment in a classroom, a teacher thinking on her feet has choices before her. Each path will have its own advantages and disadvantages and be *right* in some way. If teaching is looked at in this way, as a series of options, then the diagram in Figure 81 can be used to strengthen the idea of different paths through a lesson. The options diagram can be used during lesson planning or during feedback after a lesson. The options that were chosen by the teacher can be discussed, weighed up and kept in mind for future use in different situations. Options that were not chosen can be discussed simply as other possible ways of achieving the same aims, rather than being seen as the only right way or the trainer's way of achieving the same aims (Woodward, 1989*b*).

OBSERVATION SHEETS

Most trainers, while watching trainees teach, have a hard job getting down all the points they wish to record, legibly, and in a reasonable format. Notes written down by trainers and trainees whilst watching other people teach can, however, be given visual impact by organising the page before you start writing (or by having feedback sheets duplicated ready for use) as in Figure 82.

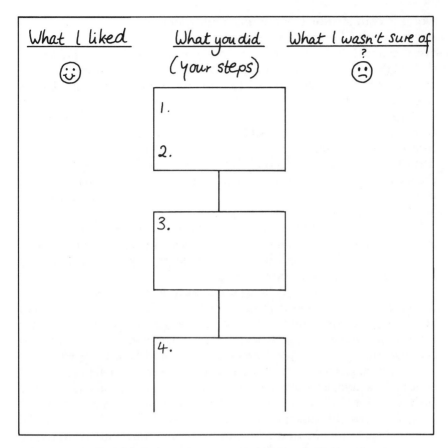

Figure 82   The little boxes observation sheet

As the teacher makes her way through the lesson, the observer writes in the central box the steps of the lesson as objectively as possible. Comments go to the left and right as appropriate (Rushton, 1987).

The choice between harmony and challenge

So far in this experiment I have discussed how we can harmonise with trainee preference. I have taken an imaginary group of trainees with a strong visual preference and have harmonised with their preference by working on lesson planning, observation, feedback, language awareness and input in as visually interesting a way as possible.

There are other ways of harmonising with trainees. Those interested in Neurolinguistic Programming (NLP) often discuss how rapport can be gained with other people in conversations, business meetings or therapy sessions. To gain rapport you match voice tone and tempo, breathing, movement, rhythms and body postures. You can also deliberately choose words in conversation to harmonise with your partner's representational system. By this I mean that if someone responds particularly well in the visual channel they may tend to use phrases such as, 'I get the picture', 'I see', 'Let's focus on . . .', 'the outlook is bright', 'it's looking good' and so on, rather than phrases such as 'I hear what you're saying' and 'hit the wrong note', which might indicate a preference for the auditory channel, or 'I don't know if I can handle it' or 'Let's keep in touch', which might show a preference for the kinesthetic channel. A tendency to respond well to visual stimuli could be supported by a trainer using expressions such as, 'Let's focus now on . . .', 'Is that clear?' and so on. The visual strength of the trainees is thus supported in speech and listening comprehension by using words and metaphors with strong reference to the visual channel and likely to throw up images of images.

Harmonising with trainees is one possible choice of reaction to them. It is also possible to choose quite deliberately to challenge their preferences, to work against their established habits and to try to broaden their normal types of communication and learning.

To provide challenge for these particular trainees, that is, to use other channels of presentation than the visual for each of the training issues above, one could give out jigsaw reading passages on classroom management, give interactive lectures on lesson planning, listen to a taped dialogue on syllabus types, discuss course models with reference to trainees' own memories, analyse student homework for language awareness, make sound tapes of teaching practice, and use ordinary linear notes as the basis for feedback sessions. All these alternatives include, of course, a visual element, for example, the sight of a text, the look of a lecturer, the home movie inside the trainee's head, the visual experience of watching other colleagues at work, and so on. It would be extremely difficult to cut out the visual element completely even if one wanted to. But it is possible to select a method of transmitting or eliciting content which makes more or less obvious use of the visual channel. Stevick (1986) shows us some simple and effective ways of achieving this with texts in language learning classes.

Conclusion to Experiment 1

To recap, in this first experiment I have imagined a particular trainee group, one that responded well to visual stimulus. We have seen how a trainer could match this visual strength in trainees by giving visually strong presentations, by using visual metaphors in conversation and so on. We have also seen how one could decide quite deliberately to challenge this preference and work in other channels such as the auditory. In this experiment, then, we have taken trainee preference as our starting point and discussed how different training issues can be dealt with in the light of this preference.

It's fairly clear that this tuning in or out to the preferences of a particular trainee group depends on: (a) their being reasonably homogeneous, and (b) your knowing them well. It needs to be accompanied by a consideration of other needs and parameters at the same time too. For example, it would be counter-productive to insist on the use of a video for a particular input session on the grounds that the trainees 'prefer visuals' if the video material itself were of doubtful quality, the video machine booked out to another teacher, the trainees sleepy after a long day's work, and there were some perfectly good task sheets at hand designed to elicit roughly the same information from the group.

One-to-one matching of one parameter to one process option or set of options may be possible in the perfect world. In a training centre full of materials and equipment and staffed by responsive, creative personnel able to act *exactly* as they wish, it could be done. But apart from being a luxury, matching parameter to appropriate response is only a partial response, set within a complex web of overlapping needs or parameters.

Experiment 2: Starting from a training issue

In Experiment 1 we started from a trainee preference. This time I would like to start with a training issue, that of supervision, and treat it in the light of different considerations such as contact possibilities between trainer and trainee, and trainer aims and beliefs.

What is supervision?

The term *supervision* is used in many different ways. In General Education literature a supervisor is usually a college overseer of the teacher/ apprentice and thus the person who tries to maintain a theoretical and methodological dimension to teaching practice. In counselling, the supervisor and client work jointly as a pair in planning and supervisory conferences to help the client close the gap between her intentions and her reality. In EFL teacher training supervision has sometimes been taken to mean, simply, the times when a trainer is physically present in a trainee's classroom to watch, listen and take notes.

I see supervision as including planning discussions, teaching observation and feedback on all aspects of the teaching/learning event by both supervisor and trainee and any other helpfully involved party. I would thus like to take a broad definition of supervision. Next I'd like to look at the term *observation*. This term too can be defined narrowly or in a broad way, a way that opens up options in how to handle them on training courses.

One way of opening out definitions is by using the 'simple question' idea. This way of keeping a theme open and full of options includes asking lots of simple questions and gathering as many silly answers as possible! (See Woodward, 1989c.) Let's try it with the term *observation*.

What is observation?
Seeing with your own eyes. Watching a video, listening to a tape, reading a lesson transcript, listening to someone else's version of a lesson, talking to the students or the teacher after class, being aware as you teach yourself, reading a learner diary, listening to a radio or watching a televised lesson.

Who observes?
The teacher, the students, the trainer, peers of any of these, an outsider, an insider, a team teacher, a boss.

Who is being taught during the observation?
The teacher's own class, another teacher's class, a microclass, a peer class, a one-off class gathered together especially for the observation.

What is the observation for?
To pass an exam, to hire somebody, to fire somebody, to help the teacher with something the teacher wants to work on or something that somebody else wants the teacher to work on, to keep the teacher 'policed' and helpless, to keep the teacher alive and developing, no particular reason.

What can people do while they are observing?
Make a film, make a tape, just look, just listen, tick boxes, write a letter to the teacher, intervene, take over, write down questions, write down verbatim what teacher or students say, fill in concentration graphs and interaction diagrams, fill in observation checklists, daydream, collect data, look out of the window.

We could open out the definition of *feedback* too by asking questions such as:

When can feedback on taught lessons occur?
Discussions on taught lessons, whether based on planning support, sound tapes, filled-in graphs and diagrams or other resources can be useful at any of the following times: well before the lesson, just before the lesson, during the lesson, just after the lesson, or well after the lesson. There are occasions on extremely intensive pre-service training courses when the absence of feedback is in itself a welcome change.

Who can 'interpret' a taught lesson?
The teacher, the students, the trainer, the trainees or all of these. The interpretation can be done aloud, silently, in written or taped form. As before, there are times when the zero option, or no interpretation, can be welcome for a change.

Many other questions could be asked about feedback, such as: Who takes part? Who gives feedback to whom? What channel is used? When does it take place? What is it for? How many people are present? What language is it in? What happens before it? What happens after it? How many different feedback sessions are there after one observed teaching period? What language and communication rules are in play? What can you discuss? What can't you discuss?

By asking simple questions such as these and then brainstorming as many seemingly silly as well as sensible answers to the question as possible, you open up a theme and provide hundreds of options which can be combined in different ways to respond to the parameters and constraints that you face. This kind of enquiry prevents a training theme from narrowing in terms of process or content. It is a way of enlivening the classification of themes and of keeping them fresh.

Just in case the detour above has taken you away from the main argument, I'll recap. We're about to start our second experiment on matching process to parameter. I'm not using the word 'experiment' here in the scientific sense of isolating single variables, running control studies and so on. The number of variables present in one training/learning event would make that an impossibly complex task for the present book. Rather, I am looking informally at process choices and types that trainers can deliberately make or select in order to respond to parameters which they see as being particularly important in any training situation.

I have chosen the training issue of supervision as our starting point, hence the discussion above of what exactly supervision is. Next, we'll look at supervision in the light of two parameters or constraints. The first is lack of contact possibilities between trainer and trainees. The second will be the trainer's own aims and beliefs.

The experiment starts

CONTACT POSSIBILITY

Let's imagine a situation where a trainer lives in a capital city and is responsible for training about 600 teachers in areas hundreds of miles from the base headquarters. The trainer can only actually meet each teacher once every couple of years unless they happen to bump into each other by chance at a movie festival! In this sort of situation the trainer's options are very limited. She really only has the chance to be an initial or occasional spur to a teacher's development. Provided she accepts this happily she could choose to write to the teachers or phone them to establish contact and confirm some basic details. She can ask the teachers to sound tape two short and different kinds of sections from two of their own lessons. The teachers are asked to listen to the tapes and to pick out two things about their own teaching that they like and one thing they would like to work on. When the trainer visits a particular teacher and watches the lesson, she does not know what the teacher has picked out, but simply watches the lesson and makes her own notes on strengths and weaknesses. After the lesson, the teacher explains the conclusions drawn from listening to the tape and together they share opinions, ideas and plans for the future. A follow-up task is set, also involving sound taping, and the teacher is required to write or phone the trainer when it is completed with some comments on their own work. The face-to-face contact possibilities in this situation are so very few that the trainer has to select options that would be quite inappropriate for another trainer in another situation. But for our trainer, phone calls and tapes would be workable options.

TRAINER AIMS AND BELIEFS

Let's imagine a trainer who works on a course where aims are based on output and expressed in terms of performance ability. She works intensively every day for a month with her pre-service teacher trainees and has decided that by the end of the second week they must all be able to write new words clearly onto the board, in context, and with the stress marked on them, *after* there has been some concept checking and choral practice of the word by language students. Unlike our previous trainer working from her capital city, the trainer this time has no problem getting enough face-to-face contact. Different options thus become available to her. Out of the choices she could make, let us imagine that her tactics so far have been:

- To write up on the board, in context and with stress clearly marked all new pieces of teaching terminology that come up in input sessions *after* there has been some concept checking and choral practice of the terminology by trainees;
- To lecture on the advisability of this practice, giving rational reasons for it;
- To ask trainees to write assignments on what to do when new words come up in class;
- To ask trainees to practise writing on the board in coffee and lunch breaks and to stand at the back of the room and look at each other's work;
- To give support reading from teacher's handbooks.

Since she wants to see for herself whether trainees actually have this behavioural sequence in their repertoires, she is present in the room during teaching practice. She has convinced the trainee group of the importance of this work, but together they have discovered that knowing something is important is different from actually putting it into practice. Some trainees are having trouble in language classes remembering to write new words up on the board at all, or to write them up in context, or to mark the stress on them, or to concept check, or to do the writing only after students have had oral practice of the word. Together the trainees and trainer have brainstormed ideas that might help the trainees. Here are some of the suggestions:

— Trainees write 'Choral first' across the back of their pen hand so they can see it when raising their hand to write on the board.
— Trainees hold up signs at the back of the class, e.g. 'Drill it!'
— Write a note on the top left of the board above the vocabulary column, saying 'Words *in context*'.
— Force the trainee to hold two pens as a reminder that colour stress marking is required.
— Students, trainees and trainer all shout, 'Drill!', or 'Board!', or 'Context!' or 'Stress!' if any of the stages is missed.
— A close friend holds the back of the teacher's jumper so that she cannot get to the board before drilling the new word.
— Observers write down how many times the sequence does or does not happen when particular teachers are teaching.
— Make videos of vocabulary slots so people can see later what they did.
— During feedback and lesson-planning sessions, trainees mime the sequence: (1) elicitation, (2) concept check, (3) drill, (4) board, to get it into their body memories. They write it in colour on their lesson plans and wander around the room chanting the order.
— Have a discussion about the security that writing on the board brings to teachers and the problems caused to students by writing words down out of context.

We can now, perhaps, sketch out how this trainer feels about training. She knows what she wants in behavioural terms, she doesn't have time for the idea of a trainee's 'natural syllabus' and she wants to force change of performance into trainee repertoires in a given period of time. She still has a huge choice of tactics open to her, as can be seen above. All the tactics are concerned with the external imposition of observable behavioural change in a short time but, as we can gauge from the above, the trainer is convinced of the importance of rational appeal, trainee involvement, group support, visual reinforcement, kinesthetic and auditory memory, practising what she preaches, written testing of input absorption, trainee practice, visual memory prompts and discussion of observed data.

The work she does reflects her own beliefs, attitudes and aims, is shaped by the kind of course she is on, depends to a great extent on trainee willingness to go along with her, and yet she still has a huge range of options with which to face these parameters and constraints.

Conclusion to Experiment 2

In this second experiment we started from the theme of supervision and have seen how enormously it can change in mode and style depending on the trainer's own attitudes and beliefs, the contact possibilities and the aims realistically attainable in the training situation. Our first trainer lived in a capital city and had to travel hundreds of miles to meet teachers. She did not know the teachers well enough to find out anything about preferred learning styles. Our second trainer, given a large group and a short intensive course whose aims were stated mainly in performance terms, decided to harness learning ideas from the group and carry them out for the aims she has interpreted from the syllabus. Given this huge disparity between contact types and trainer aims and beliefs, supervision was carried out using wildly different processes[4].

Summary

For those who like a brief recap of the main points, I offer the following summary statements.

- There are many different process options available in teacher training; a few were outlined.
- External parameters are viewed and mentally ordered differently by different people.
- It is unlikely that there will be one best or most effective process option for every situation.
- Different process options can be selected and tried out depending on trainer and trainee preferences and other variables. So far, then, we have many different parameters to respond to and plenty of process options to respond with.
- Two possible metaphors for two basic types of response to external variables are 'harmony' and 'challenge'.
- We do not know which type of response is best any more than we know which parameter will be most important or which process option will be most popular on our next course.
- We can start to juggle ways of training with parameters.
- We can choose to respond to a particular parameter by selecting different modes of training in a spirit of harmony or challenge.
- Our first experiment was around the area of trainee preference. Given an imaginary and homogeneous group of trainees, all with a liking for visual presentation, how could we harmonise with or challenge that preference?

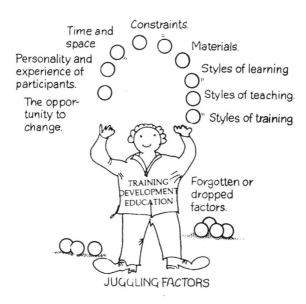

Figure 83   The juggler

- Our second experiment was around a training issue, namely supervision. How could we change our method of supervision to suit (a) a situation where contact possibilities are very limited, and (b) a particular trainer's aims and beliefs?
- In both experiments, different ways of training and different process choices were used as go-betweens, as a means of negotiating between content and trainee preference in the first experiment and between training issue and external constraints in the second experiment.
- One-to-one matching in these very clearly defined, imaginary situations was found to be possible. In reality, it would be a partial response to a very complex situation.

POSTSCRIPT

How does this relate to your training? You may find yourself in a training situation that has a very clear profile in some respect. For example:
- You only have one hour with the trainees; or you have the same trainees for three years.
- There are too many people in the group for you to get to know them all really well personally; or you are just one teacher and one trainee sharing a class and all your lunch hours for the next three months.
- The training 'centre' is an old garage and there are no facilities; or you are in a custom-made building with every resource you have ever dreamed of.

In any of these examples, you may decide to respond in harmony with your main constraint, or you may decide to respond with a challenge and meet your constraint head-on. Of all the things inside and outside yourself with which you can respond, process is one intermediary. It can be an ally, a non-constant factor in a tight situation. It is, by itself, no guarantee of success, but it's there as a go-between for you to use – to form, inform and transform your training situation.

1. Further reading on **process options**:

Bligh, D., Jacques, D. & Warren-Piper, D. (1975). *Seven Decisions when Teaching Students*. Exeter University Teaching Services.

Hess, N. (1987). The interview as a teacher training tool. *The Teacher Trainer*, 1, 3.

Lavery, M. (1988). Human resources development. *The Teacher Trainer*, 2, 1.

Marks, J. (1989). Poster presentations on teacher training courses. *The Teacher Trainer*, 3, 3.

Sturtridge, G. (1987). Using posters in teacher education. *The Teacher Trainer*, 1, 2.

Woodward, T. (1987). The buzz group lecture. *The Teacher Trainer*, 1, 3.

Woodward, T. (1988). The starter question circle. *The Teacher Trainer*, 2, 1.

Woodward, T. (1989). Observation tasks for pre-service trainees. *The Teacher Trainer*, 3, 1.

Woodward, T. (1989). Taking the stress out of post-lesson feedback. *The Teacher Trainer*, 3, 2.

There is a regular 'Process Options' column in *The Teacher Trainer*.

2. Thanks to Mario Rinvolucri for this idea.

3. Figures 71 and 72 are taken in essence from Hubbard et al. (1983, pp. 11 and 246).

4. Further reading on **supervision**:

Allwright, D. (1988). *Observation in the Language Classroom*. Longman.

Bowers, R. (1987). Developing perceptions in the classroom. In *ELT Document 125 Language Teacher Education: An integrated programme for ELT teacher training*. The British Council / Modern English Publications.

Fanselow, J. (1967). *Breaking Rules*. Longman.

Gebhard, J. (1984). Models of supervision: choices. *TESOL Quarterly*, 18, 3.

Stones, E. (1984). *Supervision in Teacher Education*. Methuen.

Woodward, T. (1989). Taking the stress out of post-lesson feedback. *The Teacher Trainer*, 3, 2.

There is a regular 'Observation and Feedback' column in *The Teacher Trainer*.

21 The evaluation of effectiveness

In this chapter I'll start by looking at two main models for evaluation. After discussing both these models and the problems they carry with them, I'll open up the definition of the word *evaluation*. This, I hope, will free us to look at alternative ways of evaluating our effectiveness.

When the word *evaluation* comes up in connection with teacher training, two things spring to mind: (a) the assessment of trainees on a teacher training course, and (b) feedback by trainees on the teacher training course they have been attending. The first area, the assessment of trainees, is a thorny one that many would love to be able to forget, and the second area, in my experience, *is* often forgotten or, at least, left until the last minute and done rather hastily. If we take the assessment of course participants first, we can identify two main models for evaluation, thanks to the clear work of Stenhouse (1975) and Romiszowski (1981), from whom I draw heavily in parts of the first two sections, and other writers who are cited individually[1].

TWO MODELS FOR EVALUATION

Evaluation of trainees: the objectives model

We can decide to see teaching as primarily concerned with the performance of skills. This was the view of the trainer in the second experiment in Chapter 20. Looking at teaching this way makes it comparatively easy to evaluate trainees since all we have to do is state the aims of the course in terms of observable trainee behaviour, then (a) find out what levels of performance trainees are capable of on entry to the course, (b) find out what level they are capable of at the end of the course, and (c) make sure that the course includes educational procedures that are designed to bring about the desired end product.

To give a concrete example, if one of the performance skills we feel a language teacher should have is the ability to give learners intensive oral practice by using choral repetition drills, then all we have to do is find out if or how well trainees can drill when they start the course, put trainees through a number of educational procedures and then find out how well they can drill at the end of the course. To make things easier, the skill of

211

drilling can be broken down into constituent skills such as: attracting students' attention, giving a model sentence, decontracting the model sentence and highlighting its form, saying the model sentence again naturally, indicating to the students that they should speak, and so on. All these constituent skills can be tested by observation. Quite simply, can trainees be seen to be doing these things with real students by the end of the course?

This *objectives* model is very tempting in its apparent clarity and practicality. It rests, however, on a large number of assumptions which, when we look at them more closely, we may have trouble agreeing with. Some of the assumptions are: that teaching is a skill or set of skills rather than a mixture of skills, attitudes, values, beliefs, knowledge areas and affective responses; that the objectives of a teacher training course can be specified before the course takes place in behavioural terms and by people such as the trainers and syllabus writers; that it is justifiable to give more weight to measurable skills than less measurable ones; that analysing performance skills into constituent skills aids the learning of each constituent and does not disrupt smooth performance of whole skills; that the progress on the course that counts is the progress towards predictable, measurable outcomes rather than any more spontaneous or unpredictable outcomes. The *objectives* model also tends to measure candidates at the end of a course rather than some time later in order to check retention of ideas, skills or values gained on the course. A course that wishes to play safe need accept only those candidates that have most of the skills necessary to pass a course when they arrive on the course. It can then boast a high pass rate. If candidates finish a course with more or better skills than they had when they started, the tendency is to assume that the course is responsible for the improvement. If participants come onto the course with their own goals, they will, if these are different from the goals the course designers had in mind, have to achieve them 'on the side'. On top of all this, the *objectives* model assumes that we already know which educational procedures lead to the required results and how long it takes to achieve them. This is clearly beyond our grasp at present. It also ignores matters such as individual learner style and learner preference for certain educational procedures over others.

Nevertheless, it is possible to define end goals on a training course and to try out different trainers, trainer styles, process options and materials, to see which bring measurably better results. Chapters 19 and 20, however, will have reminded us of the great complexity of parameters surrounding any training event. It is unlikely in our present state of knowledge that we would be able to isolate factors such as trainer style, process option and material type and find out that, for whatever reason, a certain mix and balance of these factors achieves a better result than other mixes and balances. For some, however, this setting up of end goals and the attempt to measure them, while testing out different factors in the equation, will sound an interesting endeavour and worth a try.

There are certain advantages for trainees evaluated according to an *objectives* model: they may have the feeling that they know what is expected of them from the outset; there is likely to be an entry test or interview and exit test or tutorial; grades or marks are specific and definite; failure can be explained *relatively* painlessly by stating that change of behaviour *had* taken place, but just not quite fast enough to achieve the terminal objectives by the end of the course; bad grades, although galling, are given by relative strangers and relate to behavioural skills only.

Evaluation of trainees: the process model

Although the *objectives* model will be attractive to some, others will argue that good teaching is not measurable since it is based on knowledge, awareness and understanding, concepts that are either undefinable or, at least, unobservable behaviourally. Others again will feel that while some parts of a course could be evaluated using an *objectives* model, other parts of the course definitely should not be.

A *process* model of evaluation looks at a course less as an input-output equation and more as a joint learning endeavour involving trainees and trainers in a mutual adventure. The aims of the course are learning and understanding. Thus, although these twin aims may be started off on the course, with the trainer perhaps acting as a sort of catalyst, they can go on deepening long after the course is over. They are not thought to have been achieved simply because certain training events have been attended.

In the *process* model of evaluation, the trainees are seen as developing at their own speeds and gradually becoming able to evaluate their own development. Assessment, if applied to the course at all, will tend to be continuous, negotiated by trainer and trainee, and based on non-observable, non-behavioural criteria such as 'attitude change' and 'degree of personal development', which will be evidenced by, for example, learner diaries or group, individual or self-assessment. Exams may be taken as a by-product of the course, but will be seen as a definite underestimate of the whole state of the candidate's knowledge at any one time. Rather than specific marks out of a hundred or 'A', 'B', 'C', 'D' grades, assessment will be couched in more general terms such as 'satisfactory' or 'unsatisfactory' or in profile sentences detailing abilities and potential for future development. The course is not angled towards an exam, although there may be one. On this sort of course there can be different possible reactions to an exam: (a) if the exam is seen as a partial, obligatory and formal measure, then last-minute cramming and exam preparation can be done quite explicitly and in collusion with the test setters by using take-home papers, discussion or seeing exam questions before the exam; (b) if the exam is itself seen as a learning tool and a register of progress so far, without the sting of hard and fast grades or public certification, then no last minute cramming will be necessary, desirable or even possible – the exam is simply seen as a temperature-taking exercise.

The *process* model will appeal to trainees who see evaluation as an exercise giving them valuable information about themselves from colleagues, tutors, and their own reflections, from a number of different mirrors.

Some trainees who are used to an *objectives* model may find the *process* model hard to settle to. They may complain that they have no clear guidelines as to what they are expected to achieve and that the course is too vague, that it is too easy to bluff their way through, or that it is undignified to be judged by peers.

Failure can come hard on a process oriented course since it cannot be written off as having had a 'bad day'. The judgement will have been made over a long period of time and by many people, peers, not strangers. It is not external skills one has failed, but rather a process of internal change.

Just as the *objectives* model can be accused of ignoring attitudes and personal development, so the *process* model can be accused of concentrating too little on the practical grasp of skills. Cynically, trainers using one model can hide behind performance skills with no real depth, while trainers using the other model can hide behind 'development' that has no clear practical substance. There are then, as we might have guessed, strong advantages and disadvantages to both models. It's also possible for evaluation of a course to be an uneasy mixture of the two different models, with trainers and trainees feeling rather unclear about which yardstick to use at what time.

Evaluation of a course by trainees

Informally, trainees can express their view of a course by working hard, skipping sessions or dropping out. On some courses, other channels are available, such as tutorials where trainees are encouraged to say what they feel. Questionnaires and feedback forms, graffiti walls and group discussions are all ways of encouraging trainees to share their view of the course during, at the end, or sometimes after a course. Trainers who encourage feedback sometimes isolate features such as 'course content', 'accommodation' or 'trainers'. It is rare, in my experience, for trainers to encourage trainees to use the same system of evaluation for the course as is used by trainers on the trainees.

If, for example, a course evaluates trainees according to an *objectives* model, then the following idea from Herbert Puchta[2] comes close to allowing trainees an equivalent chance to evaluate their trainers as they themselves are evaluated.

Participants are asked to get together as a group and decide what makes a good lecturer. They are requested to write down what a lecturer would have to do in order to get an 'A', 'B', 'C', 'D' or 'Fail' grade from the trainees. After group discussion and writing, without tutors present, the trainees go to a few lectures and think about the process of lecturing for a few days. They meet again and change anything they wish in their original grading points. They then type those points up and make them available to the tutors so that the tutors know what is expected of them. At certain points during or at the end of the course, trainees can anonymously write grades on slips of paper and pop them into separate ballot boxes carrying different lecturers' names.

If a more *process* based model of evaluation is used on a course, then lecturers can be asked by trainees to write lecturers' diaries, for use as the basis of group discussion and group, peer and self-assessment of their lecturing skill development. They are required to hand them in to the trainees every so often. Agreement could be reached by all concerned on the level of a lecturer's understanding of trainee needs, ability to respond to trainee questions, and so on, and this could be expressed in general terms such as 'satisfactory' or 'unsatisfactory'. Living through evaluations such as these, perhaps for the first time in many years, can really help a lecturer's development, especially in the area of empathy for course participants.

The problems inherent in the two models of evaluation

There is no getting away from the fact that people need to know whether or not a course is any good, whether a would-be teacher has had any training, and whether a trainee teacher is stable, competent and pleasant. Life is too short to find out all these things by experiencing them for oneself and coming to one's own opinions every time. Personal recommendations of courses, tutors and trainees are asked for, offered, and taken all the time. If you don't know the person recommending, and if they don't know you and what you want, then you will need to fall back on other more public and more formal measures of quality such as 'consumer guides' and 'grades'.

Employing institutions and trainees usually demand clear, definite grades at the end of a course. In many countries there is competition for teaching posts. Employers need different ways of whittling down huge piles of applications for one job. Grades are one way of whittling, but for an educational centre to give clear grades is tantamount to stating that it knows what good learning and teaching are. We may not feel sure about this. Evaluation done in a different way, however, without one-off exams and grades, but by continuous, joint assessment of unobservable factors may seem too vague to trainees and employers and may create an image of an exclusive group granting and withholding privileges on the basis of undefined and ever shifting personal criteria.

Evaluation of a course by course participants has a few catches too. If grades have already been given to the course participants, there may be a tendency for trainees who have obtained high grades to rate the course highly and vice versa. If grades have not yet been given out, course participants may be unwilling to say what they feel for fear it will prejudice tutor assessment of their performance.

Another possibility is the zero option: no evaluation at all of anything by anybody. In my experience, course participants will very rarely let their tutors get away with giving no opinion at all as to the value of their work. I have recently been on courses, however, where tutors did no soliciting whatsoever of trainee views on anything at all, at any time, before, during or after the course!

EVALUATION OF THE EFFECTIVENESS OF PROCESS

I'd like to discuss here ways of gauging whether our work in the area of process is effective. In weighing up choices and in taking different paths how can we check to see how we are doing? How can we evaluate the effectiveness of our training process? As we have just seen there are some problems attached to the two main evaluation models. Before trying to pick a path between them, around the paradoxes and over the problems, let's look at the issue of evaluation afresh. I would like to open out our definition of *evaluation* in a similar way to our earlier opening out of the definition of *feedback* (see Chapter 20), that is, by using the silly and sensible question and answer technique.

Some basic questions about evaluation

The questions I would like to ask here are: (1) What is evaluation? (2) Who carries out the evaluation and who is it for? (3) What is the purpose of evaluation? (4) What is evaluated? (5) When is the evaluation done? (6) How is the evaluation done? (7) How is the evaluation reported, who interprets the report, and what happens then?

I'll go through these questions one by one as a way of opening up our definition of evaluation and finding more options and possibilities for evaluating process work.

What is evaluation?

According to different sources, *evaluation* means: to 'ascertain the amount of', 'find numerical expression for', 'assess the value in the present and in the future of a certain activity or product of a system', 'decide on the significance, value or quality of something after carefully studying its good and bad features', 'to express in terms of the known', 'to reckon up'. Perhaps we can take an amalgam of these definitions for the purposes of this book and say that we need to ascertain the present and future significance, value or quality of our process work after carefully studying the good and bad features of particular options and to express all this in terms of the known. We may find, however, that that's rather a lot to handle!

A useful diagram schematically expressing what evaluation is composed of occurs in Harlen (1978):

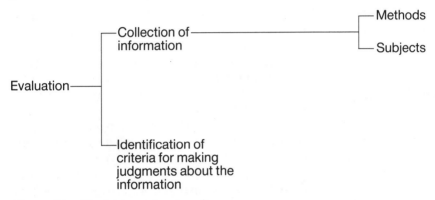

Figure 84   Harlen's evaluation diagram

'This explicitness of criteria distinguishes evaluation from the notion of "pure" reporting of evaluation, from the making of judgements when criteria are not made explicit, and from the falsely claimed "objectivity" of information expressed numerically.'

Harlen, 1978.

Who carries out the evaluation and who is it for?

There are many possible answers here as so many people, insiders and outsiders, are interested in the training encounter. Coursebook writers, syllabus designers, trainees, trainers, accounts departments and employing institutions will all be keen, at different times, to evaluate different parts of the course for different reasons. If the central event in the world of EFL is seen as the language classroom encounter, then all other groups (materials writers, syllabus designers, teacher trainers, applied linguists,

H

publishers and examining bodies) can be seen as ' "service providers" to the teaching procession: essentially parasites who depend on the classroom encounter, on the teaching/learning activity, for their very existence' (Bolitho, 1988). Bolitho makes this point in order to help teachers to take 'a more robust view of their own worth and to increase their self-esteem', and it is a useful point of view for our purposes here too. It can remind us that in a training classroom event it is the trainers, trainees and language students who are absolutely central to the encounter. Whilst not discounting the natural interest of other groups dependent on the training event for their existence, we can perhaps focus here on the central groups who will want to make their own enquiries into the process of training for their own purposes.

What is the purpose of evaluation?

The evaluation can be, simply, to assess success or failure without explanation. A trainee may sit an exam or teach a lesson watched by an examiner, be told some time later that they have failed and then have to depend on their own musings for an explanation. Alternatively, they can be told that they have passed and thus that they are, in a sense, 'licensed' to practise the profession. Some trainees may be equally surprised by this news.

A different purpose of evaluation can be to hold things still, to try to control them and measure them accurately so that others may interpret, judge and make decisions. I'll give an example of this type of evaluation. Let us say that a publisher would like to pilot or trial certain materials. A trainer is chosen and asked to use the materials in as similar a way as possible with two different groups of trainees. Both groups are non-native speakers on in-service courses. One group teach children; the other group teach adults. Both groups have similar input, assignments and back-up reading tasks based on the materials being piloted. At the end of the course, both trainer and trainees are given extensive interviews or questionnaires designed to bring out their feelings on the usefulness of the materials for training teachers of adults and teachers of children. The publishers work their way through the interview transcriptions or filled-in questionnaires and decide whether to scrap the materials, rewrite them in part, retrial them, or publish them, though marketed for a more narrowly defined target group such as teachers of children. There is an attempt here to hold some things still, in control.

Another completely different purpose of evaluation can be to watch and wait unobtrusively gathering information. A trainer may do this, for example, during a discussion activity on a course in order to learn what issues come up naturally and, thus, what input seems to be in trainees' repertoires or, alternatively, to discover what areas of language trainees will need to work on during the course.

Evaluation can be concerned with describing adaptations and side-effects as well as the planned outcomes of various choices. A trainee may take an idea from a training course and happen to be using it next time the trainer comes in to observe her teaching. From watching the trainee's and the students' spontaneous adaptations of the idea and the unpredictable side-effects of the idea on such things as teacher style, classroom atmosphere and learner contributions, the trainer can learn a lot about the idea itself, her teaching of it to the trainees and the students' powers of adaptation. The trainee will learn a lot about how far the activity will stretch in terms of her own situation and about the activity's power or lack of it.

Evaluation can be carried out to explore various responses to a problem so that the range and type of responses may change and develop. One example of this might be to video a number of secondary school classes over a period of days or weeks. The tapes can then be viewed for teacher responses to discipline problems. The responses seen can be reported on in detail at a teachers' meeting without mentioning names. The repertoire of responses already in use can be discussed, adapted and developed, and new responses brainstormed by the group who might then like to try them out in class.

Evaluation can be aimed at testing hypotheses. A trainer may feel that the women in her trainee group are contributing less often to discussion than the men. By taping a training session and counting up, utterance for utterance, how often women and men speak in her session, she may find to her surprise that the utterance counts are in fact very similar. This may lead her to hypothesise that perhaps it is the length or type of utterance that differs within the group. Again, she can test this hypothesis by going back to the data on the tape recording.

Evaluation may be carried out primarily to understand why certain effects are produced. Participants on a teacher training course may be doing an extremely small amount of homework. Evaluation here can set about trying to find out whether the causes are an overload of work on participants generally, misunderstanding by them of what is required, lack of motivation due to discouraging marking of past assignments or some other factor.

Evaluation may be done in order to motivate students by giving them a deadline to work to. In the build-up to the evaluation, adrenalin will run high and trainees may either find themselves making new connections between old data or becoming nervous wrecks.

As can be seen from the above discussion, evaluation can be carried out for a large number of very different purposes. Evaluation of the effectiveness of process and process choices in teacher training can be done in the spirit of the different purposes outlined above, that is, to hold things still as far as possible and measure them, to assess success and failure, to watch and wait and gather information unobtrusively, to describe outcomes both spontaneous and planned, to develop a range of responses, to test hypotheses, and to understand why certain effects are produced. Keeping the different purposes of evaluation in mind may help us to integrate into it description, control, measurement, patience, collection and innovation, as well as to involve all parties in the central event.

We can turn our attention away from the evaluation of individuals entering a profession and the evaluation of trainees of a training course towards the issue of effectiveness of the teacher training process. We can see trainers and trainees as joint adventurers engaged in an exploration of process types in order to find out which are enjoyable, effective, economic, harmonious or challenging, as well as which are best when learning performance skills, cramming for exams or when working within other constraints. In this spirit, trainers and trainees can integrate innovation, evaluation and development in a spirit of joint research. Both sides can give their views on the effectiveness of process options. This can take the personal sting out of evaluation, for it then ceases to be the branding of an individual with a grade, or the euphoric or depressed reaction of a tired candidate at the end of a course, and can become an ongoing piece of research with interest to both main parties in the training event. In this view, evaluation is less of the actors than of the action.

What is evaluated?

What is evaluated obviously depends on what is considered important. As mentioned earlier, evaluation in EFL teacher training has perhaps been mostly concerned until now with changes in performance of language and teaching skills and with individual likes, dislikes and attitudes. Almost anything *can* be evaluated, however, from materials to methods, from costs to values, from stress loading to creche facilities. What you choose to evaluate will depend on what you see as important in teacher training. What you 'see', what is visible to you, depends on how you have mentally structured or categorised teacher training. If you see this field as 'teacher development' where the important person is the teacher, the most important process is independent work within the teacher and between teachers, and the important result is the building of self-confidence and a robust sense of self-esteem, then what you choose to evaluate might be your own self-confidence and the amount it does or does not improve during a series of meetings with colleagues in your town.

If you see running a particular teacher training course at your centre as a way of making money and improving the status of your centre in the community, then you might choose to evaluate local opinion of the centre before and after the course as well as the total financial costs and revenues to the centre.

My point here is that we will tend to 'see' our main interests and concerns. These concerns exist for us in our mental view of things and we will remember to evaluate them. Some of our concerns and interests, however, will be so deep within us that they are too near to be seen. It might be as well before choosing what to evaluate, then, to ask people concerned centrally and tangentially with a training event what *they* see as important. This may give us a greater pool of possibilities from which to choose what to evaluate, and may uncover some of our own deepest assumptions. What I might choose to evaluate first are: trainer and trainee awareness of process and process options. But that's just what I see. What do you see?

When is the evaluation done?

Evaluation can take place before, at the start of, during, at the end and/or after the end of a course. If evaluation only occurs at the end, its value is really limited to summing up. It may perhaps be used as a basis for adaptation of future courses of the same type. But participants on the present course may not know or realise that this is going to be done, participants on future courses will not know that this has been done and, in any case, participants on future courses will be different people with, perhaps, different needs and preferences. If evaluation is only used at the end of a course, all the hard work has already been completed. Those involved may be tired and have a strong feeling of energy having been spent. An evaluation at this stage can be strongly influenced by this fatigue. The evaluation can be experienced as a test or judgement of the level of achievement, when what is really needed is a recognition of the hard work that has been put in. If evaluation takes place during the course, then modifications can be made as the course continues. Levels of fatigue are likely to be lower and different adjustments can be tried out to see which works best.

Thinking about evaluation before a course starts and initiating it from the start can mean that an open-minded flexible view is set up from the outset. With an initial sequence of 'consider', 'try out', 'evaluate', 'adapt', and 'try out again', a course can be consistently and quickly responsive to daily changes in parameters without anybody suffering a loss of face or feeling resentful.

Evaluating or re-evaluating some time after a course has finished is more likely to uncover the long term effects of the course. Although administratively it may be difficult to keep track over time of those involved in the course, and although it demands time, effort and money, there are advantages to post-course evaluation. Initial euphoria or discouragement are tempered by a more considered distillation of good and bad effects. Pressure and influence from those involved in the course have waned and individual opinions plus the opinions of outsiders have strengthened and altered the participants' viewpoints. If change is the issue, then only post-course evaluation can verify whether long-term change has occurred or whether there has been 'recidivism'!

How is evaluation done?

The methods available for evaluating are many, including:

- Those designed to test, for example, written exams, essays, multiple choice tests, oral questions, finding solutions to familiar and unfamiliar problems, and planning strategies for tackling tasks.
- Those drawing on direct observation, for example, displays of speed or skill, rapport, good or varied behaviour as evidenced by observation records of given types (e.g. frequency counts, supervisor reports, observer diaries, video and sound tapes, analyses and descriptions).
- Those designed to elicit information directly, for example, questionnaires, surveys and discussions with oral and written reports, projects including texts, diagrams, drawings, letters and plans.
- Those designed to elicit information indirectly, for example, calculating turnover and drop-out rates, sales figures, or changes in speed or quality as seen from collections of data.

How is the evaluation reported, who interprets the report, and what happens then?

Sometimes evaluation is not reported at all; it is simply noted mentally. If reports are made, they are usually oral or written and prepared in meetings of two or more people. They may be passed around amongst decision makers who then decide to pass, fail or promote individuals, rewrite materials, adjust course components, continue, stop or increase funding, gain insight into the overall course model and course principles, or go on to do more evaluation so as to reveal more exactly where and why success or failure has occurred.

If we posit a situation, as we did earlier, of trainees and trainers working together on process as researchers, innovators and evaluators, oral and written reports could be kept informally between trainers and trainees and any other interested support group.

There may, however, be good professional reasons for making the work of these trainee-trainer process teams more public. It's possible that the trainees and trainers feel they would like the discipline of setting these ideas down more formally. Some may be interested in doing research in the subject at university, some may wish to write articles, some may want to explain the work to others in their centre, to heads of departments and to other departments and centres in order to gain support for the work and encourage similar work in different departments or centres.

Process evaluation may thus act not only as an enrichment of process on a particular course by its thoughtful checking quality, but it may also have a more formal, public role. If process is seen as important, as worth spending time, thought, energy and resources on, then it will need to enter as a relatively new element in formal, accredited assessment. It will need to enter the imagination and the personal construction of training reality and be 'seen'. Once seen, it will enter discussions of what is to be evaluated, when and how.

The questions raised above are fundamental and each one has a host of very varied answers. What you choose to evaluate will depend on what you see as important. What you think evaluation is and how and when you carry it out will depend on your aims and beliefs. I have not discussed how such factors as personality, age, sex, attitudes towards assessment, and student tactics affect assessment. We can see, however, even from the partial discussion above, that our usual repertoire of thoughts on evaluation in EFL teacher training could perhaps be expanded. A lot more is possible than simply the imposition of an *objectives* model or *process* model onto a course in order to evaluate trainees or trainers. Before discussing the question 'What happens next in evaluation?', I'd like to take the pretty way home.

TEACHERS AND TRAINERS AS RESEARCHERS

I would like to posit a particular situation. Let's imagine that you are a busy trainer in the middle of your work. You have started to become interested in process and have recently been watching or experimenting with your own and trainee reactions to different process options. You have no particularly strong research knowledge and no extra budget for research into process options or for evaluation of experiments. You would like to increase your work on process, perhaps by thinking about what you do already and evaluating it, perhaps by creating and collecting some process options, perhaps by trying out some new options or by matching some options to other training parameters and evaluating the results. You may want a few possible routes mapped out for you and a variety of quick, flexible, cheap evaluative tools that are appropriate to your own aim and interests and, most importantly, non-destructive of your usual training work. If this description fits you, at least in part, then you are, perhaps, the kind of trainer who parallels the teacher interested in classroom research.

The research metaphor

Where does the metaphor come from?

The 'teacher as researcher' metaphor in Chapter 18 can be traced back in the United Kingdom to the Humanities Curriculum Project started in 1967 at the Centre for Applied Research in Education, the University of East Anglia, popularised by Stenhouse (1975) and interpreted by the Ford Teaching Project directed by John Nixon. The Schools Council Programme Two – Helping individual teachers to become more effective – spread the action research movement beyond those who had had contact with the first two projects. There has been a teacher research movement since the late 1960s and some very readable and useful books and articles have emerged in the United Kingdom and Australia[3].

Many different terms have come up in connection with the 'teacher as researcher' metaphor. Included among them are: 'teacher research', 'classroom research', 'action research'. There are a number of parallel definitions available for each term too. I have outlined a couple of definitions below.

What is 'action research'?

' "Action research" is simply a form of self-reflective enquiry undertaken by participants in social situations in order to improve the rationality and justice of their own practices, their understanding of these practices, and the situations in which the practices are carried out' (Carr and Kemmis, 1986).

Hopkins (1985) defines 'action research' as a kind of research 'in which teachers look critically at their own classrooms primarily for the purpose of improving their teaching and the quality of life in their classrooms.'

This kind of professional activism is similar, perhaps, to that mentioned by Prabhu[4] in his description of enabling procedures: 'success in training is accordingly to be assessed not by the approximation of teachers' behaviour or belief to those of the trainer but by the increase in teachers' ability to interpret experience, relate perceptions to practical procedures, articulate emerging perceptions and interact productively with other perceptions.'

The differences between action research and traditional education research

Some see action research as an antidote to traditional education research. Carr and Kemmis (1986) refine things further, detailing eight general traditions in the study of education: 'Philosophy', 'Grand Theorising', 'The Foundations Approach', 'Educational Theory', 'The Applied Science Teacher's Perspective and the New Practicality', 'The Practical', 'Teachers as Researchers' and 'The Emerging Critical Tradition'. Action research is seen then as a phase in the history of educational study and as being both formed and informed by past traditions.

From a survey of the literature on action research, the main differences between mainstream academic research and action or teacher research are those listed below:

Mainstream educational research	Action research
Verbose, general, large scale, abstract	Brief, specific, small scale, practical, empirical, and implemented within the constraints of one's own school
The testing of hypotheses derived from prior theories	The improving of theory by observing practice
One observer	Some collaborative actors
Objectivity comes from observing	Objectivity comes from discussing interpretations with other teachers
Isolation of individual factors for study	No attempt to isolate individual factors for study from their context
Done by experts distant from schools to people in schools for the benefit of those outside schools	Done by practising teachers inside the classroom from their own strengths and using self-criticism for the benefit of insiders
Bureaucratic, authoritarian	Democratic, participatory
Outside contacts act as devil's advocates within an adversarial model	Outside contacts support and refine work with descriptions, suggestions
Results should be generalisable	Results not necessarily generalisable
Priorities are objectivity, acceptance of findings by fellow researchers, ethical experiments	Priorities are speed, practicability, acceptability within the school, adding to teachers' functional change, social change, and ethical experiments

Action research is seen then to be distinct from traditional, academic education research. Again, from Carr and Kemmis (op. cit.), we are helped to understand that in action research the objective study is the teacher's own educational practices and situation, but these are not seen as scientific phenomena, that is, they are not independent of the teacher/researcher nor are they governed by universal laws. Thus action research is distinct from the approach taken in some physical sciences.

In action research the area of study is not thought to consist solely, or most importantly, of the teacher/researcher's intentions, perspectives, values and understandings. It is understood that external constraints and conditions are very important too. Thus action research is distinct from the strongly 'interpretative approach' of some social sciences.

Models for action research

We are moving gradually to an understanding of action research as being distinct in some ways from physical and social sciences and from traditional educational research. As the name *action research* implies, there is a social process of transforming practices, understandings and situations through thinking, learning, reading, discussing, planning and acting. Some authors and teachers concentrate more on the action and others more on the research. Most authors and teachers seem, however, to see action research as a blend of, on the one hand, perspectives, values, intentions and mental schemata and, on the other, external conditions and parameters. This could then be our second 'go-between', our second way of reconciling inner life and outer life in teacher training (process was our first go-between).

There are even more differences in the number and names of stages of action research than names for the work as a whole. The most simple is, perhaps, planning, fact-finding and execution (Lewin, 1946). But whatever the numbers and names of the stages, most authors agree that action research involves the following activities, although not necessarily in this order:

- There is thinking and watching, listening and discussing in order to arrive at an issue, a problem or general area to investigate. The issue shouldn't be too large. It needn't stay exactly the same throughout the work but can be refined gradually. Next, hypotheses are discussed and developed. There are good descriptions in the action research literature[3] of how to refine and clarify the topics, problems or hypotheses by discussion, reading, and so on.
- Information is gathered using an appropriate method chosen from a large number of possible techniques such as video and audio tape recordings, observation, interviews, learner diaries, questionnaires and field notes.
- The data is analysed. There is reflection and interpretation.
- Evaluation (this happens continuously) and action. There is action in the form of writing up, discussion, collaborative action or formulation of new plans.

Despite the criticisms that have been levelled at action research by those used to mainstream academic education or research, it is recognised that whenever 'specific knowledge is required for a specific problem in a specific situation . . . or when a new approach is to be grafted on to an existing system . . . action research is fitting and appropriate' (Cohen and Manion, 1984). They go on to say that teaching *methods* are an area of school life where action research could be used.

Action research is brought into EFL teacher training

I'd like to borrow the idea of teacher/classroom action research, outlined very briefly above, and bring it into the training classroom for use by trainers and trainees. I would thus like to borrow an idea from one level in *The stack* (see Figure 1) and use it at another level. The 'trainer as researcher' metaphor could be applied to any content area. Trainers could do action research into any issue that interested them. I'd like to apply the idea here to the specific content area of process in EFL teacher training.

Using action research methods in evaluating process

Different trainees and trainers will want to work on different types of process investigation. Some possible areas are: the extent of awareness amongst trainers and trainees of process in training and the existing attitudes to training process; the relative costs of different process options; the amount of 'harmony' or 'challenge' in different options used with different people; the short-term versus long-term retention of ideas that seems to result from the use of different process options. Exactly what you wish to concentrate on will obviously depend on the aspect that has struck you as most important or fundamental so far. You may be interested in spotting patterns of recurrence (how often you do something), proximity to training norms in your institution (how does what you do compare with what other people do), patterns significant in terms of a training theory (for example, how often you give or refrain from giving your opinion). A discussion of tactics follows that could be used by trainers and trainees to investigate some of these issues.

Discovering trainer awareness of process

A trainer can invite another trainer into her training room (or, alternatively, video/audio recordings or oral recall can be used) so that one or more session is 'observed' by another trainer. Next, the observer can interview the observed trainer using a questionnaire similar to the following (adapted from Woodward, 1989*d*):

1. What were your main content aims in the session?
2. What methods/vehicles did you use to work with this content?
3. Did you deliberately choose the methods for the session or would you say they were a combination that you quite often use, that is, a combination that's in your repertoire?
4. If you chose deliberately, what criteria did you use for their selection?
5. Looking back now, how appropriate do you think the methods were for the particular group, input and situation that you had?
6. Did you like using these tactics?
7. Where and when did you first learn how to use these tactics?
8. Since then, have you had the time, opportunity or inclination to do any reading, thinking or discussion of these input methods?
9. Do you feel you would know where to get information on these or other methods if you wanted some?
10. Do you know of any other methods for working with content? Could you list them or describe them to me?
11. Have you ever seen any of these methods being used?
12. If not, where did you find out about them?
13. Are there any methods you've never actually seen but think might work? Given the perfect circumstances and enough space, time and money, are there any new ways you'd like to try?
14. Did you make any session notes when planning? Could I possibly see them?

It is vital that questionnaires such as this are not used to assess or evaluate (in a narrow sense) the person questioned. Under threat of judgement most trainers, like all normal human beings, will tend to give fashionably 'right' answers and little will be learnt by either party.

Discovery of trainee awareness of process

Using questionnaires, interviews or discussions one-to-one, in small groups or as whole classes, trainees can be encouraged to give their thoughts on the 'way' that content is handled on their course. They can be asked to list the processes they think have been used or not used.

Discovery of what process options are already in use

Training sessions can be observed to see what process options are being used by the trainer or teams of trainers, or what process types are pressed for by the trainees.

One basic model for this observation is called *participant observation* and involves the observer talking to and participating in activities with the people being studied. This model is often used in situations of face-to-face interaction rather than when artificial experiments are being conducted. An example given here by Delamont (1976) is of a hospital ward orderly gradually learning the duties of her job by observing, talking and trying out. On the face of it this looks like a useful model for our purposes since teacher training involves face-to-face interaction. The problem is that we are trying to discover what processes are already in use. If we join in, by talking and participating with the trainers or trainees, we may possibly affect the process of the session even more than by sitting quietly and observing.

Interaction analysis is another possible model of observation. This involves a coding of events using pre-specified categories. Although originally used to categorise public talk in classroom situations, as in Flander's 'Interaction analysis' and Boydell's 'Teacher record' (Delamont, op. cit.), one problem with its use for our purposes is that the categories are pre-defined and will reflect the definer's knowledge and predispositions. The categories have to be of finite number, for example, from five to fifteen, otherwise it will be hard for the observer to decide at speed in which category an event should be recorded. There could be an 'any other event' category tacked on at the end, but this method of observation works from a standpoint of interaction *already* classified. If a trainer goes into another's training room to discover what the trainer knows how to do, then it is likely that pre-defined categories will only reflect what the trainer who observes knows how to do. New types of process will not show up on the observation record.

Interaction analysis is also concerned with counting how often a particular event happens. This could be useful later on in finding out the number of times a trainer uses a particular process option, but is not of primary importance in a situation where the main aim is to find out how many different things a trainer does. For a full and interesting treatment of the many different systems available in classroom observation, including the use of observation in teacher training, see Allwright (1988).

My own system of observation of process options in training sessions is to see as many trainers as possible at work as many times as possible, to have only part of my concentration on content, to look for 'ways' and to note them down. In order to set as much information down as possible I use a number of simple formats such as the one below:

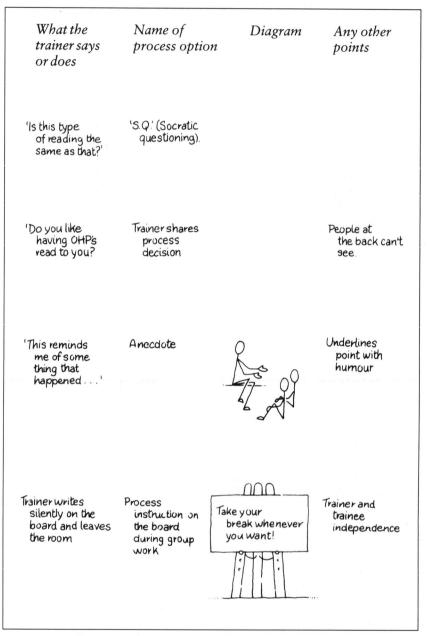

What the trainer says or does	*Name of process option*	*Diagram*	*Any other points*
'Is this type of reading the same as that?'	'S.Q.' (Socratic questioning).		
'Do you like having OHP's read to you?	Trainer shares process decision		People at the back can't see.
'This reminds me of something that happened...'	Anecdote		Underlines point with humour
Trainer writes silently on the board and leaves the room	Process instruction on the board during group work		Trainer and trainee independence

Figure 85   Process options observation sheet

Whenever possible I follow up this sort of simple notation work by talk-ing with trainers and trainees to try to understand what they saw, heard and experienced and to see how this relates to my experience.

Trainer criteria for choosing and using process options

Trainers can keep a process diary, jotting down in note, verbatim, diagram or pictorial form – before, during or after their sessions – the choices they feel were available to them at certain times, the decisions they made and the reasons for making those decisions (see Elliot, 1978 and McGrath, 1988). Here, the emphasis is less on the visibility of recording externals and more on the recording of internal decisions and unobservable factors, as recalled and understood by the person undergoing them.

Trainer experience of new options

After watching another trainer at work and spotting a new process option as an observer, a trainer might wish to join in a session where this particular process option is used again so as to experience its effect on a participant more directly. After watching and joining in, the trainer learning the new technique might like to talk to the other trainer and trainees in order to find out their reactions to using the option.

The systems of recording mentioned so far have included oral and written recall, video and audio recording, question and answer, and diagrams, notes, checklists, counts and quotations. These and other systems such as photos or drawings of critical moments and stages can be used and later analysed for any element that might seem to throw light on the effectiveness of a process option, for example: the number, type and length of trainer questions; the number, type and length of trainee offerings; the amount of verbal recall of content by trainees; the length of thinking time allowed; the number of uninitiated trainee utterances; the number of participants apparently participating at any one time; what the trainer did; what the trainees did; and where people were positioned in relation to each other.

With the help of learner diaries, letters, questionnaires and one-to-one chats, trainees can describe their reactions to process decisions made by trainers. Time can be allowed for this in class, as well as for trainee-to-trainee interviews. Regular informal checks can be made on everybody's opinions, and on the amount of change in motivation, stimulation, learning, understanding or skill produced by the use of different options. Records can be kept of preparation time, in-class time, after-class time, cost of materials and so forth, incurred by the use of different options.

We have posited here a trainer not only as a researcher but also as a learner – someone interested in learning about process from their own and other people's practice, from trainee initiatives and reactions, and from reading and thinking. The point was made earlier (see Figure 1, *The stack*) that any of the people involved in teacher training can have the twin roles of learner and teacher. Here the practising trainer is experiencing two complements to her usual role: she is learner and researcher as well.

What happens next within the 'trainer as researcher' model?

Once some data has been collected using any of the tactics mentioned above, you might want to double check it to make sure that it is valid and representative. The idea of getting more than one view on something or, more precisely, getting three different viewpoints on a situation is sometimes called triangulation or multiple method research. The idea is to use contrasting perceptions of an event to flesh out the details, prevent bias and ensure authenticity. For triangulation you will need three sources. For example, let's imagine that, as a trainer, you know that you have a tendency to use the Socratic questioning technique – that is, you try, by asking trainees questions, to lead them to discover points not exactly for themselves, since they have been led or guided, but to *state* points for themselves rather than listen to you stating the points for them. You have, let's imagine, never been taught how to do this, nor have you read very much about it, it is just something that you know you do. Let's imagine, too, that you have become aware – via trainee faces (droll smiles), trainee remarks ('Do you really want an answer to that?!'), and even your own asides to yourself ('OK, I'll ask you another obvious question then . . . ') – that your Socratic questioning doesn't seem to be reminding anyone of Socrates! You decide to tape yourself during a session. Afterwards you listen to the tape and find out that your questions are often loaded ('Now this technique is different from the other one, isn't it?') or obvious ('Is "extensive" the same as "intensive"?'), we well as being asked in what seems to you a rather patronising tone, asked one after the other in rapid succession with no answering time being given, and asked rather often during the session. At this point, then, you have your opinion and a tape of yourself using a questioning technique. In order to get two other perceptions of your work, i.e. to triangulate the data, you could (1) ask an observer to watch you teach or to listen to your tape and comment, and (2) ask the trainees to comment on or fill in a form about your questioning techniques. Using these two other sources you can see if your own conclusions are matched by other people's.

Once you have all the data in from all three sources, you will want to ponder it. You may have had a hypothesis before you collected the data and analysed it as in the example above. Alternatively, ideas may occur to you while you are collecting and analysing data. Whichever way round the ideas arise, you'll need time to think, read, discuss, plan some strategies and try them out before re-evaluating.

Tentative conclusions

By considering only the two main models for assessing courses and course participants (that is, the *objectives* model and the *process* model) together with their attendant assumptions and paradoxes, we are limiting ourselves. When it comes to a consideration of teacher training process, we don't have to take either route. Alternative routes exist, one of which is trainer action research. This very informal, independent and peer-supportive method can be used in evaluating our work in teacher training process. Action research can approximate the *objectives* model, if, for example, we set ourselves to 'use ten different process options in the first month of the course', but it doesn't have to. It can also, if done without collaboration, discussion, reading and triangulation, become very vague, personal and cosy. It is not, then, without its own dangers. But busy trainers wishing to preserve their autonomy, wanting to make their own decisions about their work and willing to follow the stages of an action research model from the original thinking to the final writing up may well find it useful. It can involve trainers finding out where they and their trainees are regarding awareness of process, actively learning more options together and putting more into practice, and seeing how everyone feels about the old and the new options once they've been tried out. What happens next will depend on what has been discovered. It could be reading, writing, thinking, collaborative action or discussion. Since it is their own project, run for their purposes, they will, after opening themselves to ideas from outside, decide from the inside.

There has been a very carefully argued account of the distinction between educational research and evaluation. An important distinction between the two, according to MacDonald (1976) is in the selection of the problems which are at the focus of the study. 'The researcher is free to select his questions, and to seek answers to them. He will naturally select questions which are susceptible to the problem-solving techniques of his craft. The evaluator, on the other hand, must never fall into the error of answering questions which no one but he is asking. He must first identify the significant questions and only then address the technological problems which they raise.'

Thus, as Cohen and Manion (1984) say after quoting this paragraph from MacDonald, 'Evaluation must respond to the situation which exists and the decisions which have to be taken. It may mean that crude techniques are more appropriate than sophisticated measurement technology . . . '

Summary

Perhaps some summary statements would be helpful at this stage. In this chapter I have raised the following points:

- Normally, when thinking about evaluation and teacher training, we may tend to think first of (a) assessing trainees, or (b) trainees assessing courses they've been on.
- When it comes to assessing trainees, two possible evaluative models are (a) the *objectives* model, and (b) the *process* model.
- When trainees assess or give feedback on courses, they are rarely given the chance to apply these models even though the models may be applied to them.
- There are advantages and disadvantages to both models.
- Before thinking about how to evaluate teacher training process, we need, perhaps, to open out our definition of *evaluation*.
- One way of opening out the definition is by asking lots of simple questions and brainstorming answers to them.
- By doing this we can see that a lot more is possible than the imposition of a *process* or *objectives* model of assessment on trainees by course leaders.
- One alternative to this imposition is *action research*, an idea taken from the teaching classroom and applied to the training classroom.
- Tactics that can be used within the classroom/action research model are discussed as they relate to discovering trainer and trainee awareness of process.
- The issue of triangulation of data is important.
- When involved in this kind of evaluation, the trainer is both researcher and learner.
- A good researcher would need to be someone interested in and committed to finding out more about classroom encounters, thinking, reading, discussing issues, collecting data, formulating theories, planning action, executing changes, writing up and evaluating the research.
- We have here an alternative set of sub-skills or abilities comprising a 'good' teacher or 'good' trainer.

We are focussing on the teacher or trainer as a researcher and learner able to both reflect and act. If this developmental view is preferred to the previous view of a merely skilled, competent, content-proficient teacher, then perhaps this too will in time become tightly defined in terms of desirable sub-skills! Input on training courses will then not only include slots on 'data collection', 'triangulation', 'hypothesising' and 'professional practice' – laudable and interesting enough in themselves – but these abilities and skills might then be tested for within an *objectives* or a *process* model. If this happens, we will have moved once more from an undefined outcome back to a defined outcome and to an outcome defined by the trainer rather than the trainee.

If we are indeed moving towards the idea of the 'good' teacher or trainer as one who can observe, reflect (see Schön, 1983), theorise, plan, execute and evaluate independently, then surely all we can do is to give the tools for this approach to a trainee. The true evaluation, the true test of whether this model of a good teacher has been grasped and interpreted individually by each trainee is whether in 20, 30 or 40 years' time the individual, other things being equal, is still enjoying teaching with students who are enjoying learning and still developing and experimenting with whatever is relevant to them at that time.

If we are moving towards the view that true professional activism and development lies in teachers becoming aware of their own practice, grasping routines, but not becoming over-routinised, open to outside ideas, but not in awe of them, and able to move easily between practice, reflection and research, then the true test of a good teacher will be: (a) if a teacher can conceptualise or offer models or explanations for aspects of their work, and (b) if a teacher can interact with other ideas, admitting some, rejecting some, and changing their own. If this view of a good teacher were accepted, it would blow apart the principles and practice of many established training courses and would change our view of who evaluates who or what, when and how.

1. Further reading on **evaluation**:

Elliot, J. (1978). Classroom Accountability. In W. Harlen (ed.), *Evaluation and the Teacher's Role*. Schools Council Research Studies. Macmillan Education.

Harlen, W. (ed.) (1978). *Evaluation and the Teacher's Role*. Schools Council Research Studies. Macmillan Education.

Macdonald, B. M. (1976). Evaluation and the Control of Education. In D. Tawney (ed.), Schools Council Research Studies. Macmillan Education.

Romiszowski, A. J. (1981). *Designing Instructional Systems: Decision making in course planning and curriculum design*. Kogan Page.

Stenhouse, L. (1975). *An Introduction to Curriculum Research and Development*. Heinemann Educational.

Stranghan, R. & Wrigley, J. (eds.) (1980). *Values and Evaluation in Education*. Harper & Row.

2. I gained the idea from a conversation with Herbert Puchta.

3. Further reading on **action research**:

Carr, W. & Kemmis, S. (1986). *Becoming Critical*. Falmer Press.

Cohen, L. & Manion, L. (1984). Action Research. In J. Bell et al. (eds.), *Conducting Small Scale Investigations in Educational Management*. Harper & Row.

Delamont, S. (1976). *Interaction in the Language Classroom*. Methuen.

Hopkins, D. (1985). *A Teacher's Guide to Classroom Research*. Open University Press.

Hustler, D., Cassidy, A. & Cuft, E. C. (eds.) (1986). *Action Research in Classrooms and Schools*. Allen and Unwin.

Lewin, K. (1946). Action research and minority problems. *Journal of Social Issues*, **2**.

McGrath, I. (1988). An exercise in autonomy. *The Teacher Trainer*, **2**, 3.

Prabhu, N. S. (1987). *Second Language Pedagogy*. Oxford University Press.

Roberts, J. (1987). A bibliography on action research. *Teacher Development*, 7.

Schön, D. (1983). *The Reflective Practitioner: How Professionals Think in Action*. Temple Smith.

4. Dr N. S. Prabhu, 'Language education: equipping or enabling', a paper given at the Regional Language Centre Seminar in Singapore in April 1987.

Conclusion to Part Two

In this part of the book I have discussed options inside the trainer's head (mental schemata for organising training), outside the trainer's head (external parameters), options for negotiating between the two (process options), and for evaluating the negotiations. I have stated that I don't feel that it's meaningful to talk about *one* form of categorisation, one course model, one process option, one matching technique, or one method of evaluation as being the best for all situations. I've said we need a broad definition of each of the features in order to open up a range of possibilities from which we can choose at different times, for different reasons, and with the expectation of very different results.

To some, a proliferation of options may, to paraphrase Prabhu, have the philosophical glow of an espousal of plurality. The argument that there is no one best way may, however, be used to support the detailing of a plethora of variables that obscures the many similarities between events, undermines the faith of those who believe in one method, and halts or blocks useful enquiry into which parts of which methods are, in fact, most pedagogically powerful in some situations for some people. Eclecticism is repugnant to those who see it as a sign that teachers and trainers are shallow, superficial dabblers incapable of real depth and application.

Given a hectic working life, however, classes full of different individuals with different needs and preferences, and given trainers and teachers with moods of their own, what's the point of sticking to one approach, method or tactic through thick and thin? Looked at this way, eclecticism can be seen as a rational response to the rich, fast, chaotic and unplanned nature of real life.

What we need then is not a diffuse and unsystematic hotch-potch of bits and pieces, but principled eclecticism. We need the space and time for trainers and teachers to think and talk about what they want to work on, to find new ethical ways of gathering and triangulating data, and to think about what adjustments would be appropriate to their own aims.

There has been much discussion in this book of different mental models and classifications. Ways of thinking about training, observation, evaluation, and adaptation of parameter to parameter have all been discussed via metaphor, diagram, model or alternative scheme.

To my mind it is this continual effort to classify and reclassify into categories, to make and break models, to learn and unlearn routines, together with the drawing out each time of the insights, assumptions, advantages and disadvantages of each schema that is the unifying developmental tool in eclecticism. Variety is good, I believe, and unifying schemata are good, I believe. To have a variety of unifying schemata is, for me, the perfect mix. To be open to variety, aware of unifying principles and able to think about, discuss and change them, in the light of work experience, is my own personal definition of a 'good' learner, teacher or trainer.

Conclusion to the whole book

I started this book with a detailed description of one particular process option. When I started developing loop input, it was the first answer I had found to my personal research question, 'How can I give input without lecturing?' At the time I had never heard of 'action research' or 'classroom research'. I was just doing what was interesting to me. Now equipped with new terminology, I can look back and say, 'I was involved in a personal research cycle!'

In Part Two I stepped back from my personal picture of training and looked at other people's ways of classifying the event. Each classification adds an insight and also carries assumptions and disadvantages. So we can say that describing the training event in any particular way throws a light and shadow on the event, just as the sun and clouds throw light and moving shadow on a hillside. The hill is there come rain or shine, but it looks different in different weather.

Regardless of how we personally describe training, there are numerous external parameters. We have to connect the vision we have of the event with the external realities. One way of matching inside with outside, internal description with external reality, is by playing with process. We can use process as a go-between in order to harmonise with or challenge the parameter. 'Harmony' and 'challenge' are themselves metaphors. We could have experimented with other metaphors such as 'simplicity' / 'extravagance' or 'broad sketch' / 'fine detail'. But I'll leave that to you, for you will have your own chosen metaphors.

With all the juggling of parameter with parameter, how can we tell if we're being effective? This was the issue of the last chapter. Again, with evaluation, there are different visions of it inside people's heads, different external realities, and different connections possible between these two, that is, between the value and the evaluation. My own personal favourite connection is trainer action research or the posing of one personal research question . . . which is where I came in.

239

Bibliography

(Those books and articles which are used for further reading at the end of each chapter, but not referred to in the text, are not listed in this Bibliography.)

Aeberbard, P. (1988). People who train people. *The Teacher Trainer*, **2**, 2.

Allwright, D. (1988). *Observation in the Language Classroom*. Longman.

Alston, W. P. (1964). *The Philosophy of Language*. Prentice-Hall.

Argondizzo, C., Aiello, A. & Romiti, R. (1986/7). Teachers' centres and the continuing education and training of language teachers. In *English in School: Teacher Education*. The British Council 1986 Sorrento Conference Report.

Ashton-Warner, S. (1980). *Teacher*. Virago.

Baddeley, A. (1982). *Your Memory: A User's Guide*. Sidgwick and Jackson.

Bandler, R. & Grinder, J. (1979). *Frogs into Princes*. Real People Press.

Belbin, E., Downs, S. & Perry, P. (1981). *How Do I Learn?* Further Education Curriculum Reviews and Development Unit.

Berer, M. & Rinvolucri, M. (1981). *Mazes*. Heinemann Educational.

Bligh, D., Jaques, D. & Warren-Piper, D. (1975). *Seven Decisions when Teaching Students*. Exeter University Teaching Services.

Bolitho, R. & Tomlinson, B. (1980). *Discover English*. Heinemann Educational.

Bolitho, R. (1988). Teaching, teacher training and applied linguistics. *The Teacher Trainer*, **2**, 3.

Bowers, R. (1989*a*). Where do ideas come from? In *Creativity in Language Teaching*. The British Council 1988 Milan Conference Report. Modern English Publications.

Bowers, R. (1989*b*). An interview with Roger Bowers. *The Teacher Trainer*, **3**, 2.

Brumfit, C. & Rossner, R. (1982). The 'Decision Pyramid' and teacher training for ELT. *ELT Journal*, **36**, 4.

Bruner, J. S. & Postman, Z. (1949). On the perception of incongruity: a paradigm. *Journal of Personality*, **18**.

Buzan, T. (1974, revised and extended edition first published 1982). *Use Your Head*. BBC Publications.

Calderhead, J. (1989). Reflecting teaching and teacher education. *Teaching and Teacher Education*, 5, 1.

Carr, W. & Kemmis, W. (1986). *Becoming Critical*. Falmer Press.

Cohen, L. & Manion, L. (1984). Action Research. In J. Bell et al. (eds.), *Conducting Small Scale Investigations in Educational Management*. Harper & Row.

Davis, P. & Rinvolucri, M.(1988). *Dictation: New methods, new possibilities*. Cambridge University Press.

Davis, R. L. (ed.) (1979). *RSA Cert. TEFL Courses: Teacher Training Techniques and Problem Areas*. Hilderstone English Language Centre.

Delamont, S. (1976). *Interaction in the Language Classroom*. Methuen.

Deller, S. (1987). Observation – the pluses and minuses. *The Teacher Trainer*, 1, 1.

Elliot, J. (1978). Classroom Accountability. In W. Harlen (ed.), *Evaluation and the Teacher's Role*. Schools Council Research Studies. Macmillan Education.

Evans, C. (1988). *Language People*. Open University Press.

Farthing, J. (1981). *Business Mazes*. Hart-Davis Educational.

Frank, C. & Rinvolucri, M. (1983). *Grammar in Action*. Pergamon Press.

Gairns, R. & Redman, S. (1986). *Working with Words: A guide to teaching and learning vocabulary*. Cambridge University Press.

Golębiowska, A. (1985). Once a teacher always a teacher. *ELT Journal*, 39, 4.

Gower, R. & Walters, S. (1983). *Teaching Practice Handbook*. Heinemann Educational.

Harlen, W. (ed.) (1978). Chapter 5 in *Evaluation and the Teacher's Role*. Schools Council Research Studies. Macmillan Education.

Harmer, J. (1983). *The Practice of English Language Teaching*. Longman.

Hess, N. (1987). The interview as a teacher training tool. *The Teacher Trainer*, 1, 3.

Hofstadter, Douglas R. (1979). *Gödel, Escher, Bach: An Eternal Golden Braid*. Harvester Press.

Hopkins, D. (1985). *A Teacher's Guide to Classroom Research*. Open University Press.

Hubbard, P., Jones, H., Thornton, B. & Wheeler, R. (1983). *A Training Course for the Teaching of English as a Foreign Language*. Oxford University Press.

Johnson-Laird, P. N. (1983). *Mental Models: Towards a cognitive science of language, inference and consciousness*. Cambridge University Press.

Jones, K. (1982). *Simulations in Language Teaching*. Cambridge University Press.

Krumm, H. J. (1973). Interaction Analysis. Microteaching for the training of modern language teachers. *IRAL*, XI, 2.

Bibliography

Lakoff, G. & Johnson, M. (1980). *Metaphors We Live By*. University of Chicago Press.

Lavery, M. (1985). Graffitti Wall. In C. Sion (ed.), *Recipes for Tired Teachers: Well-seasoned activities for the ESOL classroom*. Addison-Wesley.

Lavery, M. (1988). Human resources development. *The Teacher Trainer*, 2, 1.

Leveton, E. (1977). *Psychodrama for the Timid Clinician*. Springer Publishers.

Lewin, K. (1946). Action research and minority problems. *Journal of Social Issues*, 2.

Lindstromberg, S. (1985). Schemata for ordering the teaching and learning of vocabulary. *ELT Journal*, 39, 4.

MacDonald, B. M. (1976). Evaluation and the Control of Education. In D. Tawney (ed.), *Curriculum Evaluation Today: Trends and Implications*. Schools Council Research Studies. Macmillan Education.

McGrath, I. (1988). An exercise in autonomy. *The Teacher Trainer*, 2, 3.

Maley, A. (1987). Teacher-oriented processes for stimulating innovation in education (TOPSIE). *Focus on English*, 3, 4.

Marks, J. (1989). Poster presentations on teacher training courses. *The Teacher Trainer*, 3, 3.

Morgan, J. & Rinvolucri, M. (1986). *Vocabulary*. Oxford University Press.

Mugglestone, P. (1979). Mirroring classroom procedures. In S. Holden (ed.), *Teacher Training*. Modern English Publications.

Neisser, U. (1967). *Cognitive Psychology*. Appleton-Century-Crofts.

Peterson, P. & Comeaux, M. (1987). Teachers' schemata for classroom events: the mental scaffolding of teachers' thinking during classroom instruction. *Teaching and Teacher Education*, 3, 4.

Prabhu, N. S. (1987). *Second Language Pedagogy*. Oxford University Press.

Romiszowski, A. J. (1981). *Designing Instructional Systems: Decision making in course planning and curriculum design*. Kogan Page.

Rushton, L. (1987). Little boxes observation sheet. *The Teacher Trainer*, 12.

Schön, D. (1983). *The Reflective Practitioner: How Professionals Think in Action*. Temple Smith.

Spencer, D. H. (1967). *Guided Composition Exercises*. Longman.

Stenhouse, L. (1975). *An Introduction to Curriculum Research and Development*. Heinemann Educational.

Stevick, E. (1976). *Memory, Meaning and Method*. Newbury House.

Stevick, E. (1986). *Images and Options in the Language Classroom*. Cambridge University Press.

Strain, J. E. (1986). Method: design-procedure vs method-technique. *System*, 14, 3.

Sturtridge, G. (1987). Using posters in teacher education. *The Teacher Trainer*, 1, 2.

Tomlinson, B. (1984). A glossary of basic EFL terms. In A. Cunningsworth, *Evaluating and Selecting EFL Materials*. Heinemann Educational.

Underhill, A. (1980). *Use Your Dictionary*. Oxford University Press.

Widdowson, H. (1983). *Learning Purpose and Language Use*. Oxford University Press.

Willis, J. (1981). *Teaching English Through English: A course in classroom and language techniques*. Longman.

Woodward, T. (1985). A vocabulary review game. *Modern English Teacher*, **12**, 4.

Woodward, T. (1986). Loop input. *The Teacher Trainer*, 0.

Woodward, T. (1987). The buzz group lecture. *The Teacher Trainer*, **1**, 3.

Woodward, T. (1988*a*). Loop input, *System*, **16**, 1.

Woodward, T. (1988*b*). The starter question circle. *The Teacher Trainer*, **2**, 1.

Woodward, T. (1989*a*). Observation tasks for pre-service trainees. *The Teacher Trainer*, **3**, 1.

Woodward, T. (1989*b*). Taking the stress out of post-lesson feedback. *The Teacher Trainer*, **3**, 2.

Woodward, T. (1989*c*, December). Component questions. *Practical English Teaching*.

Woodward, T. (1989*d*). Styles of EFL teacher training input. *System*, **17**, 1.

Woodward, T. (1990). Good Names, Bad Names. *Teaching English*, summer issue, published by Reporter, Milan, Italy.

Index

action research, 224–35
  and traditional education research, 224–5
  as a go-between, 226
  definition of, 224
  in EFL teacher training, 227, 239
  models for, 226
Alston, W. P., 129
approach, method, tactic, see model(s), three-tiered
Argondizzo, C., Aiello, A. and Romiti, R., 9
Ashton-Warner, S., 104
awareness activities, 10–11

back chaining, 18
background and foreground, 15–16, 160
Baddeley, A., 156
Bandler, R. and Grinder, J., 134
being a beginner, 68–73
Belbin, E., Downs S. and Perry, P., 73
bi-polar scales, 146–50, 156, 157, 159, 161
Bligh, D., Jacques, D. and Warren-Piper, D., 181
Bolitho, R., 146, 218
Bolitho, R. and Tomlinson, B., 10
bottom-up, top-down, 144–6, 154
Bruner, J. S. and Postman, Z., 157, 158
Buzan, Tony, 73

Carr, W. and Kemmis, W., 224
categorising, 136, 138–62, 220, 237–8
challenge, see harmony and challenge
chunking, 19, 131, 156
classifying, see categorising
classroom
  atmosphere, 11
  language, 57–8
  management, 18, 50–60, 190–2

spatial arrangement, 12
Cohen, L. and Manion, L., 226, 233
community language learning, see counselling learning
content
  definition of, 4
  in Part One, 17
  in the process, 43
controlled practice, 18
  see also drills
correction, 53, 149–50
counselling learning, 44–8, 76
course components, 170–6
course models and metaphors, classification of, 152–6, 157, 159, 161
cummings, e. e., 130

Davis, Robin, 59
Davis, Paul and Rinvolucri, Mario, 42
deep-end model, 47, 118, 197
Delamont, S., 229
Deller, Sheelagh, 71
Dickens, Charles, 10–11
dictation, 16, 18, 30–42
  gap, 36–7
  mixed ability, 37–9
  mutual, 39–41
  picture, 35–6
  standard form, 32
  student power, 34
drills, 18, 74–82, 118–19, 211–12
  cues for, 80–2
  interesting, 79–82
  nonsense, 80–1
  simple repetition, 78
  substitution, 78–9

equipping and enabling procedures, 141, 224
evaluation, 19

244

Index